# Motivational Interviewing in Schools

**Keith C. Herman, PhD,** is a professor in counseling psychology at the University of Missouri and codirects the Missouri Prevention Center. He is a member of the Motivational Interviewing Network of Trainers (MINT). Prior to his faculty appointment he worked as a school psychologist in an Oregon school district. He presents nationally and has published over 80 peer-reviewed articles and chapters. He serves on the editorial boards of *School Psychology Quarterly* and *Journal of Counseling Psychology* and is coauthor of two professional books: *Academic and Behavior Supports for At-Risk Students: Tier 2 Intervention* (2012) and *Motivational Interviewing for Effective Classroom Management: The Classroom Check-Up* (2011). Much of his research and applied work focuses on using motivational interviewing (MI) with teachers and families to promote effective environments for youth. He is a coinvestigator with Johns Hopkins Center for Prevention and Early Intervention, where his primary role has been to develop MI-based consultation strategies for school professionals working with teachers, parents, and students; train these school professionals to deliver these methods with high fidelity; and evaluate the impact of the use of these methods on teacher, parent, and student outcomes.

**Wendy M. Reinke, PhD,** is an associate professor in school psychology at the University of Missouri and codirector of the Missouri Prevention Center. She has worked in a variety of school consultation settings, including as a school psychologist in an elementary school and as a behavior consultant in the Baltimore City School District. She developed the Classroom Check-Up, an assessment-based classwide teacher consultation model. Her research focuses on the prevention of disruptive behavior problems in children and increasing school-based implementation of evidence-based practices. She presents nationally, has published dozens of peer-reviewed articles, and has coauthored two books, *Academic and Behavior Supports for At-Risk Students: Tier 2 Intervention* (2012) and *Motivational Interviewing for Effective Classroom Management: The Classroom Check-Up* (2011). She is the principal investigator on a multimillion-dollar trial funded by the U.S. Institute of Education Sciences to evaluate the efficacy of a teacher classroom management intervention. She is also a coinvestigator with the Center for Prevention and Early Invervention. She is charged with developing and evaluating MI methods for promoting school engagement.

**Andy J. Frey, PhD,** earned his MSW from the University of Michigan in 1994 and his PhD from the University of Denver in 2000. He is currently an associate professor at the Kent School of Social Work at the University of Louisville. Before joining the faculty at the University of Louisville, he was a school social worker and behavioral consultant in Douglas County Schools, Colorado. He is the author of over 30 book chapters and peer-reviewed journal articles and serves on the editorial board of *Children and Schools*. His primary interest areas include positive behavior support, social and emotional competence in preschoolers, early intervention, and the provision of school social work services. He has a developmental grant from the U.S. Institute of Education Sciences to integrate MI consultation strategies with the First Step to Success program. As part of this project, his team has developed protocols for training school personnel to use MI with families and teachers and for monitoring implementation fidelity.

**Stephanie A. Shepard, PhD,** is an assistant professor with Brown University's School of Medicine. She received a Career Development Award from the National Institute of Mental Health to integrate the MI-based Family Check-Up and other engagement strategies with the well-established parenting intervention, the Incredible Years. She has authored over 30 book chapters and articles in peer-reviewed publications. She has trained a cadre of school professionals across the nation to use these methods to promote parent and staff involvement and motivation.

# Motivational Interviewing in Schools
## *Strategies for Engaging Parents, Teachers, and Students*

*Keith C. Herman, PhD*

*Wendy M. Reinke, PhD*

*Andy J. Frey, PhD*

*Stephanie A. Shepard, PhD*

SPRINGER PUBLISHING COMPANY

NEW YORK

Springer Publishing Company, LLC
11 West 42nd Street
New York, NY 10036
www.springerpub.com

*Acquisitions Editor:* Nancy Hale
*Composition:* Newgen Imaging

*ISBN:* 978-0-8261-3072-3
*e-book ISBN:* 978-0-8261-3073-0
*Handouts ISBN:* 978-0-8261-2169-1

*Handouts are available from www.springerpub.com/herman-ancillary*

14 15 16 17/ 5 4 3 2

The author and the publisher of this Work have made every effort to use sources believed to be reliable to provide information that is accurate and compatible with the standards generally accepted at the time of publication. The author and publisher shall not be liable for any special, consequential, or exemplary damages resulting, in whole or in part, from the readers' use of, or reliance on, the information contained in this book. The publisher has no responsibility for the persistence or accuracy of URLs for external or third-party Internet websites referred to in this publication and does not guarantee that any content on such websites is, or will remain, accurate or appropriate.

**Library of Congress Cataloging-in-Publication Data**

Herman, Keith C.
  Motivational interviewing in schools : strategies for engaging parents, teachers, and students / Keith C. Herman, Ph.D., University of Missouri, Wendy M. Reinke, Ph.D., University of Missouri, Andy Frey, University of Louisville, Stephanie Shepard, Brown University.
      pages cm
  Includes bibliographical references and index.
  ISBN 978-0-8261-3072-3 (alk. paper)
  1. Educational counseling. 2. Motivational interviewing. 3. Motivation in education.  I. Reinke, Wendy M. II. Frey, Andy. III. Shepard, Stephanie. IV. Title.
  LB1027.5.H4367 2014
  371.4—dc23                                                                                                2013032725

Printed in the United States of America by Bradford & Bigelow.

# Contents

# Preface

It is fun when life comes full circle. The story of how this book came to be is full of circles. The earliest beginnings of this book can be traced to Providence, Rhode Island, in the late 1990s. Keith Herman and Wendy Reinke were working on a set of research projects at Brown University, one of them involving the use of motivational interviewing (MI) to encourage teens to quit smoking cigarettes. Keith was a research therapist on the project and was trained to use MI by Jacki Hecht, an early member of the Motivational Interviewing Network of Trainers. Like most people when they first learn this method, Keith caught the MI bug immediately. Once you catch it and then really learn MI, it forever permeates everything you do and how you think about the world.

Fast forward a few years to a dinner conversation between Wendy and Keith at a convention in New Orleans. Wendy was now a graduate student at the University of Oregon, and she was working with Tom Dishion, who had developed a family application of MI called the Family Check-Up. In her work as a school psychologist, Wendy sensed that there was a need for a similar type of approach for teachers. While Wendy and Keith were brainstorming over dinner and during walks throughout the city, the Classroom Check-Up (the CCU) was born. The CCU is now an empirically supported teacher consultation model based on MI.

As fate would have it, Stephanie Shepard was working with Tom Dishion at the University of Oregon around the same time as Wendy, but the two hadn't met in Oregon. The year Wendy began her training with Tom, Stephanie departed for her internship at Boston University Consortium. She then completed her fellowship at Brown University in the same lab Wendy had worked in many years before (noticing the circles yet?). Stephanie continued on in a faculty position at Brown and became an expert at integrating the Family Check-Up with family interventions, especially the well-established parenting program, the Incredible Years.

Fast forward a few years again, when Wendy and Keith were working as part of the Center for Prevention and Early Intervention (CPEI) at Johns Hopkins. The CPEI was in part intended to bring together scholars who were developing integrated school-based interventions. They learned of Stephanie's work on a career development award she received from the National Institute of Mental Health and invited her to a center meeting. During her visit, it became obvious how much the three of us had in common, and how we were all trying to tackle the same challenges of improving services in schools.

The final member of our team, Andy Frey, came to us as a gift from Hill Walker. Wendy worked with Hill during her time at the University of Oregon, and they stayed in touch over the years. Hill, ever generous with his time and committed to supporting the next generation of scholars, contacted her out of the blue one day and said he had someone he wanted her to meet. Hill sensed that Wendy and Andy would hit it off, and he was right. Andy had been working with Hill on a grant to improve parent engagement in the First Step to Success program. He encountered some challenges in teacher engagement to the intervention as well. Hill knew of Wendy's work with the CCU and thought she would have some insights that Andy would find helpful. As with Stephanie, it was clear that Andy had been working on some of the same challenges in promoting involvement with school-based services.

All four of us believed the MI approach filled an important gap in school-based intervention research and practice. Barely a week would pass without one of us hearing from someone requesting information about school-based MI and a manual for how to do it. While MI has now been around for over two decades, we are just beginning to understand its potential in school settings. Each of us had separately adapted the methods for specific application in our school consultation work ranging from Head Start to high school settings. We decided to write a book together to capitalize on the wide range of experiences each of us has had with MI. We wanted to create a highly accessible resource for school practitioners. **Toward that end, the handouts for the book are available for download and use from the Springer Publishing Company website (www. springerpub.com/herman-ancillary).**

As you read this book, we hope that you too experience the MI bug, the excitement that comes with realizing the simplicity and truth behind the technique. There is something about it that resonates with people, a realization that the way we have been going about trying to influence people in the past may have been misguided, and a hope that this new way of being with people will make a difference. There is something empowering and exciting about this method that gives you concrete points of leverage to help people make important changes in their lives. Enjoy the journey. May yours be filled with gratifying circles!

# Acknowledgments

Wendy Reinke and Keith Herman are grateful to all the teachers, parents, and students who allowed us to pilot elements of the methods described here over the years; we are especially grateful to those who have participated in the studies that formed the foundation for our work.

We also must acknowledge the amazing coaches and school-based consultants who have inspired us over the years. Jennifer Keperling and Sandy Hardee have been two exceptional coaches and long-time champions of the Classroom Check-Up (CCU). They each have inspired us to identify key qualities of effective coaches. In particular, Jenn has an unyielding belief in teachers and their ability to enact change plans. Her spirit of conveying this moves most teachers to action. Sandy displays such a spirit of comfort and ease in her interactions with teachers that nearly all are willing to trust and work with her as their guide, even on the most difficult topics. Lana Asuncion-Bates has emerged as an exemplary CCU coach as well and has made many thoughtful contributions to the model. Jennifer Cox, Kelly Dunn, Courtney Vaughan, and Dana Darney also have provided valuable services and insights based on their efforts at implementing the Family Check-Up and Coping Power programs in urban school settings. Dana and several doctoral students at the University of Missouri, including Lindsay Borden, Tia Shultz, and Nidhi Goel, provided motivational interviewing (MI)-related services to parents, students, and teachers and completed innovative dissertations on MI topics. Each helped advance our thinking about MI and its application in schools. Dr. Lori Newcomer continues to inspire us with her amazing teacher consultation skills and her commitment to teachers and students.

We also would like to acknowledge the Center for Prevention and Early Intervention at Johns Hopkins School of Public Health for ongoing support in the development, adaptation, and evaluation of the various MI applications described in this book. The National Institute of Mental Health and the National Institute on Drug Abuse provided ongoing funding for the center and some of the projects described in this book. We are grateful to Dr. Nick Ialongo, center director, for his ongoing support and encouragement.

Dr. Catherine Bradshaw, the associate dean of research at the University of Virginia, has been a valued colleague who has supported our work and encouraged us to think bigger and better. Her recent adaptations of the CCU to various new applications are exciting and innovative. Dr. John Lochman has been incredibly gracious in allowing us to tinker with his Coping Power program as we tried to create an integrated model of support for families in schools.

We have been very fortunate to have had many amazing mentors over the years who have influenced many of the ideas we express in this book. Dr. Carolyn Webster-Stratton has inspired and encouraged us for years. Although she does not use the terminology of MI to describe her work or her exceptional clinical skills, her style and extraordinary gifts of connecting and sparking change in others are very much in line with MI. Dr. Tom Dishion has supported us over the years as we attempted to extend his brilliant efforts to apply MI with families. Drs. Randy Sprick and George Sugai have long inspired us with their incredible school consultation skills and the vast positive influence they have had on schools in the United States. Of course, we would be remiss not to acknowledge the original work of Drs. William Miller and Stephen Rollnick, the developers of MI. All MI extensions are merely adaptations of their groundbreaking work.

Finally, we would like to acknowledge our parents and families, especially Wendy and Keith's daughter, Kennedy, who has attended more professional conferences in her 6 years of life than many adult scholars.

Andy Frey would like to acknowledge his wife (Shannon), parents (Larry Frey and Maureen Frey), and children (Sam and Amelia) for their support and encouragement. He is also grateful for the mentorship he has received from Dr. Hill Walker. Without his support, this work would not have been possible. Additionally, Andy is thankful for Dr. Terri Moyers's guidance and encouragement. He is also grateful for his many colleagues at the University of Louisville and University of Oregon who have been influential in helping to transport the MI approach to school settings. Finally, he is grateful for the support of the Jefferson County and Greater Clark County Public School Systems. The administrators, teachers, and families he collaborated with to better understand how to use MI were outstanding. It has been an honor to work with them and learn from them. Andy's work has been supported by an Institute of Education Sciences, U.S. Department of Education grant that allowed him to develop the enhancements to the First Step to Success program and the Motivational Interviewing Navigation Guide described in this book.

Stephanie Shepard is grateful to all the children, parents, and staff at the Head Start programs in Rhode Island (RI) who participated in her research and helped develop and pilot some of the methods and strategies described in this book. In particular, those at East Bay Community Action Program, Children's Friend and Service, and the Comprehensive Community Action Program of Cranston. Stephanie also acknowledges the outstanding team of research assistants and students at the Bradley/Hasbro Children's Research Center, and is particularly grateful to colleagues and trainees who made substantive contributions to the development and testing of the integration of family-, program-, and classroom-level check-ups with the Incredible Years programs, including Drs. Laura Armstrong, Lisa Costello, Leandra Godoy, Megan Beers, and Rebecca Silver. Finally, Stephanie is especially appreciative of mentors who influenced this work and who have supported her professional development. She thanks Drs. Carolyn Webster-Stratton, Tom Dishion, Elizabeth Stormshak, Ron Seifer, Nancy Eisenberg, and the late John Reid for their guidance, inspiration, encouragement, and generosity with their time and resources. The work that Stephanie describes in this book has been supported by a career development award from the National Institute of Mental Health and grants from the Substance Abuse and Mental Health Services Administration; the RI Department of Health; and the RI Department of Behavioral Healthcare, Developmental Disabilities and Hospitals.

# I

# Overview of Motivational Interviewing

# Background and Rationale

We all know from personal experience that adopting new behaviors and attitudes can be a complicated endeavor. Changing well-established personal behaviors, habits, and routines requires a great deal of commitment and persistence. Thus, it should come as no surprise to us to be met with pushback and resistance when we attempt to stimulate change in complex systems such as schools and families. These systems are composed of individuals with long-standing preferences and habits that have been reinforced, sometimes for years, by the context in which they occur. Expecting these behaviors to change simply because it makes sense to do so runs against the tide of behavioral patterns and usually only

> On a personal level, we know that changing a behavior is not often as easy as simply wanting to do so.

leads to frustration when the intended change never happens. Quite often, no amount of education, information exchange, or encouragement is enough to create enduring change in people.

Thus, many school professionals find themselves in a predicament, tasked with improving student outcomes by encouraging adults in their lives to behave differently. Administrators, school psychologists and consultants, special educators, teachers, instructional coaches, and behavior consultants encounter the challenge of trying to influence change at some point in the course of their work with others. If only it were enough to explain to a parent about research showing the benefits of being involved in education to produce an increase in his or her homework participation. If only it were as easy as telling a teacher about the importance of using high rates of specific praise in the classroom to alter their positive to negative ratio of interactions. On the other hand, if it were that easy, the challenges we encounter in schools would likely never have existed in the first place.

We actually know a lot about the types of environments that are healthy and that promote student learning and positive adjustment (see Biglan, Flay, Embry, & Sandler, 2012). The irony is that we have devoted most of our science to identifying the characteristics of nurturing environments and much less of it to figuring out how to get people to actually create them. It is as though we have assumed that people will change because it is logical to do so. In this sense, our science has lagged behind common sense. On a personal level, we know that changing a behavior is not often as easy as simply wanting to do so.

Fortunately, a strand of research has surfaced in the last two decades focused on this critical aspect of change. From this research comes a new perspective on motivation, an understanding of common factors that undermine readiness to change, and an approach to help move people toward change. The approach, called motivational interviewing (MI), has been developed to address barriers to motivation, foster compliance and engagement with services, and increase the likelihood that positive change will occur. This book is about the application of MI in schools.

## THE GOOD AND BAD NEWS

The good news is that if and when people want to change, we actually have a wide range of behavioral technologies to help them be successful. Unfortunately, for much of the 20th century, psychologists excluded from study one of the most important precursors to change: motivation. That is, behavior change technologies too often begin with the assumption that people are ready, willing, and able to change. The reality is that motivation to do anything fluctuates over time. Most people are ambivalent about changing their behavior. Consider these examples:

> The good news is that if and when people want to change, we actually have a wide range of behavioral technologies to help them be successful.

- A school psychologist checks in with a teacher on the progress of a behavior support plan in the classroom. The teacher responds, "I'm sorry I haven't gotten to it. It's the end of the school year, and we are in the midst of testing. Filling out these point sheets is not at the top of my list of things to do."
- A special educator wants to contact the parents of a student in her class to create a home–school communication system. A colleague who has worked with the parents in prior years tells her, "Good luck with those parents. They've never been involved. As far as I can tell, they just don't care."
- An administrator tries to meet with another parent to discuss ways the school could support her child. Despite setting up appointments to meet, the parent fails to attend the scheduled appointments twice in a row.
- A teacher is frustrated by the lack of effort from several of her students. She confronts them with the likely reality that they will be unable to achieve any

of their aspirations without being successful in school. Her warnings fall on deaf ears and the students she was trying to reach continue to neglect their homework.

Each of these situations involves an element of motivation. From the perspective of the school psychologist, special educator, teacher, and administrator, they have a plan they believe will work, if only the adult or student would implement it. It's as though they are at the mercy of happenstance and can do nothing but wait for the teacher, parent, or student to really want to change. In other words, often school professionals feel helpless to motivate others to actively engage in services.

## A MODERN VIEW OF MOTIVATION

A modern view of motivation, however, flips these assumptions about how and why people change on their head. In the modern approach, motivation is not dichotomous (i.e., either people are motivated or they are not) but rather it is dynamic and evolving. At noon, a teacher may be very motivated to improve his classroom-management skills after a morning of referring four students to the office for serious behavior violations. By the end of the day, that same teacher may be exhausted and thinking little about ways to improve the classroom environment. Similarly, a parent may be motivated to be involved in school matters after her child is suspended. Within a few days, though, her sense of energy toward changing the situation may be replaced by concerns at work or meeting the daily needs of her family.

> Motivation resides in an interpersonal and ecological context rather than simply dwelling inside the person.

In this conceptualization, motivation resides in an interpersonal and ecological context rather than simply dwelling inside the person. The world around us influences and shapes our desire to change. On some level, we all know this. We know that certain pictures or images can evoke motivational responses from us; some people put pictures of a beach on their mirror to motivate their diet or exercise behaviors, whereas others put prompts or verbal messages in their kitchen to spark their interest in eating healthfully. We also know the way we talk about things with others can influence how motivated we are to change. Think of a teenager whose parents regularly nag him about doing well in school, but who routinely does the opposite. The types of conversations we have with people who are considering change can have a strong influence over whether their interest in changing waxes or wanes. In the modern view of motivation, the more these conversations draw out of the person the reasons for wanting to change and the benefits of possible changes, the more likely it is that the motivation will persist. However, the more these conversations encourage the person to defend the status quo, essentially arguing against change, the less likely it is that change will occur.

## WHAT IS MI?

MI represents this modern view of motivation. MI attempts to help people resolve their ambivalence about behavior change by highlighting discrepancies between their values and their behaviors. It is grounded in social psychology research and client-centered counseling principles. A basic tenet of this approach is that people are much more likely to do things that they say they will do versus things they are told to do. The role of the consultant is to ask questions that make it more likely that the teacher or parent will talk about change (*change talk*) rather than spending much time telling them what to do. Effective questions ask about problems with the status quo ("What makes you concerned about your classroom right now?"), advantages of changing ("How would your life be better if you reduced disruptive classroom behaviors?"), disadvantages of not changing ("If you don't do anything, what might be some bad things that could happen?"), and intention to change ("How certain are you that you will follow through on this plan by next week?"). Conversely, arguing and telling the parent, student, or teacher the reasons they need to change generally has the opposite effect. A rule of thumb in this approach is if you hear yourself arguing for change, do something different. You want the parent, student, or teacher making that argument.

> A basic tenet of this approach is that people are much more likely to do things that they say they will do versus things they are told to do.

In a broader sense, MI approaches are also attentive to the well-established principles of effective brief interactions, denoted by the acronym FRAMES (Miller & Rollnick, 2002). These principles that can be useful in helping people become more motivated to change include the following: First, person-specific and individualized Feedback about their behavior can often be motivating to people. Daily-performance feedback toward a targeted goal is one example. For example, providing a teacher trying to increase his positive to negative ratio of interactions with information about the frequency of praise statements and reprimands that he uses based on direct observations can inspire continued improvement or satisfaction with progress. Second, leaving Responsibility for change with each individual is also important ("It's ultimately up to you whether you want to do anything about this problem."). Third, giving Advice selectively and only with permission can help people initiate the change process, especially when it is delivered within the context of a collaborative relationship. Fourth, if individuals express an interest in changing a behavior, providing them with a Menu of options can make it more likely that he or she will remain motivated ("There are several ways that other teachers have been successful in reducing disruptions. Let me tell you about a couple and you let me know which one sounds best to you."). Fifth, expressing Empathy throughout these discussions is essential to promoting their likelihood of moving forward. Sixth, supporting people's Self-efficacy, their belief that they can make the intended changes if they choose to do so, is another element of effective consultation. Two ways to do this are to note their current successes in changing ("How did you make that happen?") and to ask about times in the past that they have successfully managed challenging situations ("Tell me about the last time you had a disruptive class and how you were able to get control of it.").

## CHECK-UPS

Some specific consultation models based on MI have been developed in recent years for application in schools. These models are extensions of the classic "check-up" strategies that emerged in substance-use counseling in the 1990s (e.g., the "Drinker Check-Up"). Check-Ups are motivational enhancement approaches that employ all of the MI-related strategies to deliver personalized feedback about particular areas of functioning. Dishion and Kavanagh (2003) developed the Family Check-Up (FCU) to provide a platform for brief assessment and tailored feedback to foster parent motivation to access and participate in services. The original model was intended for use in school settings as part of a comprehensive school-wide model for working with families. More recently, Reinke and colleagues (2011) developed the Classroom Check-Up (CCU) as a brief motivational enhancement intervention for consulting with teachers about classroom behavior management skills. Check-Ups provide a method for using MI within an explicit framework for working with teachers, families, and youth in schools. Both the FCU and CCU involve two to three session meetings, ecological assessments, personalized feedback, and action planning based on the feedback. Each assumes that the foundation for motivating consultees to change is a collaborative relationship and attention is paid to the well-established factors that promote motivation, including those emphasized in MI.

## DOES IT WORK?

Aside from its intuitive appeal, the use of MI has blossomed during the past two decades in large part because of the vast evidence base that has been accumulated about it as a method for helping people change (Miller & Rollnick, 2013). The watershed moment occurred in the mid-1990s with the release of findings from the largest therapy study ever conducted, Project MATCH. MI was one of the three treatments in the study. As MI included far fewer sessions than the other two treatments, the study authors expected participants who received it to fare worse, except for those with less severe problems. In fact, they found those who received MI did as well as those in the other treatments, regardless of problem severity. Due to MI's brevity, researchers, clinicians, and policymakers latched onto it as an innovative method. Since that time, research on MI has mushroomed with over 200 randomized trials now supporting its efficacy in a wide variety of settings (Miller & Rollnick, 2002, 2013). Moreover, MI has been extended to address a seemingly limitless array of problems in health care settings, the corrections system, and education. In one of its most novel applications, Thevos (2000) found that MI could be used to improve the likelihood of water purification practices in east African villages. The common thread of applications has been to any problem where compliance or adherence is an issue; in other words, virtually any situation that requires human change.

In education settings, several studies have now showed that MI-based interventions improve outcomes for parents, teachers, and students (see Reinke, Herman, & Sprick, 2011, 2010; Stormshak & Dishion, 2002; Strait et al., 2012). Furthermore, because it can be used alone or as a tool for connecting parents, teachers, and students to other evidence-based interventions, MI is a value-added method. Simply increasing participation in high-quality services (such as teacher or parent training programs) by fostering motivation to do so is a valued outcome in itself. Finally, the use of MI as a strategy for promoting everyday conversations about change is supported by the wealth of research on the importance of the helping relationship. Over 1,500 studies conducted during the past half century have repeatedly confirmed that the most important determinant of successful consultation or counseling interventions is the quality of the relationship between the consultant and the consultee (see Bergin & Garfield, 1994). It is one of the most consistent findings in research. The effect of the relationship quality on outcomes dwarfs the effects of other factors, including the model or type of approach (e.g., behaviorism, cognitive, psychodynamic). As you will see, the foundation of MI is a collaborative, respectful relationship in line with these findings.

## WHAT IS THE PURPOSE OF THIS BOOK?

This book is intended to foster everyday conversations about change in schools. It is designed to provide practice guidelines for any school professional who attempts to build engagement in school-based supports and services. This includes any professional working on school-based support teams in which parent, student, or staff involvement is required for success. The goal is to provide a useful model for consultation that will lead to increased use of effective practices in schools.

Additionally, we aim to describe ways to connect these skills and strategies to other established behavior support and parenting programs such as the Incredible Years Series, Positive Behavior Interventions and Supports, First Step to Success, and programs in the Safe and Civil Schools Series. These strategies also can be used to combine motivational principles with academic and instructional programs.

Part I provides an overview of MI and related engagement strategies. Chapter 2 describes contextual strategies that promote willingness to attend meetings or engage in consultation discussions. As MI requires that people actually attend meetings or become willing to have conversations, Chapter 2 provides methods for successfully accessing consultees. Chapter 3 describes specific MI techniques that can be used across school contexts. We provide a summary of the evidence base underlying MI and then describe specific MI-related strategies. Additionally, this part provides details about the critical elements of effective feedback and support planning that may lead to increased engagement.

Part II describes applications of MI for specific targeted participants. Separate chapters describe using MI with parents, teachers, and students. Additionally, we provide a detailed description of the FCU as an example of a structured MI-based model that integrates parent, teacher, and student perspectives.

Additionally, Chapter 8 in Part II describes a model for using MI to support the activities of school-based problem-solving teams.

Part III discusses other aspects of implementation and dissemination. We describe efforts to integrate MI with other evidence-based practices and programs. We also describe methods for monitoring fidelity of implementation to ensure that the school staff implements MI strategies correctly.

This book is intended to produce five primary outcomes: (a) describe research-based strategies for building teacher, parent, and student engagement in school-based services; (b) identify consultation skills related to MI, providing objective feedback, and using data to tailor interventions to the specific needs of parents, teachers, and students; (c) illustrate in explicit detail effective consultation models based in MI for supporting teachers, parents, and students; (d) identify methods for infusing MI into other school-based intervention models; and (e) define procedures for building the capacity to implement MI within a school or across an entire district.

## FOR WHOM IS THIS BOOK WRITTEN?

This book is written for educational personnel (school psychologists, consultants, special educators, behavior specialists, teachers, and others) who consult with individuals within the school, where motivation and engagement are important. The book also has value for administrators and school-based teams who have the task of designing effective behavior support systems and resources for students in their building or district.

> This book is intended to help any school professional have *more effective everyday conversations about change.*

We intend the book to be useful for two levels of MI skill development. First, this book is intended to help any school professional have *more effective everyday conversations about change.* The principles of MI apply in every interaction in which changing behavior is of interest. Ignoring these principles or acting counter to them increases the probability that school professionals will have unsatisfying conversations about change. However, attending to and adopting the principles of MI even in small ways is likely to positively shift the nature of these conversations. In this regard, any school professional can benefit from reading and applying the spirit of MI along with some of the strategies that align with it. Throughout the text, we have included pullout examples, called *Everyday Conversations About Change,* to illustrate the use of MI principles in very brief encounters that occur during a typical school day.

Second, many school professionals will already have a solid foundation in basic listening skills and effective consultation. For these professionals, the book is intended to sharpen their consultation skills, allowing them to target areas for further professional development. Some of these school professionals may want to invest more time in becoming fully fluent in an MI-consistent mode of consultation and to use it as a structured clinical technique. The detailed descriptions of the various Check-Up approaches provide a useful framework for applying a structured MI approach. Additionally, Chapter 11 describes further steps and additional resources in developing fluency in MI as a clinical technique.

## A CAVEAT

After learning of our work with MI, a colleague encouraged us to write a book about how to motivate anyone to do anything. Although this would be useful (and likely a best seller!) it calls to mind a secretive, manipulative approach to world dominance. The methods described in this book are not a magical elixir nor are they intended to solve all problems. Rather, these methods are best used as part of a broader consultation relationship.

> MI strategies only work in the context of a supportive relationship.

As we will repeat regularly throughout the book, MI strategies only work in the context of a supportive relationship. The foundation of MI work is referred to as the "spirit of MI" (Miller & Rollnick, 2013). Part of this spirit involves trusting that the people who you consult with will make the best decisions for themselves. Becoming overly attached to a single-minded goal (e.g., getting a parent to attend school meetings) is counter to an MI approach and likely will undermine the relationship. Compassion is another critical aspect of the MI spirit, that is, an abiding concern about the welfare and interests of the person with whom you are consulting. This aspect of MI is what distinguishes it from self-interested socially manipulative practices such as those found in sales and advertising.

Aside from the specific techniques of MI, there are foundational qualities and skills that are prerequisites for effective consultation. As noted above, one finding repeatedly observed in the helping literature is that the strongest predictor of whether consultation will be helpful is the quality of the relationship rather than specific methods and models. Not surprisingly, the attitudes, personal qualities, and style of the consultant play a major role in whether helping alliances form. The same is true in virtually any successful consultation relationship, be it counseling and supporting families, consulting with teachers, or guiding students. Thus, a key place to start with any consultation model is awareness of these relationship-building qualities.

We discuss how these qualities facilitate effective consultation in greater detail throughout the book. We conceptualize these factors in a hierarchical manner with some serving as the foundation for increasingly complex skills.

## MI PLUS WHAT?

A final important point is that although MI in itself is a great approach to help people move forward with plans to change, it may not be enough. For many people, this gentle push may evoke significant behavior changes. Keep in mind, however, that many people will also need help in making the desired change. In other words, motivation and intention to change are only one part of the equation, albeit a very important part. The other part involves the skills needed to make the change happen. A consultant may be effective in using MI to get a teacher to *want* to improve her instructional pacing, but the teacher may not know *how* to do it. Thus, another part of being an effective consultant is knowing how to help people produce the changes they want to see. Understanding the theory and research behind how best to help people make changes once they have decided to do so is a necessity for a well-rounded consultant. The behavior technology knowledge base is comprehensive and beyond the scope of this book. However, there are many resources that can be helpful to a consultant and even to a parent or teacher if they prefer to work on developing the skills alone. These additional resources will be listed throughout the book for each topical area.

# Getting Your Foot in the Door:
# The Context of Motivation

Motivational interviewing (MI) occurs in the context of conversation; thus, it requires that people be willing and able to engage in social interaction. Unfortunately, many of the less involved families, teachers, and students are inaccessible in some way, either unwilling or unable to attend school meetings or simply unwilling or unable to talk about change. A prerequisite for reaching these individuals so as to have more effective interactions with them is to create a broader context that invites conversations about change.

Engaging stakeholders (i.e., parents, teachers, students, etc.) in any initiative requires collaboration. At the end of the day, successful initiatives depend on proactively building relationships at every level of a system and involving stakeholders in decision making, rather than imposing an initiative on them or waiting until problems arise to establish relationships. To build relationships with stakeholders, we need to attend to the myriad motivational, cognitive, and pragmatic barriers that individuals face when presented with the potential for change.

In this chapter, we present a model for examining the common contextual barriers to change in schools and for overcoming these barriers. As will be a recurring theme in this book, the personal qualities of the consultant or liaisons for the school are the foundation for successful invitations and discussions about change. We describe some of these qualities in this chapter and will revisit them in subsequent chapters. We also introduce literature that provides carefully documented methods for reaching even the most challenging families in order to get our foot in the door and to initiate meaningful conversations about change.

## A MODEL FOR CONSIDERING CONTEXTUAL BARRIERS TO MOTIVATION

Contextual barriers to motivation can exist at every level of a system. When thinking about motivation, we typically only focus on the individual subsystem. That is, the within-person factors that contribute to motivation, like whether an individual *wants* to do it. As noted in Chapter 1, a common misconception is the belief that motivation is an internal process that only can be altered by an individual's active decision to change. In fact, an individual's motivation to do anything is dynamic and always exists in a context influenced by the setting, interactions with others, and messages he or she receives about change. MI attempts to capitalize on this dynamic by interacting in ways that elicit motivation from others, and thereby increasing the probability that change will occur.

## MOTIVATIONAL BARRIERS AT SCHOOL

Many potential contextual, relational, and intrapersonal barriers may be present within schools that can interfere with the likelihood of these new motivating interactions ever taking place. Take a moment to reflect on the following questions, and try to think of at least two or three responses for each:

> One valid reason a teacher, parent, or student might have for not talking about change is that the person offering to listen has predetermined that he or she has no interest in changing.

- What are some valid reasons that a parent may decide not to become involved at school?
- Why might a teacher legitimately decide not to work with an instructional coach?
- Why might a student appropriately decide not to talk to a school consultant?

We asked you to reflect on "valid" and "legitimate" reasons so that we could take off the table any variant of the response "because they don't care." For any effective conversation about change to occur, the consultant or listener has to begin with the assumption that people do care. Inviting someone to have a conversation about change when we have already decided that the person really has no intention to do so is a waste of time. People know when they are being judged, and they will decide rightly not to accept invitations offered under this pretense. Therefore, one valid reason a teacher, parent, or student might have for not talking about change is that the person offering to listen has predetermined that he or she has no interest in changing.

There are many other legitimate reasons. A reasonable list might include the following:

- Lack of trust
- Past negative experiences with… (the educational or mental health systems)
- Not feeling valued, like a member of the team
- Language barriers
- Lack of support from other family members, teachers, and/or friends

- Lack of support from providers to carve out the time
- Not knowing what to say or do
- Lack of appreciation for the importance of parent involvement, school success, or coaching
- Competing or incompatible agendas
- Cultural beliefs about the roles of parents, teachers, or children
- Lack of available time and competing demands (yours and theirs)
- Lack of awareness or understanding when problems arise
- Lack of shared problem definition and/or shared understanding as to whose problem it is to solve
- Parent, teacher, or student stress or mental health issues (e.g., depression)
- Low expectations that involvement will actually help

We can think of all these reasons as barriers to getting our foot in the door to have conversations about change. Many of these barriers are perceptual and historical. For instance, parents' decisions about whether to become involved in school are influenced by their past interactions with school professionals, their own experiences as students in school, messages they have received from society about their role in schools, and their beliefs about whether being an active participant will make a difference. If the parents have only had prior negative interactions with teachers, they might legitimately want to avoid having these interactions occur again. If a student has tried talking to a school consultant in the past but did not find it helpful, this would be a valid reason for not seeking out the consultant in the future. Overcoming perceptual barriers requires the formation of new perceptions.

Other barriers have to do with constraints on time, money, and resources. For instance, many parents and teachers might be willing to engage in these conversations, but life circumstances prevent them. A parent may not be able to take time off work or arrange child care to make it to school, or teachers may not have any time during their workday to meet with a consultant. Still other barriers include lack of skills or information. If parents do not know how to become involved in school, if teachers don't receive training on how to effectively engage parents, and/or if parents, teachers, or students don't know how to seek help or use available resources, then they are unlikely to do so.

Considering reasons why people might avoid change conversations, and acknowledging they are valid, gives us some clues to the most immediate causes of their decisions to act. If we understand the causes, we can identify barriers and tailor our solutions.

## UNIFIED THEORY OF BEHAVIOR CHANGE

A helpful way of thinking about all of these influences on behavior is with a widely used and studied model called the unified theory of behavior change (UTB). Many years ago, the National Institutes of Health commissioned a panel to combine all existing theories of behavior change into a single integrated model resulting in the creation of the UTB (see Jaccard, Dodge, & Dittus, 2002; Olin et al., 2010). In this well-supported framework, many factors determine

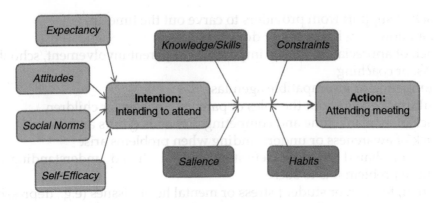

**Figure 2.1** Unified Theory of Behavior Change.

whether or not people decide to change their behavior and also whether they are ultimately successful in doing so. Figure 2.1 presents the most important determinants of behavior change.

## Building Intention to Act

As we are focused on getting our foot in the door in this chapter, the behavior of interest may be attending a school meeting, which indicates willingness to have a conversation about change. The most immediate cause of a person attending a meeting is his or her intention to do so. This book is about building people's intention to engage in a desired behavior, which in turn builds the likelihood that they will take action. A primary goal of MI is to foster intention and commitment to change. The four factors on the left side of Figure 2.1—expectancy, attitudes, social norms, and self-efficacy—all directly influence a person's intention to act and thus are primary targets of MI.

### Expectancies

Prominent among these are people's beliefs and expectancies about the behavior. When we personally believe that a behavior has a high likelihood of benefit if we engage in it, we are more likely to intend to perform that behavior. Moreover, intention is increased when we perceive the relative cost of engaging in the behavior as lower than the expected benefit. So a person's intention to attend a meeting is in part determined by whether he or she personally believes that attending will yield positive results. A parent who has to take time off from work and arrange child care to attend a school meeting has to believe that the potential benefit of doing so will exceed the time, effort, and money expended to get there.

> A person's intention to attend a meeting is in part determined by whether he or she personally believes that attending will yield positive results.

Therefore, one key consideration as we create environments to invite change is to find ways to reduce the costs associated with the new behavior while increasing its perceived benefits. Sticking with the example of getting a parent to attend a school meeting, actions to reduce costs might include arranging the meeting outside of school hours and providing child care and transportation. Building beliefs about likely benefits might involve explicitly communicating possible benefits, asking parents who have had positive experiences with meetings to communicate these with other parents, and so on.

## Attitudes

Related to expectancies about success, our attitudes about a behavior influence our intention to engage in it. If we believe a behavior is desirable and accept-able, it is more likely that we will consider doing it, certainly more so than if we view the behavior in a less positive light. A parent who believes that it is not his or her place to attend school meetings (perhaps because of cultural beliefs or past experiences)

> If we believe a behavior is desirable and acceptable, it makes it more likely we will consider doing it.

will probably not participate. Likewise, a teacher who does not see it as his or her role to address behavior problems in the classroom will be unlikely to work on improving classroom-management skills. Our attitudes about the topic of conversation or the potential outcomes of the behavior are also influ-ential. Talking about behavior problems or the emotional adjustment of their child will tap parents' attitudes about mental health. If parents have stigma associated with mental health concerns or treatment or have had negative past interactions with mental health providers, they will be less inclined to engage in conversations about these related topics. If we do not directly address these perceptions in our efforts to involve parents, the likelihood of parent involve-ment decreases.

## Social Norms

Returning to Figure 2.1, another key influence on intention includes the person's perception of social norms; that is, the belief that others perceive the person's behavior as typical and acceptable. If parents believe that the social norm is for parents to attend meetings, they are more likely to attend. They make this estimate of social norms based on their perceptions of key opinion groups that matter most to them. Often this means they estimate the opin-ions of their closest friends and family. Our perception of social norms are also influenced by broader messages, especially from the media. To the extent these messages convey to us that the behavior is acceptable or desired, we are more likely to intend to engage in the behavior. Unfortunately, the social-norm messages many people receive hinder their intention to participate in school-based discussions of change. For instance, some parents, especially those whose participation is most needed, believe that it is not typical or acceptable to talk about change at school.

## Self-Efficacy

Peoples' self-efficacy, or the belief that they can actually engage in the targeted behavior if they so choose, directly influences their intention to act. Students who believe that they can have a productive conversation with an adult about a new behavior and that they can directly influence the outcome of such conversations are more likely to engage in them. Conversely, when students believe that the outcome of the conversation will be predetermined (i.e., that they don't have influence), it should not surprise us that they are unwilling participants in conversations.

Consideration of all of these factors can help us understand barriers to change and also suggest ways to restructure environments and practices in ways that support change. As we will discuss in subsequent chapters, MI directly targets all of these precursors to intention and captures them under the umbrella term "change talk."

## Constraints, Skills, Salience, and Habits

Even when intention exists, there are several other potential influences that might interfere with action. These factors are depicted in Figure 2.1 by lines that intersect the arrow from Intention to Action. Notable among these are environmental *constraints* that make the behavior change difficult, if not impossible. For instance, many parents work during school hours and are penalized for taking time off from work; thus, even if a parent fully intends to attend school meetings, this environmental constraint may make it impossible for the parent to actually engage in the behavior. Common constraints for parents include work, child care, and transportation. For teachers, a major constraint is time. Teachers have increasingly limited time for self-reflection or supportive coaching conversations, as their free time is filled with planning or paperwork. Likewise, many teachers feel like they have little time to focus on improving their relationships with parents.

> Often we mistake lack of skill for low intention or motivation. A good place to start is with the assumption that parents, students, and teachers may simply need support in acquiring new knowledge or skills for the behavior to occur.

Other potential factors that could undermine an intention to change include skill or performance deficits, salience, and habits. Thus, a person may decide to change a behavior but *lack the knowledge or skills* for how to do it. For example, a parent may decide to become more involved in school but may have no model for what effective involvement looks like. If his or her parents had not been involved in school or if their involvement was ineffective (e.g., conflictual relationships with school professionals, nagging a child about homework, excessively punishing a child for school failures), their good intentions will be unlikely to result in effective behavior change. Likewise, a teacher may intend to change his or her classroom management but lack the skills or knowledge to be successful with the intended change. A student may want to talk to someone about a problem but may not know how to access resources, or he or she may intend to get better grades but lack the organizational skills to do so.

When people intend to change but lack the knowledge or skills to make it happen, school professionals need to be prepared to accurately assess this and provide the supports necessary to facilitate the process (i.e., provide the knowledge and/or help them develop the skills). Often we mistake lack of skill for low intention or motivation. A good place to start is with the assumption that parents, students, and teachers may simply need support in acquiring new knowledge or skills for the behavior to occur. Mislabeling skill or knowledge deficits as lack of intention only serves to undermine relationship building, effective conversations about change, and behavior change.

*Salience* refers to the perceived prominence of the behavior. Essentially, a person may intend to engage in a behavior but if it does not stand out to him or her as memorable or important relative to other intentions in the moment when action is required, it is unlikely to be enacted. Without prompts or reminder calls, some parents who initially intended to attend a school meeting may not have attended simply because the behavior was not salient relative to their other commitments or concerns at the time of the meeting.

Finally, enduring *habits* may interfere with the successful implementation of an intended behavior. Parents may intend to attend a school meeting but may forget because of enduring habits and routines, of which attendance at school is not one. Changing teaching behaviors can be disrupted by enduring classroom-management habits such as using a loud voice and reprimanding students when misbehavior occurs. Changing these habits requires persistence and planning that disrupts behavior patterns that are automatic and routine, but not desired.

Attending to all of these factors increases our likelihood of accessing people in ways that may lead to helpful conversations about change. The bottom line implication of this model is that if we want to make conversations about change accessible to more people, we must be attentive to their perceptions and attitudes about us, the environment (the school), the behavior (attending a meeting), and the likelihood of success along with constraints that may interfere with their intention to act.

In the remainder of this chapter, we examine barriers to change conversations and strategies to overcome these barriers within this framework. We spend most of the chapter focusing on engaging parents and families as the literature is more robust for this population. However, the principles apply equally well to students and teachers.

## PROVIDING A CONTEXT FOR PARENT ENGAGEMENT IN SCHOOL

Schools are ideal for proactive identification and recruitment of families who would benefit from family-centered supports. Embedding these services for families in schools addresses some key barriers to parent engagement because schools are, for many caretakers, a familiar and trusted service delivery system. The feelings of safety and community fostered in schools can be leveraged to increase parent access to, and reduce stigma associated with, these services.

Yet, family-support services delivered in schools are often characterized by low involvement and high attrition rates. Typically, only a small percentage of parents become involved, and even fewer follow through to completion due to inconsistent attendance, poor compliance, and/or premature dropout. Substantial time and resources are therefore wasted supporting underused services, diminishing the promise of this approach in schools. In addition, participation barriers present in high-risk, multiproblem families impede the participation of families most in need of services. Parents' lack of engagement remains a major obstacle to their fully realizing the benefits of school-support services.

## Reflecting on Parents

A good place to start in considering the context of parent motivation at your school is to first reflect on a common parent experience. How does a parent feel when approached with questions or concerns about his or her child? Take a moment to list several feelings that being approached by a teacher might elicit (or does elicit, if you have experienced this directly).

Parents experience a wide range of feelings when approached about concerns with their child. The first emotional reactions are usually negative. Common emotions are listed in Table 2.1.

Parents worry about their children and want them to be successful. News that their child is not succeeding can arouse strong emotions, and often these emotions can be mixed. Parents may be worried about their child and angry with the child at the same time. They might be embarrassed and sense that the teacher is judging them to be bad parents. They might be angry with the teacher for not helping the child be more successful. The news is surely disappointing to them, and many feel helpless as to how to make things better.

> When people think about effective helpers during times of distress, the qualities they mention are nearly universal.

**Table 2.1 Common Emotional Reactions When Parents Hear Concerns About Their Child**

| | |
|---|---|
| Overwhelmed | Uncertain |
| Confused | Worried |
| Judged | Angry |
| Hopeless | Embarrassed |
| Blamed | Frustrated |
| Pressured | Punished |
| Dismayed | Skeptical |
| Stressed | Disappointed |

Now think about times in your life when you have experienced a range of upsetting emotions, and think about what you needed from others in your life during these times. Most people would say that they needed others to listen and show empathy for their situation. They wanted to be respected and supported to get through it.

When people think about effective helpers during times of distress, the qualities they mention are nearly universal. We have asked literally thousands of people from around the country to reflect on individuals who have made a difference in their lives, who have helped them through a difficult period, and they nearly always generate the same list. A sample list is given in Table 2.2.

What are the implications then for how we approach parents, especially when inviting them to discuss difficult topics? The more that we can convey these qualities of effective helpers, the more likely the parent will be willing to talk with us and learn to trust us. By focusing on strengths rather than deficits and by approaching parents collaboratively, we can facilitate positive interactions with families. MI provides a structure that increases the likelihood that conversations about change begin collaboratively, and with a keen awareness that a strong relationship is critical for behavior change.

## Strategies for Building Collaborative Relationships With Families

A definition of parent engagement in school we find most helpful comes from the National Association for the Education of Young Children (NAEYC), which defines *parent engagement* as an *ongoing, reciprocal, strengths-based, collaborative partnership* that promotes a shared responsibility for observation, decision making, and action. Supporting students' school success requires strong collaboration and frequent communication with families. The foundation for these relationships starts with the family's very first contact with the school and is encouraged by maintaining an inviting environment in which families are made by all personnel to feel welcome, supported, and valued as members of the school community. From the beginning of the year, facilitating positive relationships with families will pave the way for effective collaboration to promote positive outcomes and determine ways to intervene, should difficulties arise.

**Table 2.2 Qualities of Effective Helpers**

| | |
|---|---|
| • Nonjudgmental/accepting | • Curious |
| • Empathetic | • Asks reflective questions |
| • Caring | • Honest |
| • High expectations | • Believed in your potential |
| • Good listener | • Tenacious, persistent |
| • Genuine | • Self-assured |
| • Encouraging | • Credible |

### Start of the Year

From the outset, school staff members play a key role in engaging parents by helping them recognize the ways in which their child's school success is linked to parent involvement. Parents are more likely to engage when their involvement is not only encouraged and welcomed, but also expected. This addresses the issue of establishing a school-wide and community-wide norm about parent participation

> Parents are more likely to engage when their involvement is not only encouraged and welcomed, but also expected.

in school. This can be accomplished by explicitly communicating that expectation through newsletters and conversations with parents, by telling parents the acceptable and most beneficial ways for them to be involved, and providing support and encouragement for effective involvement.

One important strategy is to build a shared vision of success for both parents and school personnel. Parents and teachers have an equal stake in child and school outcomes. Focusing attention on these overlapping goals can build and sustain positive relationships.

Another strategy is to collect surveys from parents and/or conduct "get to know you" home visits to learn about the child and family (e.g., child's likes and dislikes, school and developmental histories, routines, cultural practices, family members, expectations of the teacher and school). This sends the message that school staff care about the child and are concerned about the family. Arranging home visits or other positive interactions at the beginning of the year can help families feel welcomed, valued, encouraged, and supported from the outset. School personnel often say that such visits are not possible in today's environment either because of lack of time or, in some settings, safety concerns. However, nearly every teacher we have talked to who has made this effort at the beginning of the year reports that the effort reaps great benefits for the remainder of the year.

During these early visits, treat the family as the experts on the child by eliciting their wealth of information and tips they have for supporting the child. Discuss systemic issues that might interfere with home–school communication and problem-solving ways to overcome these barriers (e.g., preferred mode of communication, access to phone or Internet). Encourage classroom visits and parent volunteering, but be sure to give parents specifics on your preferences for when, where, and how to engage in these behaviors. Also keep in mind that families who have input into decision making about their child's ongoing experiences in the classroom and are treated as valued members of a team are more likely to engage in discussion and planning when concerns arise.

It can also be helpful to have resources available to support parents in getting their needs met. These resources can include information on how parents can be effective participants in school. For instance, provide them with tips for how they can engage with teachers or make the most out of parent–teacher conferences. Many such tip sheets have been developed and are readily available on the Internet (see Table 2.3 for some examples). Some parent-devoted space for sharing and distributing these informational resources also conveys a sense

**Table 2.3 Sample Websites With Tip Sheets for Parents**

The SERVE Center: http://center.serve.org/tt/fp_tips.html

Reading Tip Sheets from Colorín Colorado: http://www.colorincolorado.org/guides/
readingtips

Circle of Parents: http://www.circleofparents.org/parent_resources/index.html

Parent–Teacher Conference Tip Sheet: http://www.hfrp.org/publications-resources/
browse-our-publications/parent-teacher-conference-tip-sheets-hojas-de-consejos-para-
las-reuniones-de-padres-y-maestros

Centers for Disease Control: http://www.cdc.gov/ncbddd/childdevelopment/positive-
parenting/adolescence2.html

Parenting Adolescents: http://www.ahwg.net/knowledgebase/nodates.
php?pid=80&tpid=4

that parents are welcome and that schools are a place that parents and families can be supported. Also keep in mind that many families will need support to overcome basic pragmatic barriers to engagement, like child care, transportation, and translation services.

All of these strategies connect back to the spirit of MI. The context that schools provide to parents sends messages about behaviors that are expected and whether parent participation is welcome and encouraged. When done well, this sets the stage for parents to be more willing to engage in conversations about change if and when they need to occur.

### Frequent Positive Communication

Regular communication with parents to share positive news sets a supportive foundation for when contacts may be needed regarding concerns. Keep in mind that it is easier to approach and address concerns with the family when you already have a relationship built on trust and shared positive experiences. It is essential that schools communicate more positive news than negative news to families. If a parent is only contacted when there are problems at school, he or she will come to see school and their involvement with school as aversive. Instead, set goals for yourself and for all staff in the building to communicate at least two positives for every negative to every parent in the school. In the UTB model, this serves to change attitudes and correct past misperceptions about parent involvement by replacing negative perceptions with new positive associations.

Carolyn Webster-Stratton (Webster-Stratton & Reid, 2010) describes the importance of building up the ratio of positive to negative interactions with regard to school and student interactions. This applies to school and family communication as well. Think of your interactions with each parent as a piggy bank. For every positive interaction you have with the parent, you make a deposit into

> Think of your interactions with each parent as a piggy bank. For every positive interaction you have with the parent, you make a deposit into the relationship bank account. Every negative interaction or feedback requires a withdrawal.

the relationship bank account. Every negative interaction or feedback requires a withdrawal. If you make more withdrawals than deposits, you can damage your relationship with the parent and make it less likely that he or she will be responsive to your current or future feedback.

Examples of positive communication include contacting parents on a regular basis to give positive feedback of the child's progress and performance and frequent notes home reinforcing student progress and noting parent effort (see Handout 2.1 for a sample form). Parents who receive this feedback are typically more committed to promoting learning opportunities at home and addressing problems that emerge.

Encourage communications at home about school—for example, post a "topic of the day" (in classroom, at drop off/pick up, on Facebook, daily e-mails, etc.)—and encourage family members to talk about the topic with the child. One effective strategy is to send home Table Talk notes that encourage conversations at home about topics the child is learning about at school (see Handout 2.2 for an example). Establish alternative modes of communication when in-person contacts are not possible (e-mail, listservs, Facebook/Twitter updates, 24-hour phone lines, texting, parent blogs, podcasts, or other forms of online meetings, etc.) that provide regular information on activities in the classroom.

Offer a variety of activities and opportunities from which parents can choose to participate beyond volunteering in the classroom. For example, we have found that establishing ways to encourage parent-to-parent connections within the school can be one effective way to build parents' view of the school as a welcoming and supportive environment and can motivate parent involvement. This includes having identified space for informal contacts, such as a parent resource center or "parent hub," and facilitating opportunities such as scheduling informal coffee hours, organizing fun family activities or other social events as well as educational opportunities for parents, or establishing parent leadership committees. Of course, putting notices of such events in newsletters or sending home flyers to parents will encourage some parent participation. However, we have found that parent participation greatly increases when parents receive more personalized invitations from teachers or other school staff. A note home or a call to a parent with a personal endorsement ("I have been to this before and found..." or "Other parents who have gone to this before tell me..."), a description of its personal relevance ("I thought you would enjoy this because I remember you told me..." or "I think you would find this helpful because..."), or reassurance that familiar others will be present ("I am going, too!") could make all the difference for a parent.

## ENGAGING PARENTS IN SUPPORT SERVICES AT SCHOOLS

When problems arise or students need extra support in school for academic or behavioral concerns, engaging parents in a plan to support the student becomes a key factor in determining how successful the plan can be. Establishing collaborative relationships with all parents early in the year increases the likelihood that these inevitable conversations about concerns will be helpful. Remember, parents will vary with respect to their readiness to address concerns. Their readiness will depend on the severity of the concern, their awareness of the concern, their beliefs about the need to take action, their perception of their role in the process (vs. the role of the teachers or system), their abilities as a parent to support problem resolution, support from family and friends, and their beliefs about available services. Parents have a host of existing beliefs about recommended services for their child: Can the educator or provider delivering the service be trusted? Does the service work? Are the expectations about the level of parent involvement reasonable? Moreover, any past experiences they have had with getting help and any competing demands, including the parents' own mental health/stress, will impact how receptive they will be to initial conversations about change.

## Establishing Positive Local Norms and Expectations About Supportive Services

Schools often miss opportunities for parents to participate in supportive services for their child due to how the service is marketed. Supportive services might include meeting with the school consultant, psychologist, or behavior support team; attending a behavior or academic support meeting; attending a parenting group; and any specific groups and services provided to the student during the school day. The labels we use to describe supportive

> Marketing literature clearly shows that an effective strategy for getting people to use a product or access a service is to have a respected person's endorsement.

services send a message to parents and can make it more or less likely they will use the service. What do you call the supportive services that are delivered and the person delivering the services? When considering the label for services, focus on better outcomes rather than using problem-focused language or words such as "treatment" or "intervention." The label should focus on promoting child health and wellness and include terms such as "family support" or "parent consultant."

Consider how to market the service. Involving parents as liaisons to communicate positive expectations and beliefs about the service can establish positive social norms and attitudes regarding participation. One strategy some schools have used successfully is to establish a parent engagement team tasked with finding ways to bolster parent engagement and effectively market family services offered within schools. Parents who have already participated in and benefitted from a school-based service or support are excellent candidates for spreading the word.

Marketing literature clearly indicates that an effective strategy for getting people to use a product or access a service is to have a respected person's endorsement. This can be accomplished in very brief interactions. In one successful program, teachers were asked to endorse a particular service, such as a referral to a parent consultant or a school psychologist, in a 5-minute conversation about what the service was, why the teacher believed it would be helpful, and experiences other parents have had with the service (Winslow, Poloskov, Begay, & Sandler, 2011).

Asking people to make a commitment through words or writing is also an effective strategy for getting buy-in. For instance, you might ask parents to sign a form indicating their interest in being part of the service. A formal registration form with preferred times and days for attending the service along with a signature line confirming their commitment to be involved in the service makes their attendance more likely. Combining this with the power of social influence, a good strategy would be to ask parents to sign the registration form immediately after hearing the endorsement from a teacher or parent.

Creating a brochure or newsletter that describes school services can also influence parents' decisions about whether to become involved. Including testimonials about the benefits of the service from other parents can be particularly persuasive in affecting parents' attitudes about participating and developing new perceptions about the normative value of the behavior. See Handout 2.3 for an example of a poster that incorporates many of these marketing principles.

## Effective Communication Skills

Engaging families in services requires effective communication skills on the part of school personnel. We summarize these skills with the acronym LEAP (*l*isten, *e*mpathize, *a*void blame, *p*artner), which we adapted from Amador and Johanson (2000) and Romanelli, Ramos, and Burton (2008; see Table 2.4).

*Listening* involves an attitude of respect and a willingness to truly understand the parent's perspective. A good rule of thumb for whether you are listening: you should be talking less than the person to whom you are trying to listen. You can also indicate that you are listening by inviting feedback and genuinely hearing suggestions and reactions of the parent, while appreciating that the parent is the expert on the child. Involving parents in the problem definition as well as decision making and planning requires listening and respecting their knowledge about their child's developmental history, strengths, and needs across contexts.

*Empathize* refers to honoring, respecting, and supporting the parent's perspective and appreciating the challenges of his or her circumstances, including the difficulties of parenting. Always consider your reflections above about how the parent might be feeling when faced with child or family problems, as well as the qualities of effective helpers we outlined previously. At its core, empathizing involves respecting parent's wishes for the child and respecting the family's cultural practices. It is important to be aware of culturally bound practices and communication styles to approach families in respectful ways. Remember that there are many ways to define a family, and recognize and support the

**Table 2.4 LEAP Communication Skills**

| L | Listen, collect information |
|---|---|
| E | Empathize |
| A | Avoid blame, judgment, giving unsolicited advice |
| P | Partner |

**Table 2.5** Adaptive Assumptions About Families (From Michigan Department of Education)

- All families have strengths and need to know they are important
- All families can contribute to their child's out-of-home care and education
- All families can learn how to promote their child's learning and development
- All families have useful ideas and insights about their child
- All families really do care deeply about their children

involvement of all relevant family members (e.g., siblings, grandparents, aunts, uncles, cousins, etc.). Be a support to families beyond caring for their child, such as helping families get assistance with basic needs and immediate, practical concerns. If you can't answer their questions, help identify who can.

*Avoiding* blame, judging, and giving unsolicited advice helps foster a collaborative relationship. Be aware of how your own assumptions, attitudes, beliefs, and biases influence your work with parents. Take time to reflect on your own biases about parenting and about a particular parent or family. One strategy is to remind yourself of some proactive positive beliefs about all families. You might stick this on your desk and read it prior to each of your meetings with families. Some mantras that you can use to prepare yourself for a proper perspective include assumptions set forth by the Michigan Department of Education (see Table 2.5).

Also, it is important to avoid premature problem solving. Instead, be an active listener and always ask permission prior to giving advice. "I have some thoughts about this. Do you want to hear more?" Of course, it is not your role to have all the answers; a supportive approach involves wondering *with* families rather than resolving *for* families.

Finally, *partnering* refers to your efforts to be truly collaborative with a family. It requires giving families the opportunity to take part in all levels of decision making related to the care and education of their child. It may also involve imparting knowledge about development, as appropriate, to help families make sense of their child's behavior and to inform their decision-making process. Providing parents with information and supplies for activities that families can do together at home or in the community to extend what children are learning in school is also a form of partnering. Engaging the entire school staff in welcoming families conveys a sense of partnership. Remember, family engagement is everyone's responsibility, requiring strong partnerships among bus drivers, front-office staff, teachers, school consultants, administrators, and parents.

## Strategies for Accessing the Most Challenging Families

The first contact with a family about a school-based concern and an invitation to participate in a service or plan to support the student sets the stage for whether the parent will consider becoming involved. School personnel who initiate these first conversations about the concern (e.g., teachers, school consultants, principals) need to be aware of the importance of each and every contact with a family. McKay and colleagues have extensively studied the family-engagement process and identified critical leverage points for initially engaging families in supportive services for their child and also in sustaining their participation. These include relatively simple strategies that school personnel can use at every point of contact with parents.

The first contact sets the stage for successful (or unsuccessful!) engagement. McKay and colleagues (2004) found that using systematic strategies for engaging high-risk families in the first telephone contact increases the likelihood of attendance at the first session after a phone call by 30%. They reported four key strategies, all based on the UTB framework for eliciting intention to change, that need to be followed to build successful first contacts: (a) clarify the perceived need for services by focusing the initial conversation on what the parents think their child needs; (b) attempt to maximize parents' investment and efficacy to attend the first session by acknowledging the strength it has taken for them to initiate the contact and acknowledging that the parents are doing the best they can to meet their child's needs; (c) identify attitudes about and any previous experiences with educational and mental health care, including asking direct questions about common myths that other parents have had (e.g., "Some parents have been concerned that the information they share in these meetings will be shared with others. Is that something you are worried about?"); and (d) problem solve any concrete obstacles that could interfere with their attendance to the first session, including lack of time, transportation, and child-care issues (McKay et al., 2004). See Table 2.6 for questions aligned with each of McKay's four goals.

## Ongoing Visits

Although these strategies are necessary for building initial involvement in services, they are insufficient to sustain involvement. *Attending to parent engagement is a priority at every point of contact with a parent.* Subsequent research by McKay and others (e.g., Nock & Ferriter, 2005) has shown that the following elements help maintain ongoing engagement: (a) clarifying the helping process by describing the services and discussing expectations; (b) creating a collaborative relationship by using "we" language and avoiding questions such as "How can I help you?" while allowing the family to tell their story; (c) maintaining a shared game plan, or agreed-upon goals and strategies for meeting goals; (d) focusing on practical concerns the family has that can make an immediate difference; and (e) identifying and problem solving potential barriers to continued help seeking at the end of every session. Use of these strategies nearly doubled family persistence rates over time. See Table 2.7 for a list of these key elements.

> Attending to parent engagement is a priority at every point of contact with a parent.

## Don't Give Up

Stick with parents even when they don't follow through with their commitments. Persistence is key in helping support parents at highest risk for noninvolvement

**Table 2.6 Four Goals of the First Conversations About Concerns**

1. Clarify the need for supportive services
   - What do you think your child needs?
   - Tell me about your child. What are his or her strengths?
   - Are you interested in my help?
2. Increase caregiver investment and efficacy
   - Frame parents' choices as having potential for impacting the current situation
   - Recognize parents are doing the best they can
   - Convey optimism that the concern can be resolved
   - Affirm the parents' present and past efforts to support their child
   - Help parents identify concrete steps that they can take to address the situation even before you meet
3. Discuss prior experiences with past supportive services for their child
   - How do you feel about coming to see me?
     - If they say "OK," respond with "Some families have told me that before, but later expressed that they weren't comfortable telling me their concerns the first time we met."
   - Tell me if you have any of the following questions/concerns:
     - If the concern is about the child's behavior or emotions, ask about the parents' perceptions of mental health including the following:
       - Do you worry that "mental health means something is wrong with my child?"
       - Have you had a bad experience with a mental health provider?
       - Some parents worry that discussing behavior problems will lead to a referral for medications. Is that a concern?
     - Some parents worry that information we discuss will get out/become public. Are you worried about that?
     - Sometimes schools are not friendly with parents. Has that happened to you before?
     - Have you had a bad experience with an educator?
4. Problem solve concrete barriers to care
   - Ask for a commitment to whatever the parent agrees to be the next step.
   - Ask what might get in the way of a parent fulfilling that commitment (e.g., attending a meeting).
   - What supports do the parents need to be successful in participating in the service?

**Table 2.7 Elements of Ongoing Engagement**

➤ Clarify the helping process for clients
  - Expectations (What do you expect from parents, and what do parents expect from you?)
  - Create collaborative relationship
  - Talk about how "we" are going to work together to meet the needs of their child
➤ Focus on immediate, practical concerns
  - Give parents something to take away from the first meeting
  - Establish an agreed-upon game plan and review regularly
➤ Identify and problem solve barriers to help seeking
➤ Assess whether they will come back again
  - "I'm really wondering, what the chances are that you will come back again...?"

> Can you persist too much when attempting to access a parent? No, not really.

in schools. Can you persist too much when attempting to access a parent? No, not really. McKay actually interviewed difficult-to-reach families about their perceptions of outreach by school and clinic personnel who persistently called or tried to contact them. Almost universally, parents perceived persistent efforts to reach them in a positive light. Most viewed these efforts as well-intended caring and concern. So don't give up!

## ROLE OF LEADERSHIP IN ENGAGING PARENTS

It is important that staff are supported in developing their own understanding of the advantages of parent involvement; they need to value parent involvement and see parents as assets and partners. Administrators set this tone through the policies, practices, and programs they promote. Making parent involvement a leadership priority sends a powerful message to school personnel.

> Making parent involvement a leadership priority sends a powerful message to school personnel.

Schools need written policies about involving parents. Written policies stimulate strategic planning to ensure that parent engagement is an active goal of staff in every position. Parent-engagement efforts and goals should be formalized in the written job descriptions for all staff. Family engagement is promoted to the extent that the leadership puts in place the appropriate systems to support the work it entails. For example, systems that promote cross-disciplinary communication and collaboration among staff to meet families' needs, appropriate resource allocation (e.g., protected time, space, and materials needed for family contacts), and provide sufficient training and supervision around working effectively with parents. In making hiring decisions, it is important to consider the extent to which staff reflects a multicultural school community.

Administrators communicate their values by how they devote resources toward and have supports available to staff and families alike. Teachers and other staff need dedicated time for planning activities to involve parents and for making parent contacts. At a very basic level, they need phone and computer access to offer a variety of modes of communication, and they need the means necessary for conducting home visits. Administrators must also promote communication and coordination among the various roles/disciplines in schools so that each has an interest in involving parents, and so that their shared interest in involving parents leads to coordinated efforts. All too often we see examples of well-intentioned staff scheduling different events for families at overlapping times, planning events but not informing other staff or eliciting their help in spreading the word to parents, and/or lack of awareness of other staff simultaneously planning similar opportunities for parents.

We often hear from teachers in particular that their teacher-preparation programs did not provide training on how to effectively involve and engage parents. Many do not see it as integral to their role as educators or as falling within their job description. Or, even when they value the importance of engaging parents, they feel intimidated and inadequately prepared to do so. It is therefore important to attend to the training and supervision needed to promote family engagement. Training, supervision, and ongoing coaching should include specifics on how to engage families using the LEAP skills, particularly when considering the range of emotional reactions parents experience that we generated at the beginning of the chapter. However, it is recommended that training also include developing knowledge of child development, mental health/developmental psychopathology, family dynamics, and contexts that impact child functioning in schools.

Indeed, effective family engagement requires the coordinated effort of the entire school team. To be maximally effective, we recommend establishing a parent-engagement team charged with coordinating all parent-engagement efforts. Their responsibilities might include conducting an assessment of the school's capacity to engage parents to identify unmet needs and a review of policies and procedures for parent engagement. They can also develop a shared mission around parent engagement, establish or enhance polices to execute that mission, establish plans for motivating all staff involvement, and build the systems, supports, skill sets, and channels of communication needed. Such a group could bring together key stakeholders from every level of the system (e.g., key administrators, supervisors, mental health and social service staff, teachers, parents, and, when appropriate, community representatives) to engage in collaborative decision making and assist in problem solving while executing plans.

## PARENT-INVOLVEMENT ACTIVITY

Using Handout 2.4, take a moment to reflect on what you and/or your school currently are doing well with regard to building a positive climate for engaging parents. What are your strengths or the assets of your school in this regard? Next, reflect on possible areas of improvement based on the model of change and the strategies presented in this chapter. Finally, write down three strategies that you plan to implement to foster a positive parent-involvement climate at your school.

## PROVIDING A CONTEXT FOR ENGAGING TEACHERS AND STUDENTS

Although we focused much of this chapter on parent engagement, the same model and principles apply to engaging teachers and students in services. The same factors that influence a parent's intention to change also influence teacher and student perceptions. When you approach a teacher or a student with a problem, it is likely he or she will have the same range of

> The same factors that influence a parent's intention to change also influence teacher and student perceptions.

emotional reactions that parents would have and students and teachers are likely to prefer the same types of helping responses (refer back to Table 2.2). Setting up systems of support at the beginning of the year to send messages about how a teacher or student would seek help removes one barrier to help seeking. For instance, you might attend a teacher meeting at the start of the year to advertise your consultation services and inform teachers about how they might access it. Frequent positive communication also applies equally well to creating an environment for conversations about change with teachers and students.

Consider how you could use the marketing principles discussed earlier to make teachers and students more amenable to having conversations about change. For instance, if you would like teachers to participate in a coaching-support system, you might create a brochure with testimonials about coaching and its benefits, elicit the support of influential teachers who can endorse the service, and ask teachers to make a commitment in writing to use the service. For students, you might create a student-engagement team to find ways to support student participation in school and related services. It would be helpful to explore ways to influence social norms about student and teacher support seeking to make it more common and acceptable. Collecting surveys about attitudes and barriers toward support services and publicizing the benefits of support seeking can be steps in altering student and teacher perceptions.

## TEACHER- AND STUDENT-INVOLVEMENT ACTIVITIES

Using Handouts 2.5 and 2.6, take a moment to reflect on what you and/or your school currently are doing well with regard to building a positive climate for engaging teachers and students. What are your strengths or the assets of your school in this regard? Next, reflect on possible areas of improvement based on the model of change and the strategies presented in this chapter. Finally, write down three strategies that you plan to implement to foster a positive teacher- and student-engagement climate at your school.

## SUMMARY

The communication skills and the principles for creating contexts that invite conversations about change apply to all stakeholders in schools. The framework presented in this chapter was intended to stimulate your thinking about ways that your school environment can improve so that more parents, teachers, and students are willing to engage in the MI types of conversations that are described in the next chapter.

# Handouts and Forms

**ACCOMPLISHMENTS OF THE WEEK**

Dear _____ , this week _____

1.

2.

3.

# Congratulations!

Your child earned

the  STUDENT OF THE DAY award

for

_____

_____

_____

_____

**Daily Progress Report for** _____

| Goal 1: | | Comments: |
|---------|---|-----------|
| Goal 2: | | Comments: |
| Goal 3: | | Comments: |

# HANDOUT 2.2 TABLE TALK NOTES TO FACILITATE FAMILY CONVERSATIONS ABOUT SCHOOL

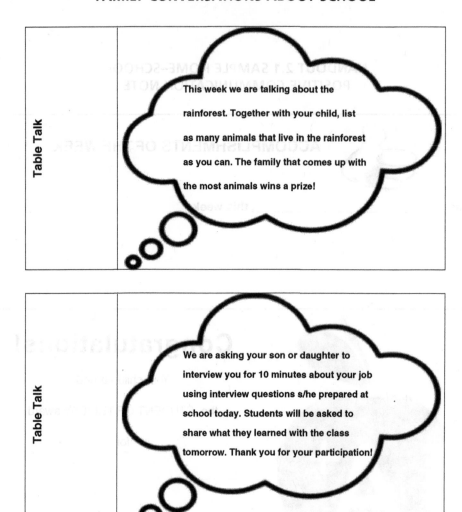

Table Talk

This week we are talking about the rainforest. Together with your child, list as many animals that live in the rainforest as you can. The family that comes up with the most animals wins a prize!

Table Talk

We are asking your son or daughter to interview you for 10 minutes about your job using interview questions s/he prepared at school today. Students will be asked to share what they learned with the class tomorrow. Thank you for your participation!

HEAD START is now offering....

# THE PARENT SURVIVAL PROGRAM

"I feel more confident, more in control. I am more able to deal with my children's behavior." (Mother of Amy, age 3)

"My children are a lot calmer, and so am I!" (Father of Kyle, age 4)

Being a parent is <u>hard work</u>. We could all use some tips and support!

## Join other Head Start parents in a program to:

- Get practical advice about common problems like temper tantrums
- Support your child's successful transition to Kindergarten
- Learn what to do at home so your children do their best at school
- Find ways to get your child to listen without having to yell
- Feel more confident and LESS STRESSED as a parent
- Meet and talk to other parents like you

### I PLAN TO ATTEND

☐ THURSDAYS 9:30am to 12pm (join us for a free lunch 11:30-12)
☐ TUESDAYS 5:00pm to 7:30pm (join us for a free dinner 5-5:30)

☐ I will need child care during that time (children's ages: _____)
☐ I will need transportation to the meeting

---

Parent Name _____     Phone Number _____
Child Name _____      Class_____

Parent Signature _____

*Please sign this form to let us know you plan to attend and give it to your family advocate. She can answer any questions you have about the program. She will also give you a reminder call the night before each meeting. We look forward to seeing you there!

---

## HANDOUT 2.4 ENGAGING PARENTS IN MY SCHOOL: GOAL-SETTING SHEET

| Things We Do Well | Things We Could Improve |
|---|---|
|  |  |

**To foster stronger parent involvement, I commit to trying the following three strategies:**

(1) _____

(2) _____

(3) _____

## HANDOUT 2.5 ENGAGING TEACHERS IN MY SCHOOL: GOAL-SETTING SHEET

| Things We Do Well | Things We Could Improve |
|---|---|
|  |  |

**To foster stronger teacher engagement, I commit to trying the following three strategies:**

(1) _____

(2) _____

(3) _____

## HANDOUT 2.6 ENGAGING STUDENTS IN MY SCHOOL: GOAL-SETTING SHEET

| Things We Do Well | Things We Could Improve |
|---|---|
| | |

**To foster stronger student engagement, I commit to trying the following three strategies:**

(1) _____

(2) _____

(3) _____

# 3

# Motivational Interviewing Principles and Strategies

Once you get people in the door and willing to have a conversation with you, then what do you do? The context described in Chapter 2 is important, if not essential, to get the attention and initial willingness of parents, teachers, and students to consider talking with you about issues that are important to them. The focus of this chapter is how to keep that momentum going.

> Our behavior change technologies too often depend on the compliance of those willing to implement our suggestions.

You may have a knowledge base that you are comfortable sharing with people about how to create effective classroom or home environments or how a student might cope better but without attending to motivational issues your suggestions and advice are unlikely to be heard.

Many school professionals and support service providers (administrators, teachers, school psychologists, school social workers, school consultants, resource teachers, and behavioral consultants) experience frustration from a simple and enduring realization. On the one hand, much is known about effective practices to address a wide range of academic and behavioral problems at school. On the other hand, it can be challenging to get people to actually use these practices. In this respect, a consultant's effectiveness hinges on the ability to influence people's motivations, decisions, and actions.

People's tendency to hold onto practices that are known and comfortable is hardly surprising, and the art and science of motivating people to change has, until recently, not been well understood or studied, at least not within the context of education. For example, think about how many "best practices" you have heard, and then consider the volume of interactional tools you employ to intentionally change the likelihood someone will engage in a target behavior? A seminal review by Dean Fixsen and colleagues examining the adoption and implementation of high-quality practices across several disciplines concluded that although the knowledge base to solve complicated social problems has increased exponentially in recent decades, our ability to effectively adopt and apply effective practices with fidelity remains limited (Fixsen, Naoom, Blase, Freidman, & Wallace, 2005).

For parents, motivational issues arise during a range of tasks that could support children's educational attainment, from the seemingly simple and mundane (e.g., attending meetings, checking backpacks, signing home–school notes) to more complicated and time-consuming tasks (e.g., daily homework support and implementation of effective family-management practices to support prosocial behavior and compliance). How many times have you heard (or said), "The parents who need to _____ (fill in the blank: attend a conference, volunteer, spend time on homework, attend a parent training workshop) are the least likely to do so," or "Those who need it the most are the least likely to participate"? A similar dynamic often unfolds between consultants and support staff, administrators, or teachers.

Much to our chagrin, it seems that the "best" consultees are the ones who solicit and implement our suggestions, attend our workshops, and adopt new practices with relative ease. In other words, our behavior-change technologies too often depend on the compliance of those willing to implement our suggestions. What if we could change this dynamic? Rather than hoping and waiting for the perfectly compliant and motivated parent, teacher, or student, what if we could influence the motivation of those least likely to participate?

Motivational interviewing (MI) provides that much-needed approach for addressing the critical component of change: motivation. At its foundation, MI is an approach that leads to effective consultant–consultee relationships, and therefore successful everyday conversations about change. Any school professional can learn the foundational skills and spirit of MI, and we believe doing so will increase their influence to support behavior change that is consistent with the values and goals of the consultee and promotes desirable academic and behavioral student outcomes. Schools would also benefit from having one or more consultants in their buildings trained in advanced MI skills, which involves the substantial effort to learn and strategically apply MI. The spirit and skills associated with MI are described in this chapter and supported by examples within the schooling process. We begin by inviting readers to "think motivationally" and then provide an overview of the MI spirit followed by a description of the four fundamental processes and skills of MI.

## THINKING MOTIVATIONALLY

Think for a moment about something in your personal life that others have been encouraging you to change, and perhaps that you have also wanted to change. It could be health habits (e.g., eating, exercise) or perhaps something about your communication style with a significant other or your child(ren). If you cannot think of anything, congratulations (and we don't believe

> MI begins with the assumption that how one interacts with others has a strong influence over one's motivation and can be used to maximize change outcomes.

you!). Then think about the person, or people, who are most and least likely to have influence over you. Who is helpful? Who just makes you mad—and probably less likely to engage in change—despite their good intentions? How would you describe these people? Do you prefer a confrontational approach—someone to point out how illogical you are and educate you on "a better way" or "what you should be doing"? Or, do you turn to someone who is more likely to suspend judgment and advice and instead facilitate a process where by you can reach a decision that best works for you given your values and goals?

Most people prefer the latter; that is, when attempting to change a behavior, we are more influenced by those who support us with open listening and encouragement rather than with confrontation and judgment. Quite often, when others tell us why we need to change, it evokes within us the opposite responses, as in all the reasons why we don't want or need to change. We argue for why it is too difficult to make the change or describe barriers to changing. This simple truth is the basis for altering consultation relationships and beginning to think motivationally.

MI is grounded in this concept of thinking motivationally. Developed, refined, and evaluated over the past 25 years by Drs. William Miller and Steve Rollnick (Miller, 1983; Miller & Rollnick, 2002, 2013; see Box 3.1), MI is a method for having effective conversations about change. MI begins with the assumption that how one interacts with others has a strong influence over one's motivation and can be used to maximize change outcomes. The lay definition of MI is "a collaborative conversation style for strengthening a person's own motivation and commitment to change" (Miller & Rollnick, 2013, p. 12). A more technical definition for advanced users is "A collaborative, goal-oriented style of communication with particular attention to the language of change. It is designed to strengthen personal motivation for and commitment to a specific goal by eliciting and exploring the person's own reasons for change within an atmosphere of acceptance and compassion" (p. 29). Implementation of MI strategies is associated with increased change talk (Glynn & Moyers, 2010; Miller, Yahne, Moyers, Martinez, Pirritano, & 2004; Moyers & Martino, 2006). In turn, goal-directed change talk is associated with subsequent behavior change (Amrhein et al., 2003; Miller et al., 1993; Sellman et al., 2001; Sellman, MacEwan, Deering, & Adamson, 2007).

---

### BOX 3.1 A BRIEF HISTORY OF MI

In the second edition of *Motivational Interviewing*, Miller and Rollnick (2002) conceptualized MI as having two phases; specifically, they described Phase 1, precommitment, in which ambivalence is resolved, and Phase 2, postcommitment, in which intrinsic motivation for change is activated to drive a collaborative change-planning process. In this conceptualization, the MI environment or treatment context was represented by three underlying constructs: evocation, collaboration, and autonomy, and four general principles (i.e., express empathy, develop discrepancy, roll with resistance, and support self-efficacy) that

*(continued)*

## BOX 3.1 A BRIEF HISTORY OF MI (*continued*)

were skillfully combined to direct a client toward change. This second itera-tive conceptualization of MI relied on the use of these constructs and prin-ciples to affect two critical requirements for change: (a) importance and (b) confidence.

Since 2003, the application of MI to other populations and settings has expanded exponentially. There are now over 2,000 individuals who have completed intensive training provided by the Motivational Interviewing Network of Trainers (MINT); non-English trainings are now provided, and regional MINT meetings also exist for supervisors (Miller & Moyers, 2012). Additionally, substantial work has been done to create fidelity measures to assess and provide clinical feedback and supervision, evaluate MI proficiency (Moyers, Martin, Manuel, Hendrickson, & Miller, 2005), and to evaluate train-ing (Miller, Moyers, Ernst, & Amrhein, 2008). Further, publications related to MI have increased from approximately 50 in 2003 to an average of 175 per year in 2008 and 2009 (Miller & Moyers, 2012). From 2003 to 2011, over 200 randomized trials have been completed, largely the result of rapid diffusion in health care and corrections. Recently, Guilford Press has published a series of books on MI related to children/youth (Naar-King/Saurez, 2011), groups (Westra, 2011), social work (Hohman, 2011) and for treatment of anxiety (Westra, 2011). A new training DVD has also been released (Miller, Moyers, & Rollnick, 2012). Finally, in the fall of 2012, the third edition of *Motivational Interviewing* was released (*MI-3*; Miller & Rollnick, 2013).

*MI-3* contains a number of changes. For example, the five principles and two phases have been eliminated. Additionally, the components of the MI "spirit" have been revised, and include partnership, acceptance, compassion, and evocation. It is important to note that the focus of MI was expanded to include not only behavior, but decision, attitude, and resolution/acceptance. Further, *MI-3* provides far more guidance than its predecessor with regard to the use of direction, aligning MI with a guiding style as opposed to the directing (e.g., behavior therapy, cognitive therapy) or following styles (e.g., client cen-tered) associated with other practices. To be considered MI practice, Miller and Rollnick suggest that three essential elements must be met: a conversation, an established collaboration, and evocation of the client's reasons for change. Whereas conversation requires no explanation, consultants seek to build a relationship with the client that embodies collaboration. To this end, consul-tants facilitate dialogue and avoid taking an "expert role," instead emphasizing choice and responsibility for change to the clients, who remain the expert on themselves. Evocation embodies the consultant's active elicitation of the cli-ent's personal reasons for change. Priority is given to the client's values and ideas about the process of change, and ideals of self and life become a central focus of the ensuing dialogue.

Perhaps the most striking feature of the new conceptualization of *MI-3* are the four fundamental processes: (a) engaging, (b) focusing, (c) evoking, and (d) planning. It is important to note that a practitioner can implement MI without

*(continued)*

---

### BOX 3.1 A BRIEF HISTORY OF MI (*continued*)

having engaged in the fourth process, but the application of the first three processes are a necessity. The core strategies associated with *MI-3* will be familiar to MI veterans (OARS: open-ended questions, affirmations, reflections, and summaries), but the strategic use of them within these four processes, as well as the addition of two levels of change talk (i.e., preparatory and mobilizing), have resulted in much more clarity about when and how to use the core skills.

---

The logic behind the MI approach is simple. People feel ambivalent about most important life- and work-related decisions. If prompted, they can usually generate compelling reasons for and against changing, or for or against remaining the same. When someone argues for change on his or her behalf, it is more likely to be met with resistance[1] than agreement, a phenomenon known as the *righting reflex*. Specifically, when directed to change, the righting reflex encourages the person to articulate the disadvantages of change and the advantages of the status quo, making it less likely that he or she will initiate change. Alternatively, if the listener resists the righting reflex, he or she may evoke within the other the advantages of change as well as the disadvantages of the status quo, and in turn make it more likely that change will occur. Although MI is more complicated than this, the intuitive appeal as well as the evidence base has resulted in its widespread adoption.

Although originally developed as a counseling approach, the style and specific interviewing strategies can be applied in a variety of settings and with diverse populations to promote behavior change. MI resembles other well-regarded behavior-change technology approaches in that it advocates for (a) developing a supportive, trusting relationship as an enabling feature of change (e.g., client-centered therapy); (b) helps others focus on specific behavior change (e.g., cognitive therapy, behaviorism, and solution-focused counseling); and (c) avoids confrontation (e.g., systemic family therapy).

MI is unique, however, because of its emphasis on evocation, or the strategic use of methods to leverage a person's motivation and commitment to engage in a target behavior. Specifically, MI involves the differential evoking and reinforcement of change talk, strategic and directive use of client-centered therapy strategies, and the sequencing of preparatory change talk and mobilizing commitment (Miller & Rollnick, 2013).

---

[1] MI no longer uses the label *resistance* because the term pathologizes ambivalence, which is after all a normal and common human reaction. Instead, language in support of the status quo or not changing is referred to as Sustain Talk.

## SUCCESS STORY

One of the most rewarding educators we have trained in MI was a special education teacher for 30 years before becoming a behavioral coach. For him, the righting reflex—the desire to "fix" or offer advice or information—was strong. The righting reflex was likely reinforced by many years of teacher education and an expert orientation. When he learned to listen before offering advice, he found that his relationships with parents and teachers changed dramatically, and the advice he offered was more likely to be heard and followed.

## UNIFIED THEORY OF BEHAVIOR CHANGE

In Chapter 2, we used the Unified Theory of Behavior Change (UTB) to consider factors that explain people's decisions to change a behavior. Recall that a primary determinant of whether people act is whether they intend to act. In this view, a key role of a consultant is to help bolster the consultee's intention to change. UTB identifies several specific ways to help grow intention. By altering expectancies of success and attitudes, social norms, and self-efficacy related to the intended behavior, consultants can affect a person's intention to engage in the behavior. In this chapter, we are primarily concerned with the language of intention.

> A key assumption of MI is that the more a person expresses language in favor of changing, including intention and commitment to do so, the more likely he or she is to change.

In MI, the language of the intention to change a behavior (and its precursors) falls under the umbrella term of *change talk*. The more a person expresses language in favor of changing, including intention and commitment to do so, the more likely he or she is to change. Thus, in MI, instead of telling others what to do and why, the consultant attempts to elicit from the person a rationale for why he or she might want to change, including desires, abilities, reasons, needs, and commitments related to changing. Figure 3.1 highlights the relationship between MI and the UTB model.

## MI SPIRIT

MI only works in the context of a collaborative relationship. Without the foundation of a trusting relationship, the MI strategies will be accurately perceived as manipulation. Miller and Rollnick (2013) take great lengths to emphasize the spirit of MI that sets the foundation for the type of relationship

> MI only works in the context of a collaborative relationship.

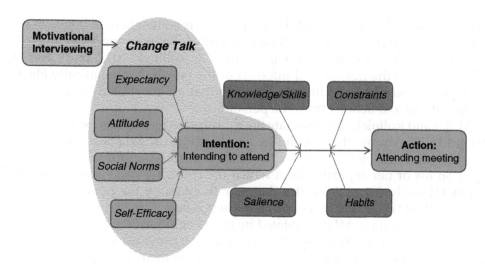

**Figure 3.1** MI unified theory of behavior.

required for MI to be successful. The components of the MI spirit include partnership, acceptance, compassion, and evocation. Partnership involves the recognition that MI is done with and for people, not to them, and the recognition that people "are the undisputed experts on themselves" (Miller & Rollnick, 2013, p. 15). Acceptance includes an attitude of tolerance, irrespective of whether or not the consultant approves of the consultee's behavior or beliefs. Miller and Rollnick refer to four aspects of acceptance: (a) absolute worth, (b) autonomy, (c) accurate empathy, and (d) affirmation. Compassion requires a consultant to pursue the welfare and best interests of the consultee. Finally, evocation involves the adoption of a strengths-based perspective—the belief that people already have the tools to make change consistent with their goals and values; thus, the consultant need not be concerned with providing expert information but rather calling forth this knowledge. These habits of "heart and mind with which one enters into the practice of MI" (Miller & Rollnick, 2013, p. 15) are typically not emphasized in school administration and teacher education programs nor are the client-centered counseling skills that are used in the practice of MI.

## GUIDING

Miller and Rollnick (2013) distinguish among three conversation styles, or roles, commonly taken by a helper: following, directing, and guiding. Following is in line with client-centered therapy approaches in which the helper simply listens and lets the other lead the conversation. In this role, the helper provides little if any direction and trusts that by listening he or she will allow the person to find his or her own direction. The role of directing stands in stark contrast to following. Here the helper provides explicit instructions or advice for the person to follow, including what

> The direction in MI really comes from the change talk given by the person.

to discuss and what actions to take. Guiding falls somewhere in between these two extremes, and involves a balance of both following and directing; "Not doing too much or too little to help" (Miller & Rollnick, 2013, p. 5). Here the helper listens to the desires and interests of the person, systematically eliciting and reflecting key parts of the conversation that are most likely to evoke positive intentions and actions from the person.

Miller and Rollnick (2013) situate the role of effective MI users in the activities of a guide. They write that much like a tour guide, the MI consultant attempts to understand the wishes and desires of the consultee, and then offers options based on his or her expertise from which the consultee can choose. The direction in MI really comes from the change talk given by the person. This is the language the MI consultant seeks to elicit and reflect.

Further, guiding in MI is facilitated by the recognition of the four processes or stages of an interview. The remainder of this chapter provides an overview of these processes and the strategic use of the MI skills within them. Examples of how they can be applied in schools are presented throughout, in addition to practice boxes that allow readers to test their understanding of the concepts being discussed.

## FUNDAMENTAL PROCESSES AND STRATEGIES OF MI

There are four processes in MI: engaging, focusing, evoking, and planning. The first two processes resemble other counseling approaches, and we believe using these would be desirable for a variety of school staff who serve as consultants, or at least who seek to influence the behavior of others. Evoking is uniquely MI, and requires more training, practice, and feedback to become proficient. The planning process is optional, as some people will actively choose not to change, and their autonomy should be accepted; other daily interactions are not formal enough to reach this process. The core skills associated with an MI approach are applied across all four processes, and will be familiar to those trained in any person-centered counseling approaches. They are represented by the acronym OARS: open-ended questions, affirmations, reflections, and summaries, and also include informing and advising (see Table 3.1). These core skills are applied uniquely and *strategically* during each of the four processes.

### Engaging

The purpose of the first process, engaging, is to develop an understanding of the problem from the consultee's perspective, learn about the effect the problem

**Table 3.1  OARS Plus Advice**

O:  Open-ended questions
A:  Affirmations
R:  Reflections
S:  Summaries
    Informing and advising

has on various aspects of his or her life, elicit the values that are important to the person, and develop an awareness of what the person is currently doing (or not doing) in relation to the problem. The core skills described below can all be used to develop an understanding of the consultee's perspective. The engaging process builds on nondirective approaches developed by Carl Rogers's (1959) theory regarding the critical consultant skills necessary to facilitate change. Specifically, Rogers advocated a client-centered approach whereby the consultant provides an ideal atmosphere for change by expressing empathy, warmth, and sincerity. Like the client-centered approach, those adhering to an MI approach should refrain from judging, promoting/advocating for change, or giving advice (unless invited to do so; more about that later).

> Alternating questions with reflections and summaries is a critical interviewing skill.

OARS can be used to facilitate the engaging process. *Open-ended questions* (e.g., *Tell me a little about how the adults and other children react when Nina refuses to complete her work?*) encourage elaboration, in contrast to closed-ended questions (e.g., *Do you engage with Nina when she refuses to do her work, or do you ignore her?*), which invite short, if not one word, responses. Open-ended questions help build a relationship by inviting further conversation, revealing deeper thoughts and reflection, and conveying a sense of interest and intimacy. Note, however, that they can be overused. A conversation with only open-ended questions can feel like an interrogation. Alternating questions with reflections and summaries is a critical interviewing skill.

*Affirmations* communicate acceptance or admiration for another's actions, intent, beliefs, or values. Affirmations can be expressed nonverbally such as through eye contact and head nods as well as through words. Effective affirmations require sincerity, so only affirm what you believe to be true. Likewise, people are more likely to believe that an affirmation is genuine if it is specific. For instance, "You are working so hard on this problem," rather than a general "Good job."

Although reflective listening and summaries are part of any client-centered approach, what distinguishes MI is how these strategies are used selectively and in the service of change talk. There are two types of reflections. *Simple reflections* are statements that repeat (i.e., mirror) or paraphrase what the other person has said. Reflections should be brief; a good rule of thumb is that they should be shorter than the statement(s) they are reflecting. For example, a consultee might say, "One of my values as a teacher is to create a safe environment where children are free to take risks." The following responses would constitute use of a simple reflection because each statement stays very close to the consultee's communicated intent: (a) *safety is important,* (b) *creating a safe environment is one of your responsibilities as a teacher,* or (c) *children are more likely to take risks if they believe the environment is safe.* Simple reflections are useful for allowing the conversation to continue while inviting further elaboration. As noted in using open-ended questions, basic reflections can also be overused. If you find yourself stuck in a conversation, going in circles, or not moving forward, it is possible that you are using too many simple reflections.

*Complex reflections* extend the meaning of what has been communicated, and thus can be used to go beyond the surface expressions of a conversation. This extension is typically a supposition formed from the client's current statement as well as previously shared information. Good complex reflections are essentially educated guesses about what the person is truly trying to convey, including what the person may be feeling. The following are examples of complex reflections in response to the same statement: (a) *A safe environment is the foundation for all learning;* (b) *You are willing to do whatever it takes to ensure children in your classroom take risks;* or (c) *Creating a safe environment, which includes establishing positive relationships with children, is an extremely important value of yours.*

*Summaries* include the paraphrasing of several ideas, and in this sense, they are merely a compilation of extended simple and complex reflections. Sometimes these summaries reflect recent conversation, but they can also integrate or synthesize bits and pieces of information the consultee has presented in the past. Summaries can be used to end a particular topic and transition to a new one or to strategically repeat back to the consultee an important theme or series of change talk statements.

Finally, while *advising and informing* can be overused to the detriment of motivation, they can be applied selectively and strategically within the spirit of MI. Specifically, one strategy in MI is to ask permission to advise or inform. Additionally, advice or information should be dispensed only after the consultee's perspective and needs are understood. Finally, following the giving of advice or information, the consultant should help the consultee draw his or her own conclusions about its relevance to his or her situation. Test your ability to identify OARS statements by completing Practice 3.1 and Practice 3.2.

---

### PRACTICE 3.1

To test your ability to identify OARS statements, look at the following. Here we have listed four statements. Determine whether each statement is an example of an open-ended question, affirmation, reflection, or summary, and compare your answers to the ones given below the statements.

**Teacher:** It is important for children to believe their environment is a safe one, one where they can take risks without fear of being wrong.

1. I appreciate your commitment to creating a safe environment where children feel free to take risks.
2. Can you tell me a little about what you do to make sure children feel safe taking risks?
3. If you want to be a strong teacher, it is imperative to create an environment in which children feel free to take risks.
4. Real learning can only occur when children are unafraid to fail.

Answers: *(1) Affirmation (2) Open-ended question (3) Reflection (Complex) (4) Reflection (Complex)*

---

### PRACTICE 3.2

Determine whether each school consultant statement below is a simple reflection, complex reflection, or a nonreflection, and why?

**Ms. King:**  Ms. Smith picks on Jerome constantly. If I were Jerome, I'd hate coming to school too.

**School Consultant:**

1. Ms. Smith is always on Jerome's case.
2. I was in class just the other day and Jerome and Ms. Smith were getting along well.
3. Ms. Smith does not care for Jerome.
4. It angers you that Jerome is harassed by his teacher.

Answers: *(1) Simple reflection—the meaning has not been extended, this is simply another way to say the same thing; (2) Nonreflection—this is not an attempt to understand Ms. King's perspective; (3) Complex reflection—the meaning has been extended. Ms. King did not say that, though it is very possible this is an underlying belief; (4) Complex reflection—meaning has not been extended. Specifically, emotion has been added.*

---

Reflections allow you to demonstrate your understanding of the other person's values and dilemmas, and affirmations communicate respect and acceptance, which assists in establishing a positive relationship. However, to effectively begin to effect change in a directive fashion, which is where MI differs from the client-centered approach, these skills need to be systematically and strategically applied by shaping the conversation so that one's values and motivation for change become central. This systematic and strategic application is called evocation. Whether evocation, or directional MI, is used during the engagement process depends on the context of the practice, but the use (or omission) of evocation in the engagement process should be intentional. Although you will eventually need to identify a specific target for behavior change, during engagement your focus may be considerably broader than behavior—again, depending on the context. In any event, you should be attuned to helping the other person crystallize the possible change decision to be made (e.g., allow my frustration to be seen by the other children or not; use praise to govern behavior or not; communicate support and understanding for a child you don't particularly care for) or supporting the resolution (acceptance) of the status quo, and facilitating the connection between the decision and values.

### Values Exploration

Spending time learning about another's values and beliefs is an effective engaging strategy. Not only is values exploration engaging for most people, but it provides you with important information about what inspires and motivates a person. Values are linked to our passions, and passions usually have energy behind them. It is this energy that MI seeks to capitalize on, as people make decisions about change.

Much social psychology literature has documented that humans prefer to be consistent in actions and beliefs. When we perceive discrepancies between what we do (how things are) and what we value (how things ought to be), we adjust to try to get them realigned. We have two options: to change our actions, or to change our values. As values are difficult to change, becoming aware of a value–behavior discrepancy often moves us to change our actions. MI tries to uncover and highlight such discrepancies. Thus, one important aspect of engaging with another is to understand his or her values and core beliefs. We do this by asking directly about them and through activities such as the Value Card Sort, which will be discussed in subsequent chapters.

### Using Summaries to Synthesize

Throughout the engagement process, and particularly when you believe it is time to move to the next step (focusing), a summary should be provided that synthesizes the potential focus of change, the importance of resolving it in a fashion that is consistent with the person's values, as well as his or her motivations for change. Motivations for change constitute the next important acronym—DARN: Desire, Ability, Reason, Need (Miller & Rollnick, 2013; Miller & Rose, 2009). It may be that this summary takes the form of a complex reflection followed by an open-ended question ("So, where do you think you'll go from here?" or "Tell me what you'll do with this new understanding of the situation.") to guide the client through the transition to focusing.

## Focusing

The second MI process, focusing, involves the narrowing from a general decision about change to a specific focus on a target behavior, or a change goal. Although the change goal can be considered entirely from the other person's perspective, in school settings it is likely to be defined, at least to some extent, by the context. Whereas the focus of counseling, unless it is court ordered, is typically driven by the client's desire for improved life satisfaction, the focus of interactions between someone who would be employing MI strategies in the schools is likely to be far more focused from the start.

A few examples of MI applications in school settings demonstrate a narrow starting focus, but not a target behavior. For example, in the Tertiary First Step to Success intervention (Frey, Walker, et al., 2013), participation begins with a broad focus on five universal principles of positive behavior support: (a) establish clear expectations, (b) directly teach the expectations, (c) reinforce the display of expectations, (d) minimize attention for minor inappropriate behaviors, and (e) establish clear consequences for unacceptable behavior (Sprauge & Golly, 2013). Thus, engaging begins within this context, and focusing involves the consultee's identification of a subset of these principles, which the subsequent change plan will address. Similarly, the Classroom Check-Up (Reinke, Lewis-Palmer, & Merrell, 2008) begins the engagement process in the general context of overall effective classroom-management strategies, and focusing involves the identification of specific classroom-management strategies within this general framework. Finally, Frey, Lee, et al. (2013a) propose a consultation model, the Motivational Interviewing Navigation Guide (MING), which includes a five-step process to motivate consultees to adopt evidence-based practices and to implement critical features of the intervention with fidelity. Within this application, the change goal is also predetermined and defined by the fidelity parameters of the intervention of focus. In each of these situations, the relationship begins with an agreed- upon focus and the consultant knows in advance how he or she will proceed strategically to favor the resolution of the consultee's ambivalence in a particular direction (e.g., toward practices that are known to be effective). However, in some school-based applications of the MI approach, the relationship may not begin with a general target of change or a predetermined aspiration to influence the person in a particular direction. The decision to remain neutral (or not), referred to as equipoise, has critical implications for how to proceed within the MI framework. Specifically, whether one adopts an aspirational position (i.e., favors change in a particular direction) or equipoise, determines what aspects of the conversation will be selectively amplified or minimized.

A clear understanding of the 2×2 decisional balance grid (see Figure 3.2) is critical to understanding this distinction. Conversation regarding any dilemma can be classified in one of four quadrants: (a) good things about the status quo, (b) good things about change, (c) less-good things about the status quo, and (d) less-good things about change (Miller & Moyers, 2012). It is important to note that conversation in Quadrants B and C favor behavior change, whereas conversation in Quadrants A and D favor the status quo and oppose behavior change. The former is referred to as *change talk*, whereas the latter is considered *sustain talk* (Miller & Rollnick, 2013).

A primary task of an interviewer adopting an equipoise stance is to facilitate conversation consistently across all four quadrants. When consulting with

|  | Status Quo or Option A | Change or Option B |
|---|---|---|
| Advantages + | (A) Good things about *Status Quo* or Option A Sustain Talk | (B) Good things about *Change* or Option B Change Talk |
| Disadvantages − | (C) Less-good things about *Status Quo* or Option A Change Talk | (D) Less-good things about *Change* or Option B Sustain Talk |

**Figure 3.2** Decisional balance grid.
Modified from Miller and Moyers (2012).

someone about an issue for which maintaining neutrality makes sense (e.g., a difficult decision the person needs to make, a complicated situation in which change could have unintended consequences), the interviewer would solicit the person's perspective evenly across all four quadrants; further, the interviewer's responses would be identical irrespective of which quadrant was being discussed.

Consider the following example in which a student has a complicated decision to make about whether or not to end a romantic relationship and seeks your input. The open-ended questions below demonstrate this balance of equipoise. When assuming an equipoise position, it may be most useful to think of the options more neutrally, such as Option A (staying in the relationship) and Option B (ending it).

- What advantages come to mind when you picture yourself continuing in this relationship? (Quadrant A)
- What are the benefits of ending the relationship? (Quadrant B)
- What disadvantages come to mind when you picture yourself staying in the relationship? (Quadrant C)
- What are some of the down sides of ending the relationship? (Quadrant D)

Notice that talk related to Quadrants A and D is likely to favor option A, continuing the relationship, and talk related to Quadrants B and C is likely to favor ending the relationship. When a consultant gives equal balance and responds identically to talk related to these two options, he or she is helping the consultee consider all sides of the issue equally without inserting influence on motivation in a directional fashion. We believe that most MI in school-based practice will be directional, and thus the remainder of the chapter focuses on MI applications in which the consultant has aspirations to influence motivation in a particular direction. Assess your understanding of the decisional balance grid by completing Practice 3.3.

---

### PRACTICE 3.3

In the following dialogue between the school social worker and a teacher, consider the behavior-change target for the teacher to be remaining neutral in the face of frustration with a challenging student (Max), and the status quo for the teacher as continuing to display frustration with Max. Classify each along the following dimensions: Core skill (i.e., OARS), Quadrant (i.e., A–D), and type of talk it is likely to elicit (i.e., change or sustain).

**School Social Worker:** Max is very skilled at engaging in behaviors that really push your buttons (reflection). Can you tell me what you did the last time he was tapping his pencil when you were talking?

**Teacher:** I sent him into the hallway for time out.

---

*(continued)*

---

### PRACTICE 3.3 (continued)

**School Social Worker:**

1. When Max pushes your buttons, there are times when you become frustrated, but remaining calm in the moment is more consistent with your teaching value of respect.
2. What do you suspect some of the advantages would have been if you had remained neutral, or even ignored Max on this occasion?
3. Can you think of any negative outcomes that occurred as a result of you losing your temper and sending him to time out?
4. You were really taking a stand for the entire class when you removed him.

Answers: *(1) Summary (invoking information from a previous comment), Quadrant B, change talk; (2) Open-ended question, Quadrant B, change talk; (3) Open-ended question, Quadrant C, change talk; (4) Reflection, Quadrant A, sustain talk.*

---

Applying directional MI is difficult because it requires the consultant to track the consultee's statements at a metacognitive level during the conversation and strategically apply the core MI skills (i.e., OARS) depending on whether the consultee's talk supports or opposes the desired change. Again, talk that supports behavior change is referred to as change talk, and language that opposes change is referred to as sustain talk (Miller & Rollnick, 2013).

## Evoking

A primary task of the consultant using the MI approach from a directive position is to increase change talk. To use the OARS skills strategically for this purpose, the interviewer must understand how they are likely to affect what the other person says next. Open-ended questions will likely result in the person expanding on his or her thoughts and ideas, whereas close-ended questions are likely to bring the conversational thread to a halt. Affirmations communicate acceptance and approval, and are therefore reinforcing and encouraging. Simple reflections communicate understanding, but are not likely to expand the conversation. Complex reflections communicate and deepen understanding and invite the person to make connections he or she may not have made previously, which is likely to expand the conversation. Summaries emphasize the important aspects of the conversation, and often mark a shift

> A primary task of the consultant using the MI approach from a directive position is to increase change talk.

> Research has shown that although all change talk is important and can be used to guide MI interactions, mobilizing language is the more powerful predictor of behavior change.

in the discussion. Given these likely responses, the consultant uses the OARS skills selectively in the presence of change versus sustain talk. To evoke one's motivations for change in a directional fashion, the interviewer must be able to recognize, elicit, and respond (differentially) to change talk.

### Recognizing Change Talk

There are two types of change talk: preparatory and mobilizing. Preparatory change talk is the language of why changing a behavior may be more desirable or favorable than not changing a behavior. There are four types of *preparatory change talk*, denoted by the acronym DARN. The following statements are examples of preparatory change talk from a parent in relation to teaching his or her child to share. Here it is important to note that we are interested in preparatory statements about adult behavior change. A desire for the child to change without any discussion of what the adult's role will be in the change should be classified as sustain talk.

- *Desire*: "I wish I could help Amelia learn to share with other children."
- *Ability*: "I think I can do a better job teaching Amelia how to share."
- *Reasons*: "If Amelia learns how to share, she would probably make more friends."
- *Need*: "I have to do something different. I cannot continue to leave work early to pick her up from school."

Preparatory language reflects a consultee's interest in changing. It is a precursor to mobilizing change talk and behavior change and therefore should be encouraged.

The second type of change talk involves the mobilization of change; it reflects the resolution of ambivalence in favor of change (Miller & Rollnick, 2013). Rather than simply noting advantages of changing, mobilizing language signals an intention to act. The four types of *mobilizing change talk* are represented with the acronym CATs— Commitment, Activation, and Taking steps, as demonstrated in the following examples.

- *Commitment*: "I plan to help Amelia share while we are coloring this weekend."
- *Activation*: "I've never considered it my job as a parent to teach sharing, but I'm ready to do that now."
- *Taking Steps*: "I will set up at least one play session each day in which my goal is to help her practice sharing her things."

Research has shown that although all change talk is important and can be used to guide MI interactions, mobilizing language is the more powerful predictor of behavior change. This is very much in line with the UTB model presented earlier, which maintains that intention is the direct cause of action.

DARN-CATs statements are subtle and easy to miss, yet recognizing them is necessary to use directional MI effectively. In some situations, change talk will be generated easily with little or no prompting. When it is not, however, the interviewer must be able to elicit it. Assess your understanding of preparatory versus mobilizing change talk by completing Practice 3.4.

---

### PRACTICE 3.4

Read the following statements and identify which are examples of preparatory change talk, mobilizing change talk, or sustain talk.

1. I could probably revisit the consequences I use in the classroom.
2. Having some lower-level consequences before sending children to the office would probably be good for all of the children, not just the really hard ones.
3. I'm going to revisit my consequence structure.
4. The consequences in the class are working just fine for everyone except two children.
5. I'll try whatever you suggest for class consequences.

Answers: *(1) preparatory change talk (Ability), (2) preparatory change talk (Reason), (3) mobilizing change talk (Commitment), (4) sustain talk (5) mobilizing change talk (Activation).*

---

### Eliciting Change Talk

If consultees do not offer change talk spontaneously, it can be elicited with direct questioning within the DARN-CATs framework. Evocative open-ended questions and rulers are two common strategies to evoking change talk.

*Evocative Questions.* When interspersed with reflective listening and within the spirit of MI, open-ended questions can be used to systematically evoke the language of change. Asking directly about a person's desires, reasons, abilities, and needs related to change invites him or her to express preparatory change talk. In the decision balance example above, questions were asked to elicit language about the advantages of changing and the disadvantages of staying the same. These questions

> Asking directly about a person's desires, reasons, abilities, and needs related to change invites him or her to express preparatory change talk.

will spark a conversation full of change talk. Moreover, the interviewer can ask, "To what extent is teaching Amelia to learn to share your responsibility as a parent?" (Desire) or "What is it about you that makes you think you might be able to help teach Amelia to share?" (Ability). Reasons are perhaps the easiest category to use to elicit change talk. In doing so, one elicits the advantages of teaching

Amelia to share or the disadvantages of continuing to hope she learns to share in school without parental assistance. In this case you would ask, "What are some of the positive outcomes that could occur if you were to directly teach Amelia to share?" or "What do you suspect might happen if your current strategy of hoping she grows into sharing does not produce a different result?" The answer to these questions will almost assuredly be change talk. There are no set questions in MI; the possibilities are truly unlimited. The big idea is that any question that invites the other to talk about the advantages of changing and why it is possible will evoke change talk.

*Rulers.*  Scaling rulers are used to evoke change talk in MI. Typically, rulers that are used to assess motivation to change are found in two domains: importance and confidence, although there is no reason why other domains could not be explored with this tool (commitment, priority). The format for asking ruler questions is some variant of the following:

- On a scale from 1 to 10, how important is making this change to you, where 1 is not important at all and 10 is extremely important?

Often, we use a form with the words and a rating scale to accentuate the conversation, but the conversation can happen with or without a form. Note that the first ruler question is close ended; the answer, a number, is informative but it alone is not change talk. To evoke change talk, the follow-up is key. Regardless of the number chosen, respond with the following open-ended question:

- Why a (whatever number selected) and not (a number lower)?

The answer to this question will be one or more change talk statements, essentially reasons why changing the behavior is important. Notice that the follow-up question needs to ask about a *lower* number. If you inadvertently ask why not a higher number (e.g., why it is not more important to the person), the answer will be some version of sustain talk (e.g., "Changing this behavior is not that important to me because...").

Consider the following extended dialogue illustrating the use of an importance ruler at the end of a meeting with a teacher after she has decided to use more praise statements with all of her students.

| Dialogue | | Comments |
|---|---|---|
| Consultant (C): | So we have a scale here that's from 0 to 10. So 0 would be not important at all, and 10 would be the most important thing to you. How important is it for you to meet this goal in your classroom? | 1st ruler question |

*(continued)*

| Dialogue | Comments |
|---|---|
| **Teacher (T):** Um, let's go with 9. | |
| **C:** Wow, that's pretty high, a 9. And why did you say a 9 as opposed to a 5 or a 6? | 2nd ruler question |
| **T:** I would say that meeting this goal is important to me just because I stress equality and I stress wanting students to feel good about themselves, and yet I feel like I'm not living that as much as I could be. I think it's a strength of mine, but I could be even better at it with reinforcing the good behavior. I feel like the kids who I have like this soft spot for the misbehaving kids so they get more of my, um, time and attention and affection than the kids who are doing the right thing a lot of the times. And so I even noticed at one point in the year where some of my really well-behaved kids were acting out, and I was like, "They're doing this because I'm giving all my attention to the kids who are acting out. So now they're acting out to get my attention. This is not good." So that's why I'd say it's really important, because I want to practice what I preach so to speak. | Change talk: reasons for change |
| **C:** So part of it is practical, wanting to reduce behavior problems in class, but it's even more than that for you. Giving positive attention to all is a core value of yours, to create an environment of fairness and equality. | Complex reflection highlighting value discrepancy |
| **T:** Yeah, it is a big deal to me. I don't like to be inconsistent. I want to think kids learn something about right and wrong from how I act in class. So when I'm not being fair, I don't like what I'm teaching them. I'm going to change that. | Preparatory talk<br><br>Mobilizing talk |

Notice how the consultant slightly altered the wording of the first ruler question (asking about 0–10 instead of 1–10) and the second ruler question (asking about a number well below the given rating). These nuanced changes are likely unimportant in the overall scheme of things. The key features of this task are to ask for a specific rating of importance, ask why he or she did not rate it lower, and then reflect back what he or she says. Here the consultant offered a complex reflection by noting how the teacher's current behavior (not praising all statements) violated a core value of hers (equality and fairness). This prompted more change talk, including mobilizing language ("I'm going to do this").

*Responding to Change Talk*

An important step in learning MI is to be able to hear change talk. In this regard, it is critical to differentiate change talk (in support of the target behavior) from sustain talk (in support of current practices that run counter to the target behavior) and respond selectively. When you hear change talk, the goal is to keep it flowing.

> An important step in learning MI is to be able to hear change talk.

*Listening With Your EARS.* The EARS acronym provides a useful mnemonic for selectively responding to change talk and encouraging it to continue. When responding to change talk, eliciting and strengthening confidence talk, selective use of EARS—*E*laborating, *A*ffirming, *R*eflecting, and *S*ummarizing—is likely to increase change talk and minimize sustain talk. Elaborating involves the use of open-ended questions to encourage the interviewee to say more about a topic, often about the details that may have been glossed over, that is, who, what, when, where, and why. Affirmations reinforce what has been said. Simple reflections are the least effective strategy but may be sufficient to encourage elaboration with consultees who already appear engaged and motivated. Complex reflections that link the interviewee's behavior or the child's behavior to his or her values; previously stated hopes and dreams; and/or desire, intention, and motivation to change are preferable, particularly when motivation is low. Summarizing allows the consultee to hear what he or she said while also allowing you to confirm your understanding. The examples below have a high likelihood of increasing the change talk language expressed by the consultee.

> *Parent*: "I wish I could help Amelia learn to share with other children."
> *Consultant*: "Can you say a little more about that?" (Elaboration)
> *Parent*: "I think I can do a better job teaching her how to share."
> *Consultant*: "You are confident you're able to do more to help Amelia learn this skill because it is important for her education, and that is one of the top values in your family." (Complex Reflection, tied to values)
> *Parent*: "If she learns how to share, she would probably make more friends."
> *Consultant*: "Learning to share could lead to more friends, which would likely make school a more enjoyable experience." (Complex Reflection)
> *Parent*: "I have to do something different. I cannot continue to leave work early to pick her up from school."
> *Consultant*: "In addition to making your professional life easier, what advantages could come from teaching Amelia how to share?" (Elaboration)

These responses are not only likely to generate more change talk, they are likely to move the change talk in a mobilizing direction. When mobilizing change talk is offered, the consultant's role is to affirm it. Affirming responses to the previous examples are provided below:

> *Parent*: "I plan to help Amelia share while we are coloring this weekend." (Commitment)
> *Consultant*: "Good for you! I look forward to hearing about it." (Affirmation)

*Parent*: "I've never considered it my job as a parent to teach sharing, but I'm ready to do that now." (Activation)

*Consultant*: "I love that you are embracing this new role. I really admire your commitment to Amelia's development." (Affirmation)

*Parent*: "I will set up at least one play session each day in which my goal is to help her practice sharing her things." (Taking steps)

*Consultant*: "You have a real solid plan. I think that is great!" (Affirmation)

*Enhancing Confidence.* Enhancing confidence following initial conversations about change is helpful as it draws out change talk linked to ability. As noted in the UTB model, self-efficacy, or the belief that we can make important changes if we so choose, is a precursor to behavior intention and action. Research strongly supports the role of self-efficacy as a predictor of subsequent behavior change. Thus, MI places great emphasis on attending to and drawing out statements that support self-efficacy.

We have found two strategies taken from the narrative therapy literature— anchoring and thickening—to be very helpful in enhancing confidence. Each of these strategies is designed to elicit confidence talk, which can be increased with use of the core OARS skills.

Consistent with the MI approach, narrative therapy is characterized by respect, transparency, and relentless optimism. Within this literature, the notion of identifying and getting parents to elaborate on what is referred to as unique outcomes is very similar to differentially responding to change talk during the motivational interview. Unique outcomes are examples from the past that are consistent with the target behavior. Taken from the field of narrative therapy, anchoring and thickening questions can be applied to deepen the change talk story (White, 1988, 1995; White & Epston, 1990). Anchoring examples of change from the past that are consistent with the interviewee's values provides a point of reference (typically in time—past, present, and/or future) from which they can build confidence. Inviting the interviewee to discuss successful change experiences (e.g., "Were there times when you taught your other children [or Amelia] to share?" or "What successful examples of teaching sharing can you think of?") provides an anchor with which to associate the target behavior. Once examples of successful change behaviors have been identified, these examples can be further anchored though process questions (e.g., "As you look back at how you taught your older child to share…" "What were the steps you took to teach her to share in the home with her siblings?" "What did you do first?" "Then what?" "How did you prepare yourself to teach her?") Anchoring in the present or recent past, such as in the last few days, works to protect a consultee's initial good intentions regarding change from being overly vulnerable to inevitable setbacks.

Thickening questions plot a substantial relationship between the anchored events and the teacher/parent's current life (e.g., meanings, desires, intentions, beliefs, commitments, motivations, and values). To thicken these stories of change and further instill confidence, the consultant might: (a) ask for details (e.g., "What is the significance of this possible change for you as a family?" "If you were to apply this knowledge in your life now, in what context would it make the most difference?" "What difference would it make?"); (b) include others, such as witnesses to the events (e.g., "What have others seen that would lead them to believe you can do this?" "What do you think motivated [a significant other] to make this same change?"; (c) include values (e.g., "What does this example say about your character?" "What does it say about your commitment to your values?" "What does it say about you as a person that you would do this?" "What does this new perspective tell you about yourself?" "What does this show about your goals for your life?"); or (d) include alternative perspectives (e.g., "Why does this way of acting suit you better than the old way?" "What positive effects on [significant others] do you foresee this change having?").

Miller and Rollnick (2013) also identify using the confidence ruler and soliciting hypothetical change as strategies for enhancing confidence. Using the confidence ruler, the interviewer can elicit confidence talk. The following discussion between a parent and behavioral consultant demonstrates this technique.

> *Consultant:* "On a scale from 1 to 10, with 1 being not confident at all and 10 being super confident, where would you evaluate your confidence that you can teach Amelia to share?"
> *Parent:* "I would say I am a 5 right now."
> *Consultant:* "Why are you a 5 and not a 3?"
> *Parent:* "Because I have done it before, and I think if I really focus on sharing for just a few minutes each day it may make a big difference."
> *Consultant:* "What would it take to get you to a 7?"
> *Parent:* "I am not sure. I guess I might have to try it first, see how it goes."

As with our prior discussion about the importance of ruler, the consultant's second ruler question ("Why a 5 and not a 3?") has a high probability of generating change talk, in this case, ability. A third ruler question added here asks what it would take for the person to go even higher on the scale ("What would it take to get you to a 7?"). This can also elicit change talk and provide clues as to what might be needed to support the consultee in the change process.

### Responding to Sustain (Nonchange) Talk

Responses to nonchange talk are equally important, and classified as sustain talk or discord (Miller & Rollnick, 2013). Sustain talk includes discussions related to the target behavior that fits in Quadrants A or D in Figure 3.1. It is the opposite of change talk in that it represents *Desire* for the status quo, *Ability* to change, *Reasons* for continuing with the status quo, *Need* for the status quo, and *Commitment* to the status quo (DARN-C). In addition, focusing on how the child or another person (e.g., assistant teacher, principal, relative) should change, rather than what the consultee needs to change, might also be considered sustain talk.

> More often than not, our intuitive response to sustain talk is not helpful, as it involves some version of the righting reflex.

The first rule of responding to sustain talk is to become aware of your characteristic response to it. More often than not, our intuitive response to sustain talk is not helpful, as it involves some version of the righting reflex (e.g., arguing against it). Catching yourself from arguing against change, telling others reasons they need to change—including educating them—is a first step in learning to provide a more effective response. We provide more information on ineffective responses to sustain talk in the "Don'ts" section below.

What to do instead? The first line of recommended responses to sustain talk is a simple reflection, followed by a redirection of the topic so as not to promote elaboration. If this strategy is not effective in promoting change talk, the interviewer may choose to move sequentially through strategies that carry increasing levels of risk to the relationship, such as double-sided reflections, exaggeration, and coming alongside. These strategies invite further exploration, defuse sustain talk, and avoid the trap of taking sides. Below, these strategies are described, followed by an example of a response that demonstrates this skill set. In this example, the conversation takes place between a teacher and a behavioral consultant who has suggested they collaborate on the writing of a behavior intervention plan, which was mandated by federal and state law given the child's special education status and recent history of suspensions. The consultant has explained that a behavior intervention plan is required, and the consultee responds, "I've tried behavior intervention plans before and they don't work."

*Double-sided reflections* are excellent ways to respond to sustain talk. These responses usually take the form, "On the one hand, (reflection that repeats what was recently said). ... On the other hand, (invoking a comment or value that was raised previously that is contrary to what was just said)." Double-sided reflections invite the other person to attempt to reconcile their ambivalence.

> *Consultant*: "I can see your predicament. On the one hand, you don't think this is going to work, and on the other, you're convinced things are not going to improve for Nicholas unless you do something different."

When reflecting both sides of the consultee's ambivalence, it is helpful to end with the reflection *in favor of change*, as in the example above.

The intention behind an *exaggeration response* is to amplify a sustain talk statement to evaluate how committed the speaker is to it, and one hopes, to elicit the righting reflex in the direction of change.

> *Consultant*: "It is very unlikely we will generate any strategies in this process that will be helpful to you or Nicholas."

In this example, the consultee's position is made more extreme. Regardless of the consultee's response, you will have learned something about how to proceed. Typically, the speaker will retreat from the position (e.g., "Well, it might be a little helpful. I am willing to try") and, with a little luck, add information about the specific concerns behind the more global statement ("The last time someone came in and made a bunch of suggestions, she left and then I was responsible for implementing everything. I need real help, not just someone telling me what I already know. I have 27 children in this class."). In this case, the elaboration may have revealed an underlying assumption about the type or level of support the consultee believes is necessary to be useful.

Miller and Rollnick (2002) describe a special instance of amplified reflection, *coming alongside,* in which the consultant makes a reflective statement that takes the side *against* change. Similar to exaggeration, the intent is to mobilize the righting reflex in the direction of change. This strategy should be used cautiously because it may be perceived as sarcastic, and therefore introduces a great deal of relational risk.

> *Teacher*: "I've attended your workshops; I've tried all of the strategies you are recommending."
> *Consultant*: "You have tried a lot of strategies. I'd be reluctant to accept additional advice if I were in your shoes as well."

Discord is a verbal or nonverbal signal of dissonance between the consultant and consultee (Miller & Rollnick, 2013). Like sustain talk, discord is predictive of nonchange. Although sustain talk is typically about the target behavior, discord is an interpersonal dynamic and should signal that the relationship is strained. Examples of discord include interrupting, arguing, open hostility, or withdrawal. Assess your ability to apply the OARS skills by completing Practice 3.5 and Practice 3.6.

---

### PRACTICE 3.5

Try taping a segment of an upcoming consultation meeting, or even a conversation with a friend, spouse, or partner. People are often receptive to this if you tell them it is for your benefit and no one else will listen. You will need to set an agenda, and prepare them to focus on a topic for which they have some ambivalence. For teachers, this could involve communicating with a parent they have an aversive relationship with, adopting a new practice, or discussing a conflict with a colleague/supervisor. For a friend or family member, it could be about a lifestyle change (e.g., drinking, eating, exercising), or adopting a new parenting practice. Listen to the tape and try any (or all) of the following.

1. Count the number of open versus closed-ended questions you ask.
2. Record the duration of the time you talk versus listen.
3. Identify all of the other person's comments as change or sustain talk, then determine if your response encouraged more or less of the same.

---

### PRACTICE 3.6

The following statements reflect sustain talk. Test your ability to apply the strategies below.

**Teacher:**   "I don't understand why we have to waste instruction time teaching children how to behave. They should know how to follow rules and directions before they come to school."

*(continued)*

## PRACTICE 3.6 *(continued)*

**Parent:** "I don't have the time to check Sam's backpack every day."

**Teacher:** "I've tried my best and nothing is working. I am not really open to doing much more."

Next, write a response to each resistant comment using the advanced skills listed below.

Simple Reflection:
Amplified Reflection:
Double-Side Reflection:
Coming Alongside:

## SUCCESS STORY

A resource teacher found the distinction between sustain talk and discord useful. She reported that a teacher she worked with recently accused her of being "bossy and demanding," terms that imply discord, not sustain talk. These concepts helped the resource teacher come to understand that the problem was not necessarily with the advice she was offering, but located within the relationship between the two. The solution then involved taking steps to repair the relationship and reduce the discord.

## Planning

The fourth process of MI, planning, is optional because some individuals may not commit to change. For other consultants, the interactions may not be formal enough to justify a planning process. In the planning process, the consultee's autonomy should be honored, and interaction should end with the understanding that if he or she changes his or her mind, you are more than happy to revisit the situation.

> The planning involves negotiating a change plan and consolidating commitment to the plan.

Planning involves negotiating a change plan and consolidating commitment to the plan (Miller & Rollnick, 2013). The plan should include (a) the client's values and ideals, (b) the target behavior that has served as the focal point of all discussions, (c) objectives (i.e., the specific behaviors that operationalize the goal), (d) potential barriers to adherence, and (e) a plan of action to follow when potential barriers surface (Frey, Lee, et al., 2013b). In the context of school-based MI applications with students, the change plan will likely be integrated with some type of academic and/or behavioral intervention, such as implementation of an academic or social–emotional curriculum, a classroom-management strategy, or a behavior-intervention plan. With parents, it might involve attendance at school events, strategies to get their child to school on time every day, or a plan that focuses on effective parenting strategies to support behavior or academic performance in the home setting. Implementation of the change plan will benefit from rehearsal. Role-plays using examples and non-examples of the behavioral objectives are particularly important and prepare the individual to overcome potential barriers.

If one has not given information or advice until this part of the process, it is very likely to occur while developing a change plan. Miller and Rollnick (2013) suggest that giving information or advice is acceptable within MI. However, once again, one needs permission to give it. Miller and Rollnick identified three types of permission: (a) the person asks for advice (permission is implied), (b) you ask to give advice, or (c) you give advice and emphasize autonomy. The *Elicit–Provide–Elicit* strategy (Rollnick, Miller, & Butler, 2007) is useful to ensure information and advice is delivered in a way consistent with the MI approach. In this situation, the interviewee is asked what he or she has heard or thinks he or she knows about the strategy (Elicit). Next, the interviewer provides the information or advice (Provide). This is followed up with an open-ended question to elicit the interviewee's thoughts on the information, advice, or next steps (Elicit). The following dialogue demonstrates this technique within the context of developing a classroom-management plan with a consultee.

> *School psychologist*: "One aspect of a classroom-management plan typically involves the use of consequences when children do not follow the teacher's expectations. Would it be all right if I shared a little about a strategy in the context of a classroom-management plan?"
>
> *Teacher:* "Sure, I need all the help I can get."
>
> *School psychologist*: "Great. Before I do, do you mind telling me what you have heard about consistent consequences, or even what you already do in this regard?" (Elicit)
>
> *Teacher*: "Consequences are important because it sends a message to the other children that they cannot get away with something. I'm very consistent. When a child's behavior is disrupting the class, I send the child into the hallway to work, or write a referral to the office."
>
> *School psychologist*: "That's good. You already have a plan in place that involves consequences. In addition to communicating to other students that a behavior is not acceptable, consequences involve a few additional characteristics from my perspective. For example, there should be a hierarchy of consequences—at least four to five—that are understood and agreed upon by the students; they need to be applied immediately following the violation, and they have to be consistent. Many teachers use a formal system to help them meet this requirement, but that would be entirely up to you (promote autonomy; Provide). What do you think about what I've just said regarding consequences?" (Elicit)
>
> *Teacher*: "What do you mean by 'a hierarchy'?"

When information or advice is offered in this fashion, it is likely to elicit sustain talk, preparatory change talk (DARN), or mobilizing change talk (CAT). The interviewer's responsibility is to listen carefully. If it is anything but change talk, it is likely a sign that the interviewee is not ready for the planning process. If you hear preparatory change talk, you should attempt to make it commitment talk, and if it is commitment talk, you should affirm it and begin putting a plan in place around this topic.

## SUGGESTIONS FOR GETTING STARTED

For many people, understanding the logic and strategies of MI is easy, yet applying the strategies in real conversations can be difficult. The five core skills of MI—OARS plus informing and advising—are foundational to practicing MI proficiently. Spending time learning and practicing these skills is a part of becoming more proficient in MI. Additionally, simply learning to hear and distinguish between change and sustain talk is a foundational skill. Listening to popular songs or TV shows and becoming more in tune with the language of intention will build your skill in this regard. Once you learn to hear change talk, it becomes your guide in doing MI. For those just learning MI and interested in gradually incorporating it into their daily interactions, here are some simple "dos" and "don'ts" that may be helpful.

### Dos

First, the consultee should be doing the majority of the talking. If you find yourself talking more than the other person it is unlikely that you are doing MI. One easy way to find out is to tape a few of your consultation meetings (with the permission of the other person, of course!) and listen to how much time you spend talking compared to the other person. Second, use more reflec-

> If you find yourself talking more than the other person, it is unlikely that you are doing MI.

tions than questions. Aim for a 3:1 reflection-to-question ratio. Third, keep reflections brief and use complex reflections when you can. People have a tendency to rely on simple reflections, perhaps because they are easier and require less attention. Complex reflections enrich the conversation in ways that paraphrasing cannot. Fourth, avoid affirmations that are evaluative or that communicate judgment. Evaluative statements often begin with "I," so try to use more "you" forms of affirmations. Finally, Dr. Rollnick recently suggested that consultants spend at least the first 20% of all interactions engaging others. This metric is useful because it applies equally well to short and long interactions. In a 5-minute conversation, you would be wise to spend at least the first minute focused on simply engaging the other person; in a 60-minute conversation, 10 minutes or more would be spent on engaging.

Please note that Miller and Rollnick (2013) suggest that these core skills (OARS), which are common to many person-centered counseling approaches, do not in and of themselves constitute MI. Rather, it is the strategic use of these skills to move in the direction of change that defines MI. However, applying these skills, even generally in daily conversations, is likely to dramatically alter the interaction patterns of conversations between consultants and consultees, or school staff and parents.

## Don'ts

We all have our characteristic responses to given situations, including our intuitive reactions to things that other people say. Sometimes these intuitive responses may vary by the content of the conversation. For instance, perhaps when the conversation is about improving classroom management your characteristic response is to provide education, whereas if the topic is about something more emotional for you, like social justice, you may be more inclined to respond to sustain talk with argument. Know that quite often these intuitive responses are not effective; instead, these responses can elicit more sustain talk. It is important for you to be aware of your intuitive reactions, and when they are counter to motivational speech, to prevent them. Below we describe several common intuitive responses that may actually undermine motivation.

### Argument

Perhaps the most common intuitive reaction to sustain talk is to argue against it. Miller and Rollnick refer to this tendency as the righting reflex. As we noted earlier, most of us are aware of both sides of an argument (i.e., why change would be good and why it would be bad). Our cognitive world is set up to have a reflexive response to counter any resistant speech ("I don't want to exercise") with the opposite side of the argument ("but exercise is good for you"). Keep in mind that your intuitive response to argue against the status quo will almost always elicit the opposite reaction from your consultees—to argue in favor of the status quo. This is inevitably a losing argument if you are hoping to motivate someone to change.

> Keep in mind that your intuitive response to argue against the status quo will almost always elicit the opposite reaction for your consultees—to argue in favor of the status quo.

### Education

Many well-educated people have an inclination to try to educate others as a strategy for building motivation. It should come as no surprise that this inclination may be stronger in educational settings than other settings. For example, when a parent says that he or she disagrees that praise is a useful parenting strategy, a consultant might naturally reply, "There's been a lot of research on that question and very consistently it has shown that praise is a key parenting skill." The problem with an educational response to sustain talk is that it assumes the reason a person is not motivated to change can be altered by logic and reason in a simple linear fashion. As we have already established, motivation to change is a complex and dynamic interaction among many aspects of a person's life and environment. Another problem is that this response also assumes the person has not already contemplated the educational piece of information you provide. In fact, many consultees with whom you work are already aware of many of the things you might want to teach them. More often than not, an educational response to sustain talk elicits arguments against the educational tidbit ("That research wasn't done in my home"). Finally, it is important to note the irony of an educational response. The consultant attempts to educate the listener about research on a topic yet ignores the vast research, which shows this type of response is generally ineffective in moving people toward change.

### Premature Solutions

Another intuitive response might be to shift to direct advice giving. These responses usually begin with a phrase like, "Have you tried..." or "What if you..." or the more direct, "If I were you, I would..." While giving advice can be an effective strategy, it is best used sparingly and only when invited. It is also best to pair advice giving with another MI consistent response, such as emphasizing choice.

### Self-Disclosure

Some consultants intuitively shift to disclosing their own experiences as a strategy to overcome resistance. "I have a classroom very similar to yours and the way I dealt with it was to..." or "When my child was learning to assert himself, I found the best thing I could do was..." Like advice giving, self-disclosure can be an effective consultation response. When used in a timely and thoughtful manner, self-disclosure can build rapport and the helping alliance. However, when used excessively or as a typical response to sustain talk, self-disclosure can have the effect of both eliciting more sustain talk ("Well this classroom [or my child] is different than yours") and creating discord (because the self-disclosure is now interpreted as an indication that you don't understand the person's circumstance).

### Authority/Pressure/Guilt

Another strategy some people use to influence others to become more motivated is to make them feel guilty. Although guilt can be a motivator, it is a risky strategy to use as a consultant.

### Avoidance

Many times we may want to avoid sustain talk. Discussing sustain talk can feel uncomfortable and many of us naturally steer away from uncomfortable conversations. Sometimes avoidance can be an effective strategy when used intentionally, as in shifting the focus. However, when it is a characteristic, unconscious response, a consultant can miss genuine opportunities for eliciting change talk. Willingness to broach difficult topics is a higher-order consultant skill.

### How to Know Which Way to Go

As before, the parent, teacher, or student's language will be your guide in knowing whether your education, advice giving, or self-disclosure interfered with or fostered motivation. If after your response you hear change talk, then your response was fine. If, however, you elicit more sustain talk, it is a sign to do something different. In general, we simply encourage you to be aware of your characteristic responses, practice withholding them on occasion, and monitor the effect.

### Alternate Responses

#### Catch Yourself

The two steps we recommend for changing your intuitive response are (a) catch yourself, and (b) do something different. By "catch yourself" we mean be aware of your characteristic responses and withhold them before they occur. So if you intuitively respond to sustain talk with education, notice this and pause before it happens in your next consultation meeting. The second step involves intentionally choosing a different strategy. Ideally, it would be one that is in line with MI. A simple approach as you are learning new MI strategies is to simply reflect the sustain talk. If sustain talk persists, then shift the focus.

#### Coping Statements

Sometimes your own internal dialogue can interfere with the process of learning MI skills. We encourage you to identify some positive coping statements to carry with you as you engage in the arduous process of learning a new skill or even a different way of being in your consultation relationships. Coping statements include, "I can do this" or "I'm going to treat this like a scientist and just observe what happens." In training people to use MI, we note a tendency for people to want to become immediately proficient at it. Part of this may come from the sense that this approach seems easy. In reality, most people need time and practice, so we encourage you to set realistic goals for yourself based on your own strengths and areas for growth.

#### Setting Goals

A realistic goal for most people is to simply target one new skill at a time. For instance, if you are already good at asking open-ended questions but tend not to reflect comments, then simply set a goal to increase your number of reflective comments in your next meeting. Or, if you already use a lot of simple reflections, perhaps your next goal could be to increase your number of complex reflections in your next visit. A good place to start if you are completely new to MI is simply to start paying attention to your intuitive response to sustain talk and to interrupt it. In past editions of MI, this was referred to as "rolling with resistance."

## SUMMARY

Infusion of MI techniques into school-based intervention research is in its early stages but is continuing to be adopted by researchers (Blom-Hoffman & Rose, 2007; Connell & Dishion, 2008; Dishion et al., 2008; Dishion & Stormshak, 2007; Dishion, Stormshak, & Siler, 2010; Frey et al., 2011; Gill, Hyde, Shaw, Dishion, & Wilson, 2008; Lunkenheimer et al., 2008; Moilanen, Shaw, Dishion, Gardner, & Wilson, 2010; Nock & Ferriter, 2005; Nock & Kazdin, 2001; Nock & Photos, 2006; Reinke et al., 2008; Shaw, Dishion, Supplee, Gardner, & Arnds, 2006). Within these interventions, MI is used to increase the fidelity of evidence-based interventions that depend on changes in teacher or parent behavior, such as parenting skills or classroom-management practices. Although we agree MI is a very useful approach to guide these intervention procedures, we also believe adopting the spirit and skills associated with this approach to guide everyday conversations about change could be useful. Although the evidence for MI's effective use by school personnel is still emerging, it is reasonable to expect that MI will expand within the context of school support services in the next decade. MI meets a number of needs and has numerous positive features, including strong face validity and flexibility of use.

In the next part of the book, we apply the skills and processes of MI to three common consultees in schools: parents, teachers, and students. The emphasis is on using these strategies to have more effective conversations about change in schools.

# Specific Applications of Motivational Interviewing in Schools

# 4

# Motivational Interviewing With Parents

As most educators are well aware, children benefit when their parents are involved in all aspects of their education. This is true for high-performing students as well as low-performing students, and for students with and without special needs. Unfortunately, not all parents are actively involved in school. This is especially so for students from diverse backgrounds and for those with behavior problems (Park, Pullis, Reilly, & Townsend, 1994). One of the ongoing challenges for most schools is how best to reach families and encourage their participation in educational activities and services offered through the school.

In this chapter, we explore ways of using the motivational interviewing (MI) strategies, discussed in Chapter 3, to gain greater parent involvement in schools. We first provide a rationale and discuss common challenges in achieving this goal. Next, we provide strategies that can be used at each MI process—engaging, focusing, evoking, and planning. As with earlier chapters, the goal is to describe the use of MI strategies in everyday interactions with families. In addition, we situate these strategies within a structured consultation model that can be applied in longer interactions and meetings with parents.

## RATIONALE AND CHALLENGES

There are a number of structural, contextual, and perceptual factors that can interfere with whether a parent or a caregiver participates in educational and/or psychological services. This is unfortunate, given that children with mental health and academic needs are more likely to receive services in school than anywhere else. Parents' initial decisions about whether and how to participate are influenced by their beliefs regarding their role in education, their perceptions of what causes problems, perceived barriers to participation, and their past experiences with the educational system (McKay et al., 2004). Additional factors contribute to lack of parental involvement. Socioeconomic disadvantage, ethnic minority status, severity of child problems, parental stress and depression, lack of knowledge and skills in accessing supports, and lack of confidence in becoming involved all play a significant role in determining whether a family becomes engaged in services (McKay et al., 2004; Nock & Kazdin, 2001).

Families of youth with emotional or behavioral problems tend to have many interactions with the educational and mental health service systems. These past experiences influence parents' perceptions about their role in services and their estimates of the relative risk and benefits of ongoing participation. Some minority group parents may also experience a cultural disconnect between the family and the school (McKay et al., 2004). This in turn can lead to mistrust in services due to experiences of mistreatment or marginalization (Duran & Duran, 1995). Additional structural barriers such as work/time conflicts with the typical school day, transportation, and child care may also interfere with parental involvement in school and related services (McKay et al., 2004; Nock & Kazdin, 2001).

Addressing these barriers to service participation is critical for school personnel to serve students effectively. Further, parents have become central players in many interventions for children and adolescents (Affronti & Levison-Johnson, 2009). For instance, most effective treatments for youth with emotional or behavioral problems have shifted from child-focused interventions to family-centered services that require significant parental participation and behavior change (Fauber & Long, 1991). Increasingly, parental involvement in the schooling process contributes greatly to the success of all students.

## ENGAGING

As described in Chapter 2, a growing literature has given us guidance on how best to encourage family engagement in a variety of services. These first-level methods are necessary to "get your foot in the door"—that is, to begin building a successful relationship with parents by gaining their trust and increasing their willingness to attend meetings and maintain open communication with school personnel. Once parents are willing to participate in discussion, school personnel are able to use the MI process of engaging to capitalize on this momentum.

### MI Spirit Applied to Parents: Three Key Lessons for Working With Parents

There are three important lessons to always keep in mind when working with families with the greatest service needs. First, most parents will resolve many of the structural barriers to participation (e.g., transportation, child care) if they perceive the benefits of their participation to be greater than the costs. This is not to say that schools should not provide support services. On the contrary, evidence suggests that these support services do help. These include offering services at flexible

> The most effective engagement strategies must focus on directly addressing the perceptual barriers to participation and helping parents see a high likelihood of benefit in involvement relative to cost.

times, providing meals and child care for participation in family-focused interventions, and providing incentives for participation (Webster-Stratton, 1998a). At the end of the day though, most parents will figure out a way to participate in services if they truly believe their effort will be rewarded with a better outcome for their child. Thus, in addition to support services for parents, the most effective engagement strategies must focus on directly addressing the perceptual barriers to participation and helping parents see a high likelihood of benefit in involvement relative to cost.

Second, persistence is key. Many family consultants and school personnel report worrying about bothering parents with repeated phone calls, e-mails, or notes. When researchers have asked parents about these contacts, however, rather than viewing these repeated contacts as intrusive, most parents appreciate the effort and concern. So, the second big lesson in working with difficult parents is to keep trying.

Third, check your assumptions at the door. No one likes to be judged. This is especially true when it comes to parenting behaviors. Many parents, particularly those whose children have challenging behaviors, come to school expecting to be judged. They watch for it and will leave at the first hint of social evaluation, so it behooves you to spend time monitoring your assumptions about parents you work with. If you find yourself thinking or saying negative things about a parent ("If she cared more, she would attend meetings," "He's a bad parent"), remind yourself that parents will pick up on these assumptions. Not surprisingly, parents are unlikely to work well with a provider they don't trust and by whom they feel judged. You can repair relationships that have started out with a parent feeling judged, but you must first change your assumptions and beliefs about the parent.

---

### EVERYDAY CONVERSATIONS ABOUT CHANGE

Mrs. Fitzgerald, a fifth-grade teacher at Ridgeview Elementary School, decides to talk with the mother of her student, Gerald, who is frequently tardy to class at the start of the day. She e-mails the mother, Ms. Mendoza, and asks if she can find a time to talk with her in person or by phone. Ms. Mendoza responds and indicates that she can stop by after school the next day. At the meeting, Mrs. Fitzgerald invites her into the classroom and starts the conversation:

**Teacher (T):** Thank you so much for finding time in your busy schedule to meet with me today.

**Parent (P):** No big deal. So what's the problem?

**T:** First, I want you to know that I see Gerald doing a lot of positive things at school. I can really see him trying to do well even on things that don't come as easily to him. Just yesterday, I was watching him stick with it and finish his math work before the bell rang even though students near him were distracting him. That's a huge improvement from earlier in the year when he gave up easily or got off track when he struggled with problems.

*(continued)*

---

### EVERYDAY CONVERSATIONS ABOUT CHANGE (*continued*)

P: Uh huh (tilts head).

T: That surprises you.

P: Hmm. I don't usually hear good things about what he's doing. Usually when I have to meet at school it means he's screwing up.

T: It's nice to hear about the good things.

P: Yeah.

T: I really, really want to be sure we keep this momentum going. The one thing that I see that is getting in his way right now is that he has been coming late to school.

P: Yeah, he's not good at getting moving in the morning.

T: Mornings are a struggle.

P: Hmm. I don't even mess with him anymore. I wake him up and tell him to get moving. But the more I talk, the bigger fights we have.

T: It's just easier to let him do his own thing.

P: Yeah. He's not a morning person.

T: What do you think about him being late to school?

P: I don't think it's good.

T: What bothers you about it?

P: He would probably do better at school if he came earlier. It's also not very responsible to be late. I want him to be responsible.

T: Being on time is a sign of growing up. How do you think being on time will help him be better at school?

P: I don't know. I just think it can't hurt. Plus he might be missing something.

T: That makes a lot of sense. I see that. You know on days when he's here on time, I just see him having better days. When he's late, he starts the day behind everyone else, and it's like he spends the rest of the day trying to catch up.

P: Hmm.

T: What do you think we should do?

P: I don't know. I've tried everything and it just seems to make things worse.

T: Whatever we do, it needs to be different than what you've tried and not lead to bigger fights for the two of you.

P: That's right.

T: You know I've talked to a lot of parents who have struggled with similar things, and it's pretty normal. I have some ideas about how others have made things better with getting up. It is completely up to you, but if you want, we can talk about some of those things.

P: Okay. I'm open to hearing ideas.

---

*In this example, the teacher initiated a more productive conversation by beginning with specific positive comments about the student, withholding judgments, framing the problem around their shared goal of wanting the student to be successful at school, asking evocative and open-ended questions, using reflections and affirmations, and asking permission before giving advice.*

## Initial Contact

The goal of the engaging process is to build trust with families and encourage their openness to continuing conversation; therefore, as McKay's engagement model described in Chapter 2, much emphasis is placed on the initial contact with parents. The initial contact is the time when rapport building begins and sets the stage for a positive relationship between the family and the consultant. Often, the initial contact with the parent is the phone call inviting the family to the first meeting, an interaction that marks the beginning of the intervention. During the initial phone call, it is important to begin building a relationship with the parent while carefully avoiding in-depth discussion of family issues. Addressing family problems over the phone without having met the family could unintentionally create situations that undermine later intervention work. For instance, the parent involved in the initial phone call could begin creating an alliance with the consultant, inadvertently or intentionally, against another family member by sharing information about the other family member.

## Social Conversation (Not Small Talk)

Be sure to take time at the beginning of your visit to simply engage in social conversation. Brief social conversation should not be confused with small talk about the weather or other frivolous topics, what Miller and Rollnick (2013) refer to as the Chat Trap. Small talk can interfere with rapport and motivation building if it is about trivial topics or if it persists too long. Instead, the brief introductory talk should be about something relevant to the person you are meeting, curiosity questions that their surroundings invite you to learn about. If the meeting is in the parent's home, for instance, you might comment on the house or artifacts in the house ("That's a beautiful painting") and ask about when or where they were acquired. Curiosity is an important quality for facilitating these conversations.

## Provide a Rationale for Your Meeting

Parents will want to know why they have been invited to meet with you. It is likely that you will have already explained the purpose to the parent prior to the meeting, but it is a good idea to repeat it at the beginning of the meeting. The rationale should be brief, matter-of-fact, and nonjudgmental. It should convey a sense of collaboration and commitment to a shared goal: "As I mentioned in my phone call, I wanted to share some concerns with you about some of Jeffrey's classroom behaviors and get your ideas on how to support Jeffrey at school."

## Using Your OARS

OARS (open-ended questions, affirmations, reflections, and summaries) are the primary tools for facilitating the engaging process in MI. If your primary concern is building the parent's motivation, be prepared to spend much of the early part of your meeting simply listening to the parents to understand their perspective. The emphasis on listening is not determined by how long the meeting is. Even in a brief visit, your time is much better spent building a relationship through affirmations, reflective listening, summaries, and evocative, open-ended questions.

### Affirmations: Start With the Positives

Affirmations are a wonderful way to begin any visit with a parent. Remember that affirmations are most effective if they are genuine, accurate, and specific, so be sure to take time prior to a visit with a parent to reflect on positive feedback you would like to share. For some children and families you encounter, it is easy to think of their strengths and positive attributes. For others, especially children you are struggling to help, it can sometimes be difficult to think of even a single positive characteristic. Thus, the process of taking time to think about positives before a visit is also important to get you in the right frame of mind to help the parent. Recall from prior chapters that the people who are most helpful in our lives, the ones who are most likely to support us through difficult times, are the ones we perceive as caring, genuine, and well intentioned.

An example of beginning a conversation with affirmations is given below:

> Thank you for taking the time to meet with me to talk about Jeffrey. I'm lucky to have your little boy in my class this year. He really has a spark that attracts other children to him. When I watch him on the playground, he's just having so much fun. I can see why the children want to play with him. His social relationships are going to be a real strength for him.

*Using Affirmations to Instill Hope.* Early and often during your visits with a parent, it is important to convey optimism and build the perception that something can be done to improve the situation. You want the parents to leave any meeting with you with a sense that things will improve. The ability to instill hope in others starts with your beliefs and perceptions. If you believe the situation is hopeless, your words and actions will communicate this to the parent and undermine any visit you have with them. It is important, therefore, to take time prior to a meeting and check your assumptions. For particularly challenging children and families, you may need to remind yourself of some basic truths. Reading and believing the following statements, or variations of these, may help:

- All children can learn and grow.
- Adults can work together to support the learning and growth of all children.
- Something can be done to improve any situation.
- I can do something to improve any situation.

You can convey your optimism and your commitment in words early and often during the meeting. Some things you might say to communicate this include the following:

- "I'm confident that we can figure this out."
- "I wanted to get on top of this early because it is something we can improve now."

- "By working together, I know we can help Jeffrey get the most out of learning."
- "I see great things for Jeffrey and I'm committed to helping him."

## Open-Ended Questions to Build Engagement

Open-ended questions during the engaging process are focused on learning more about the parent, his or her perceptions, values, and intentions. As we discuss below, gathering the parents' perceptions of the problem and potential solutions are also part of the focusing, evoking, and planning processes. Engagement questions that open the door for deeper understanding and rapport building include questions that examine strengths and resources; their reasons for optimism; and their general perceptions of their child, their family, and the school. Don't feel pressured to ask all of these questions, or to ask them only at the beginning of the meeting. The engaging process is active during the entire meeting.

- "What's been going well this year?"
- "What are some of (your child's) strengths?"
- "What are things that you admire about your family?"
- "What are some challenges you and your child have overcome in the past?"
- "What has been your experience of the school?"
- "What have you liked/disliked about the school this year?"
- "How can I be of most help to you? What things can I do to better support you?"

## Reflections and Summaries

Listening, truly hearing the parent and understanding his or her perspective, is an important goal of the engaging process. By asking open-ended questions about their perspective and then spending time reflecting and summarizing their comments, you have the potential to build a relationship with them. Simple reflections of content and feelings ("You are really worried about your son") encourage the conversation to continue and demonstrate that you are listening. More complex reflections of inferred deeper meanings behind what is said ("You feel stuck because it seems like if you make these changes your whole life will be different, it will be a new you") convey empathy and offer the opportunity for a closer and more trusting relationship.

Summaries can serve these functions and also help to move the conversation forward, give the conversation structure, and link ideas expressed at different points in the conversation. Summaries can provide useful transitions from one topic to another ("So far we've talked about your concerns about Cindy and how your life would be better if you made some small changes as a family. Now I want to ask you about things that are most important to you as a parent, some questions about your values."). They can also be used to collect a string of ideas, a theme, perhaps not explicitly mentioned by the parent but that you as a listener can connect the dots and present back to the parent for confirmation. Miller and Rollnick (2002) refer to this as collecting a bouquet of flowers and presenting them to a client for further discussion and consideration. For instance, midway through an interview, you might say, "You talk about how much you are working and how stuck you feel in that role. You also talk about how important school is for your children and how hard it is for you to check on your kids schoolwork. You want them to feel connected to their extended family but you have no time for that. As I'm listening to you, I get this sense of how much everything in your family's life hinges on you and how little support you have for making everything run smoothly."

## Be Willing to Ask Difficult Questions and Discuss Uncomfortable Topics

Throughout the interview, pay attention to cues from the parent about sensitive topics. It is important to bring these topics to light by asking gentle questions about them. By asking these questions you are able to gather important information that may be central to understanding the child and family. By asking in a matter-of-fact manner without showing discomfort, you gain credibility with the parent and demonstrate that you are willing and able to tackle the difficult problems. You can also think about willingness to discuss difficult topics as an example of immediacy, talking about the here and now rather than the past or future. Successful discussions about difficult topics can increase the intimacy of a relationship and build rapport. Some examples of sensitive topics include living arrangements, relationship problems, recent deaths in the family, and alternative lifestyle questions. Timing, of course, is important with these questions. You want to establish some rapport before probing too deeply. You may make a note to come back to certain topics later in the interview as you notice the family is feeling more comfortable with you.

> Note that the concept of confrontation is different in an MI approach. Rather than the confrontation occurring *between* the consultant and the parent as might occur in a more interpretive counseling approach (e.g., psychodynamic), in MI the confrontation is *within* an individual as they encounter discrepancies between their values and actions.

Note that the concept of confrontation is different in an MI approach. Rather than the confrontation occurring *between* the consultant and the parent as might occur in a more interpretive counseling approach (e.g., psychodynamic), in MI the confrontation is *within* an individual as he or she encounters discrepancies between their values and actions (Miller & Rollnick, 2013).

## Exploring Values

As described in Chapter 3, values exploration is a foundational aspect of MI. Discussions about values serves two essential functions: (a) it facilitates the engagement process by encouraging a discussion about what is important and valuable to the parent and (b) it provides valuable information to the consultant that may be used during the evoking stage to highlight any observed discrepancies between values and actions. Values discussions also provide a platform for consultants to use all of their OARS strategies as they ask open-ended questions ("Tell me about your important values") and deliver affirmations ("That makes a lot of sense"), reflections ("So providing a good role model for your children gives meaning to your life"), and summaries ("The three most important values for you are honesty, generosity, and loyalty and all of your decisions as a parent are designed to teach your children to value these as well"). The two methods we use to invite values discussions are either to simply ask values-oriented questions or to use a more structured values exercise.

### Value Questions

Part of spending time engaging a parent involves learning more about his or her values. We do this by asking open-ended questions (or statements) and listening to the responses. Questions or statements that elicit value discussions include the following:

- "Tell me about the things that are most important to you."
- "What are your hopes and wishes for your child (or family)?"
- "What things do you value most as a parent?"
- "When you look into the future, what do you most want for your child (or family)?"
- "When your child is an adult, what do you want him to say about you as a parent?"

Each of these questions taps into a personal belief or value that defines the parent. These evocative questions add to our understanding of the parent and give us access to a personal part of them. When asked with good will, with the intention of simply learning more about them, and when we truly listen to their response (showing this with reflections and summaries), we foster a positive relationship with them. We also learn about some key factors that drive them.

### A Parent Values Card Sort Exercise

Another method for engaging parents is to conduct a values exploration task during an early meeting with them (see Frey et al., 2011; Miller, de Baca, Matthews, & Wilbourne, 2001). Although you will not have time to do this with all parents, it can be a useful activity for those who you are truly committed to spending time with to build their involvement in school or services for their child. The task can take 10 to 15 minutes, but it is an investment well worth the effort. It provides a rich source of information and most parents will find it to be fun and engaging to do. We suggest you practice it with a peer or friend before doing it with a family for the first time just to experience what it is like.

---

### SUCCESS STORY USING THE VALUES CARD SORT

A school consultant met with a mother of a 7-year-old with severe behavior problems at school. The consultant had observed the parent to be inconsistent in follow-through with school appointments and commitments. Based on brief interactions with the parent and comments from other staff, the consultant hypothesized that the parent had limited organizational skills and possibly some cognitive delays.

During a first meeting the parent and the consultant effectively used the values card sort task to both engage the parent and to gather critical assessment and support planning information. The mother quickly engaged in the task and carefully processed her decision making about the importance of the various values. The fine distinctions that she was able to make between overlapping values (e.g., providing for her family vs. being a good parent) made it clear to the consultant that her original concerns about possible cognitive limitations were incorrect. The values discussion led to further revelations by the mother about her own history of abuse and concerns about her own parenting practices. The consultant was able to reflect back to the mother the following discrepancy: On the one hand, the mother identified Being a Good Parent as one of her cherished values, and, on the other hand, in her own estimation, she was falling short. The mother agreed and expressed her deep concerns about her child's behavior problems and with the growing distance and disconnect she was feeling from him. These statements were all examples of motivational statements that highlighted for the mother the discrepancy between how things were going in her life versus how she wanted them to be. Such cognitive dissonance is the source of motivation for creating positive life changes in the MI model (Miller & Rollnick, 2002).

---

The purpose of the task is to evoke a discussion about the parents' most important values so the consultant can get a better sense of their ideals, dreams, and wishes for their family. When you invite the parents to complete the task, provide a more basic overview and rationale such as, "I really find it helpful to learn more about my students' parents, especially some of the things that are most important to them. If it's okay with you, I would like you to do this card sorting game with me so I can learn more about you."

Although there are many variations of the task, the version we use involves presenting parents with a stack of 20 to 30 cards with a value statement on each (e.g., education, wealth, discipline) and asking them to sort them into three piles: Not Important, Important, and Very Important. The consultant then asks the parent to identify his or her top three values and explain why each is important to him or her; if both parents are present they can complete the task independently. This information is often useful in making the parent aware of discrepancies between his or her values and current life experiences and actions. Moreover, most parents find the task to be challenging, self-affirming, and highly engaging.

To complete the task, use the value list provided in Handout 4.1 to generate a pack of individual cards. You can do this by printing each value on a separate index card or by printing each on a label and then putting each label on an index card.

Tell the parent you would like to learn more about the important things in his or her life. Begin by laying the cards labeled "Not Important," "Important," and "Very Important" on the table. Hand the remaining cards with value statements on them to the parent and ask him or her to read each one and sort them into these three piles. Alternately, you can read the cards with parents, especially those whose literacy skills are challenged, and complete the exercise through an interactive discussion. Tell the parent that there are no right answers as everyone has personal values. Also, encourage him or her to go with their first gut response. As they complete the task, we prefer to turn away and attend to other tasks (paperwork, for instance) to give them a sense of privacy as they do their first sort. We encourage you to try the task yourself and notice how revealing it can feel.

After the parent has finished sorting all value cards, pick up the Very Important pile and ask them to re-sort these by identifying the three to five most important values. Many parents will struggle with this final task. Do not pressure them to sort them into the final five if they find the task too difficult; for instance, many parents will say the values are equally important.

Next, facilitate a discussion about their values by asking them to tell you why they choose any three to five as their most important values. Use your OARS as you listen to affirm parent values, link them to their current versus ideal parenting practices, and connect them to their goals for their child's behavior and future. Ask open-ended questions about why the client picked each value, what it means to them personally, how they know they have this value or goal (e.g., what do they see in their life that convinces them this is important), how they enact the value, and how the value relates to the target behavior. Listen for examples of child behavior and parenting practices that do not fit with their stated values and ideals. Reflect these examples by validating their struggles, affirming their commitment to their values, and evoking arguments for change. Use an MI approach (such as rolling with resistance) if the client provides answers that indicate his or her card choice is consistent with an undesirable behavior (a common one is Having Fun). Listen carefully for the presence of change talk that might occur and reinforce it as you hear it.

This exercise will facilitate a discussion of values and goals between you and the parent. It is typically done early in the relationship, during the engagement process. Done well, engaging in a values discussion will improve your relationship with the parent, and it may also provide useful information to draw on in the focusing, evoking, and planning stages. For instance, you may refer back to the values to evoke discrepancies between deeply held beliefs and a current behavior. It is important to note that the values exercise is only intended as a conduit to engagement. A common error for those who try it the first time is to be overly concerned about the procedural details, which if taken to an extreme can undermine the primary goal of building the relationship.

In the example below, notice how the consultant mixes simple reflections with complex reflections and open-ended questions to explore and affirm the parent's value while connecting it to parenting:

| Values Dialogue | | Comments |
|---|---|---|
| Consultant (C): | You picked "Doing Something Good in the World" as a top value for you. Tell me why that is so important to you. | Open-ended statement |
| Mother (M): | I just think there's enough problems in the world. I want to be part of the good. | Change talk: reasons for change |
| C: | You want to make a difference. | Reflection |
| M: | Yes, I just have always had this sense that I was here to help people, to do the right thing, to inspire others. | Values |
| C: | What are some ways that you do good in the world? | Open-ended question |
| M: | I volunteer at the local food bank. Even though I don't have a lot, I want my kids to see that I still give back. | Change talk: reasons for change |
| C: | It's really about instilling this value in your children. | Reflection |
| M: | That's right. I want them to know that they make the world through what they do, that they can make a difference. They can be part of the good. | Values |
| C: | Your work as a parent will be done if they follow your example. | Values reflection |

## FOCUSING

Focusing involves determining the direction of your work together with parents. Sometimes the focus is provided by the meeting itself. For instance, if you initiated a meeting with a parent to discuss his or her child's academic problems, the focus will be coming up with a plan to address those problems. Sometimes the focus is established by the parent, as when a parent requests a meeting for support with a problem at home involving the child. Occasionally, the focus is unclear at the outset of a meeting.

### Agenda Setting

Regardless of the scenario, it is helpful early in a visit with a parent to clarify the focus and involve him or her in establishing an agenda for your time together. When you have requested the meeting, it is a good idea to have some ideas about what you would like the focus to be and even to write down a brief agenda for the meeting. When you take the lead for setting the agenda in this way, it is critical for you to invite the parent to participate in creating the agenda. Here, the teacher invites the parent to get topics on the agenda that she wants to discuss after providing the general focus of the meeting:

> I wanted to talk to you today about helping Zelda become a better reader. I have some ideas about what I would like us to talk about today, but first wanted to see whether there were things that are important for you to talk about related to Zelda's learning.

After getting the parent's input, you can transition back to the topics that were on your agenda, highlighting any that overlapped with the parent:

> That's great. So it sounds like we're on the same page with things to talk about. I would like to (1) tell you more about what I'm seeing in the classroom, (2) get your perception of her reading skills, (3) hear more about her learning activities at home, and then (4) come up with a plan for next steps.

When the parent has initiated the meeting, you can invite the parent to provide the focus by asking open-ended questions such as, "What would you like help with today?" or "What should be the goal of our visit?" or "What would be a good outcome of our time today?"

## Ecological Assessments

The critical part of focusing is finding a common direction with a parent. In MI, this can be accomplished through conversation alone as described above. In some cases, when you commit to working with a parent over time on a particular topic you will want to collect additional assessment information on that topic. This is optional in MI and will be described in more detail in Chapter 7. Detailed assessments are not necessary for having everyday conversations about change. Here we simply introduce the idea that gathering systematic interview, observation, and rating scale information can be useful in pinpointing problem areas (e.g., sometimes parents are surprised to learn that their child is depressed after this information is gathered from a child rating scale) and accurately characterizing parenting behaviors (e.g., often parents are not particularly insightful about their parenting behaviors and so direct observations can sometimes provide enlightening information to further focus discussions about the problem).

Potential areas of focus for ongoing meetings could include home–school communication systems, setting up effective home learning environments, building effective family communication skills, and supporting parents in improving their home behavior-management skills. Structured assessments of the domains of focus for subsequent meetings can provide further clarity on the direction of your work together. For instance, when working with a parent to improve his or her

> A good rule of thumb is that any data collected should be linked to potential interventions that are available as part of a menu of options.

behavior-management system, assessments might reveal that the parent provides effective proactive parenting strategies but has not learned to deliver consequences consistently. Your work would thus be tailored to that family's particular need.

In our work with parents, when we are concerned with bolstering their motivation to participate in an ongoing intervention (e.g., a behavior support team, weekly meetings with a school consultant to learn new strategies), we collect data from the following domains: youth adjustment, family adjustment, and school adjustment. In the youth-adjustment category, we collect information about the child's emotional and behavior symptoms, his or her social skills, and his or her adaptive functioning using behavior rating scales such as the Behavior Assessment System for Children Second Edition (BASC-2; Reynolds & Kamphaus, 2004). This information can be helpful in arousing preparatory change talk in parents, especially reasons for change such as participating in a parenting group or becoming more involved in a behavior support team. Structured rating scales such as the BASC-2 have the advantage of comparing youth symptoms and behaviors to national norms. Telling parents not only about areas that their child is functioning well in but also about areas of concern and giving normative comparisons is a form of personalized feedback that can be alarming to parents. Consider feedback such as, "Your child's depressive symptoms are at the 99th percentile compared to other children his age." Most parents would be very concerned about such information and would likely be moved to do something to address the concern.

The assessments related to family and school functioning provide an ecological perspective on the area of concern. In the family domain we often assess parenting behaviors (use of praise, reprimands, consistency), quality of family relationships including parent and child bond, parent stress, and family communication through questions (asking the parent to reflect on how well the family is functioning in each of these areas), direct observations, and sometimes rating scales. School functioning is assessed through records review (grades, attendance, discipline referrals), academic assessments, and rating scales such as the BASC-2 completed by one or more teachers, which provides information on performance and behavior concerns at school.

Although the types of rating forms and assessments collected are flexible, a good rule of thumb is that any data collected should be linked to potential interventions that are available as part of a menu of options. So, only collect information about parenting skills if you are prepared to deliver a parenting intervention or if you have one to refer the parent to in the event that the assessment reveals an area of concern.

## EVOKING

Evoking can occur at any time in the collaboration process. However, sustained, focused attempts to evoke a parent's motivation to change are easier and more effective after one or more target behaviors have been identified. It involves eliciting parents' reasons and commitment for changing.

### Eliciting Change Talk

All of the OARS strategies are used to elicit change talk. Open-ended questions are the primary tool for eliciting change talk initially, and affirmations, reflections, and summaries are used to encourage more change talk. Questions that ask about desires, ability, reasons, needs, or intentions to engage in a target behavior (i.e., change) are particularly helpful to invite a conversation about change.

It is also important to distinguish between behaviors the parents have control over and those they do not. For instance, the parents only have direct influence over their own behaviors and so the behaviors targeted for change need to be within the control of the parents. This is important because many parents will come to meetings wanting you to correct or change their child's

> It is also important to distinguish between behaviors the parent has control over and those they do not.

behavior. In the initial discussions with a parent, the child's behavior may be used to evoke change talk by inviting a parent to discuss concerns about the behavior and desires for how they want it to be. Some evocative open-ended questions about a child's behavior are given in Table 4.1. These all ask about a child's behavior, but the word "academics" could be substituted throughout with the same effect.

Notice that evoking questions about the child's behavior are asked in the service of activating concern in parents and willingness to consider what actions they might take to improve the situation. Some parents may come to a meeting ready to focus on themselves, but many do not. Talking about their child's behavior and the concern it elicits is often less threatening than beginning by broaching the topic of parenting behaviors. The challenge is to help make the connection between behaviors the parent has control over and the likely benefit that will result in his or her child's behavior.

After gaining a parent's willingness to discuss these problems and activating his or her concern and desire for change, it is important to shift questions to focus on the behavior or behaviors the parent is able and willing to consider changing. One example of a behavior a parent might consider changing related to the child's behavior is the parent's level of consistency in following through with consequences for the child. The same stems of evocative questions are given in Table 4.2 except the behavior targeted for parent behavior change is substituted for the child behavior focus in Table 4.1. The sequence of questions is the same and the end result is that parents can very easily move into a goal-planning discussion after answering these evocative questions about their own behavior.

## Using Importance and Confidence Rulers

MI uses scaling tools referred to as rulers as one method to elicit motivational talk from clients. Importance and confidence rulers are the most common examples of this tool (see Table 4.3). Parents rate how important taking a particular action is on a scale of 0 (not

> Asking these questions strategically about the importance of change and the parent's confidence can draw out important change talk.

important) to 10 (very important). For instance, a consultant might ask a parent at the end of a meeting how important it is for the parent to attend their next meeting. Whatever the response, the consultant follows with, "And why that number and

**Table 4.1 Questions That Invite Change Talk Focused on Their Child's Behavior**

*Disadvantages of the Status Quo*

- How do you feel about your child's behavior? How much does that concern you?
- What worries you about your child's behavior?
- What about your child's behavior might you or other people see as reasons for concern?
- What makes you think that your child's behavior is a problem?
- What difficulties have you had in relation to your child's behavior?
- In what ways has this been a problem for you?
- What makes you feel like you should do something different?

*Concerns About the Future*

- What can you imagine happening to you as a result of your child's behavior?
- What do you think will happen if you don't make a change?

*Advantages of Change*

- How would you like things to be different?
- What would be some good things about improving your child's behavior?
- What would be the advantages of making this change?

*Envisioning a Better Future*

- What would you like your life (your child's life) to be like in 5 years?
- If you could make this change immediately, by magic, how would things be different?

*Optimism About Change*

- What makes you think that if you decide to make a change that you could do it?
- What encourages you to feel like you can change if you want to?
- What do you think would work for you, if you decided to change?
- When else in your life have you made a big change like this? How did you do it?
- What personal strengths do you have that will help you succeed?

*Questions That Invite Mobilizing Change Talk*

- What are you going to do?
- What's the next step for you?
- If you could easily make any changes, what would you do?
- Where are you in terms of changing your behavior at this point?
- Never mind the "how" for right now, what do you want to have happen?
- What would you be willing to try?
- What do you intend to do?

not one number lower?" The answer to this question is nearly always some version of change talk; that is, why change is important, needed, or desired. Next, the consultant follows by asking how confident the parent is that he or she can successfully carry out the targeted behavior (e.g., attend the next session) using the same scale. In addition to eliciting change talk, this method also invites discussion and problem solving about potential barriers to engaging in the targeted behavior.

Asking these questions strategically about the importance of change and the parent's confidence can draw out important change talk. We tend to use these questions at the end of the meeting because research has shown that the most important type of change talk (that best predicts whether people actually follow

**Table 4.2 Questions That Invite Change Talk About a Parent Behavior (Inconsistent Consequences)**

*Disadvantages of the Status Quo*

- How do you feel about your use of inconsistent consequences? How much does that concern you?
- What worries you about your use of inconsistent consequences?
- What about your use of inconsistent consequences might you or other people see as reasons for concern?
- What makes you think that your use of inconsistent consequences is a problem?
- What difficulties have you had in relation to your use of inconsistent consequences?
- In what ways has this been a problem for you?
- What makes you feel like you should do something different?

*Concerns About the Future*

- What can you imagine happening to you as a result of your use of inconsistent consequences?
- What do you think will happen if you don't make a change?

*Advantages of Change*

- How would you like things to be different?
- What would be some good things about improving your use of inconsistent consequences?
- What would be the advantages of making this change?

*Envisioning a Better Future*

- What would you like your life (your child's life) to be like in 5 years?
- If you could make this change immediately, by magic, how would things be different?

*Optimism About Change*

- What makes you think that if you decide to make a change that you could do it?
- What encourages you to feel like you can change if you want to?
- What do you think would work for you, if you decided to change?
- When else in your life have you made a big change like this? How did you do it?
- What personal strengths do you have that will help you succeed?

*Questions That Invite Mobilizing Change Talk*

- What are you going to do?
- What's the next step for you?
- If you could easily make any changes, what would you do?
- Where are you in terms of changing your behavior at this point?
- Never mind the "how" for right now, what do you want to have happen?
- What would you be willing to try?
- What do you intend to do?

through on change) is the type that occurs during the final minutes of a session. In particular, the more committed the language (e.g., "I'm going to do this"), the more likely people are to actually do what they say.

The targeted behavior is whatever was agreed to during the focusing process. Here, *it is essential that the action that is targeted in ruler questions is a parenting*

**Table 4.3 Importance and Confidence Rulers**

How important would you say it is for you to _____? On a scale from 0 to 10, where 0 is not at all important and 10 is extremely important, where would you say you are?

| 0 | 2 | 4 | 6 | 8 | 10 |
|---|---|---|---|---|----|

Not at all                Extremely
Important                 Important

Why are you at a _____ and not zero?

What would it take for you to go from ____ to (a higher number)?

And how confident would you say you are that if you decided to _____, you could do it? On the same scale from 0–10, where would you say you are?

| 0 | 2 | 4 | 6 | 8 | 10 |
|---|---|---|---|---|----|

Not at all                Extremely
Important                 Important

Why are you at a _____ and not zero?

What would it take for you to go from ____ to (a higher number)?

*behavior, not a child behavior,* because as noted previously, the focus is on gaining parent motivation for changing a behavior the parent has direct control over. It could be completing a homework assignment, getting the child to school on time, or simply attending the next meeting. For instance, Parent: "I'd say a 6." Consultant: "Great. That's pretty important. Why a 6 and not say a 5?" You could also go lower ("say a 3"). Be sure to reflect their responses here, as this will almost certainly be change talk. If a parent says 0, you can amplify and exaggerate by saying, "So this is the least important thing in the world right now to you." It also may be a sign that you need to start over and select a new goal.

Next, ask, "What would it take to go from a 6 to a 7? What would have to happen?" You can then walk them up to a 10. Write down things they say above the numbers they give. So if a parent says, "If he got another failing grade in school" to get a 7, write "failing grade" above the number 7 on the form. Continue to use active listening and reflection throughout.

Repeat this process with the confidence ruler. "How confident are you that you can make this change?" with the "one less" question and then with the "one more" question.

### SUCCESS STORIES USING RULERS WITH PARENTS

In one case with a mother who expressed strong feelings about wanting to improve her child's behavior and her own parenting, the consultant concluded the first meeting by asking her the importance question. The targeted behavior

*(continued)*

### SUCCESS STORIES USING RULERS WITH PARENTS *(continued)*

was developing clear expectations at home. The mother rated it a 10 because in her words, she wanted her child to be happy and successful in life, and she wanted to be a source of support for him rather than a burden. She also rated her confidence as a 10. When asked why not a 9, she replied that helping her son was her top priority and that she had made successful changes in the past to help her family. She added, "I never felt like a good mother because my mother didn't teach me how, but I know that I can make a difference with my son. He is very bright, and he can do the work. I just have to learn how to help him. I know he can get better. I feel like all his behaviors are my fault but also that I can change him because I'm his mother." When asked if there was any way she could feel more confident she said, "I can help my son if you teach me how to do it." The consultant responded, "So you will feel more confident by coming to meet with me each week and learn new skills." The mother agreed, "Yes, I know I can do this with some support." In this case, the rulers helped the consultant end the session on a positive note. The mother reported feeling very optimistic and empowered. She ended the session by saying, "I will definitely come back to see you." Such strong commitment language at the end of sessions has been shown to be a powerful predictor of actual behavior change (see Miller & Rose, 2009).

Using these scales at the end of a session is not only a positive way to end the meeting, but it is also a great tool for identifying obstacles to continued participation. For example, in one case, the consultant asked the parent how important it was for her to attend the next meeting, and she rated it a 10. The consultant asked why she rated it a 10 and not an 8 or a 9, the parent responded with comments such as, "I need to show up to help my child," and "I'll try anything... I just want things to get better." The parent then rated her confidence as a 5. When asked why a 5 and not a 4, the parent responded that it was important to her and that she had been successful in attending the current session. The consultant next asked whether anything could make her move to a 6 or a 7. The parent responded that if she were sure she could arrange child care for her young child at home that she would be more confident. This led to a discussion about problem solving this barrier that might have prevented the mother from attending subsequent sessions. Through this discussion, the parent was able to identify a family friend who could watch the child during future meetings.

## Providing Personalized Feedback as Evocation

Providing parents with personalized feedback about areas of strength and concern can be an important part of the evoking process. Sharing data from school records, academic assessments, rating scales, and direct observations can pull language from them about reasons for changing, optimism about changing, and intentions to change. It can be

> Detailed assessment and feedback are usually reserved for parents who are disengaged or who are ambivalent about participating.

especially helpful to give parents a point of comparison for the feedback so they can understand how common (or uncommon) the behavior or performance is.

Two important points bear mentioning. First, as we noted when we discussed the option of collecting ecological assessment data, personalized feedback is optional in MI and is not essential for having effective everyday conversations about change. Ideally, data that is already being collected by a school can be used to provide feedback without creating excessive burden for consultants. For instance, most schools collect and organize attendance/tardiness data, office discipline, curriculum-based measures, behavior report cards or start charts, homework completion, and state assessment scores for all students in a school. Students who have been referred for additional support or for a special education evaluation also usually have a rich source of data about their school performance and behavior. All of this information can be used as part of delivering personalized feedback. Second, if a parent is already motivated to participate and fully engage in services, there is no need to spend excessive time evoking their motivation with evocative questions and feedback. In fact, spending too much time eliciting change talk and evoking with people who are ready to take action can have the opposite effect. So detailed assessment and feedback are usually reserved for parents who are disengaged or who are ambivalent about participating. In these cases, personalized feedback can be especially evocative and helpful in moving parents forward toward wanting to participate in services.

Although feedback can be provided verbally, as in telling a parent his or her child has missed 12 days of school compared to the school average of two absences, when you have collected ample information about the child, parent, and family, we recommend that you compile this information onto a single form to share with the parent. Handout 4.2 provides an example of a feedback form (see www.springerpub.com/herman-ancillary for the color version of this handout).

The feedback form is an effective visual tool to concisely communicate information from the ecological assessment to the parent. The left side of the form lists various characteristics grouped into three categories: youth symptoms, family functioning, and school functioning. The x-axis of the form has a color spectrum from green to yellow to red. Prior to the feedback meeting with the parent, the consultant compiles all of the assessment data and marks each child, family, and school characteristic based on whether it is a strength/ in the normal range (green), whether it is an area of mild to moderate concern (yellow to orange), or whether it is a serious concern demanding immediate attention (red).

A benefit of the feedback form, in addition to its concise communication, is that it makes the negative feedback less conflict-inducing by drawing attention to the form and away from the consultant as the bearer of bad news. It allows the consultant to identify concrete and specific areas of the child's behavior that need to be addressed, while also highlighting identified strengths. As the feedback form compiles all assessments (from parent, teacher, and child), it takes into account everyone's point of view and provides a concise overall summary.

## SUCCESS STORY OF USING PERSONALIZED
## FEEDBACK WITH A FAMILY

In one case involving a student diagnosed with attention deficit hyperactivity disorder (ADHD), the parent was receiving persistent negative feedback from the teacher about the child's disruptive and impulsive behavior at school. The parent was also experiencing the same difficulties at home. Although these behavior problems were highlighted in the red zone on the feedback form, what elicited the most concern from the parent was that the child also rated in the orange zone (needs attention) on anxiety and depression. This allowed for a productive conversation between the parent and the consultant about anxiety and depression in children (psychoeducation) and how these symptoms often go unnoticed in children whose behavior problems are more prominent. Without the use of the assessments, including the child's self-report, these specific issues may have gone undetected or attributed to something else (inattention). The feedback form aroused the parent's concern and became the "hook" that made her determined to address these internalizing problems.

This parent was also very forthright about her difficulty managing her child's disruptive behavior and in using effective discipline techniques at home. Rather than dwelling on these concerns, which had already been discussed repeatedly at school, the feedback form highlighted other areas that were equally important to consider—the strengths of the family environment. Overall, the parent had a very loving relationship with the child, used high rates of encouragement, closely monitored her child at home, and provided him with academic support. By highlighting these strengths first and noting that these were areas where many other parents struggle, the consultant was able to praise the parent and make her more receptive to the areas of concern. The mother, who began the session feeling defeated and discouraged about her parenting practices, was visibly taken by the feedback—she smiled, sat taller, and leaned forward as she received the feedback. Drawing on information gathered from the values card sort, the consultant also commented on the fact that being a good parent was a high priority for the mother and these positive attributes provided a solid foundation for becoming the parent she wanted to be, highlighting the specific areas that could be improved. After providing feedback about parenting skills in the yellow or red zone (developing clear rules and expectations, limit setting, and stress management) the consultant checked in with the parent to get her reaction to the feedback by asking, "What do you make of that? How does that fit with what you were expecting to hear?" The parent quickly agreed and noted that she appreciated the specificity of the feedback and attention to her positive attributes. She concluded, "Geeez...I guess I'm not doing EVERYTHING wrong at home like I thought I was!"

The parent was also able to see that her ability to manage stress effectively needed attention. The consultant reflected the parent's comments about stress and then drew a connection between the two areas of concern by noting that

*(continued)*

**SUCCESS STORY OF USING PERSONALIZED
FEEDBACK WITH A FAMILY (*continued*)**

stress can undermine any parent discipline plan. The parent appreciated some of the focus being on her and commented that she enjoyed hearing statements from the consultant such as: "You need to take care of yourself." "It's important for you to have time for you." The parent reported that she often felt guilty when she scheduled any time for herself and felt validated by the consultant. She also noted that she understood the effects of her stress on her child as well as her relationship with him. In creating the action plan for next steps, the parent elected to focus on stress management before beginning to work on her parenting skills. She remarked: "I definitely need to learn how to take time for myself and chill out without feeling guilty about it."

## Responding to Change Talk

As you visit with the family, pay close attention to any language they use indicating their willingness to change behaviors or their concerns about current circumstances. As you hear these comments, make note of them and use affirmations, reflections, and summaries to amplify them and encourage more change talk. You might also probe for more details to make the concerns more concrete. For instance, a father might say about his son, "He does have a lot of friends, but I will say one thing, he definitely is a follower. He'll do what other kids are doing even if it gets him into trouble." You could respond, "What do you see happening if..." or "You're happy that he has friends and you would like him be more of a leader in some of his relationships."

> As you visit with the family, pay close attention to any language they use indicating their willingness to change behaviors or their concerns about current circumstances.

## Responding to Sustain Talk

When sustain talk occurs it is important to roll with it rather than challenge it. A common response when we hear others talking about reasons that they don't need or want to change is to argue against and tell them why change is important. As is clear by now, such a response is almost always counterproductive as it invites more sustain talk from the parent. An important first step in learning to adopt an MI approach is to halt your intuitive response to argue against sustain talk. Instead, try using one of the OARS strategies when you hear sustain talk and see how it alters the interaction.

## EVERYDAY CONVERSATIONS ABOUT CHANGE

Mr. Douglas stops in to complain to Mrs. Reese, the school principal at his son's high school. Mr. Douglas believes his son's math teacher has been unfairly targeting his son as a troublemaker. Mrs. Reese knows the story is more complicated than that. Mr. Douglas's son is frequently off task in class and has had several office discipline referrals for serious rule violations (threatening peers, stealing). Mrs. Reese has been hoping to get Mr. Douglas involved in creating a behavior-support plan for his son and has left him many messages at home.

**Father (F):** Look, it just ain't fair. She has something against him. She just thinks he's a bad kid up to no good.

**Principal (P):** It's frustrating because you don't see him getting a fair shake and you really just want the best for him.

**F:** That's right. I don't want him to have problems at school. But I don't see how he can do well when he has a teacher who doesn't like him.

**P:** You are mad at his teacher and also you are just really disappointed that he's not doing well in school.

**F:** Both.

**P:** Let's look 4 years down the road here. Sidney is 14 now. What's your big worry about what's going to happen if we don't get a handle on this?

**F:** That he's not gonna make it. That he's gonna drop out or get booted out. That he'll be on the street, doing no good.

**P:** You don't want that to happen.

**F:** No! He has to graduate.

**P:** You are going to make sure that happens.

**F:** That's right.

**P:** I admire your commitment to him and his success. What if we come up with a plan and talked about ways that we all can best support Sydney.

**F:** I would like that.

---

*In this example, the principal facilitates a positive discussion with the father by first listening to his concerns, reflecting them, and then asking evocative questions to tap the father's core values. The discussion helps connect the father to the goal of creating a plan to help the son be successful in school.*

## PLANNING

### Transition to Planning

Once a target behavior has been identified and parents have expressed high levels of motivation to engage in that behavior—as indicated by spontaneous and free-flowing change talk and limited sustain talk—it is time for the planning process. For parents who are willing to develop a plan, provide a summary of the discussion and a transition to start talking about next steps. It is helpful to ask the family to summarize their "take home points." For instance, you might ask, "Based on all the information we've covered tonight, what stands out to you the most?" or "What do you see as the most important thing we've discussed tonight?"

As you start moving toward discussing next steps, ask the parents to identify their greatest area of concern or the target behavior they want to work on first ("Where do you want to start?" or "What is your biggest concern right now?" or "What do you think is the most important thing to focus on first?"). Spend some time reflecting their comments, as all of these questions will yield some form of change talk.

## Menu of Options

Providing people with more than one option for how a goal might be met makes it more likely they will follow through on a plan. Thus, it is a good idea to generate a list of possible options, a menu, from which the parent can choose. You can co-create the menu with the parents by asking them what they have considered doing. You can also ask their permission to help generate items on the menu. Here, the process is very collaborative and should focus on brainstorming to identify potential solutions. Invite the parents to offer suggestions for addressing the problem. Depending on the problem, options could include (a) continuing to meet with you, (b) setting up a time to meet with members of a school support team, and (c) referral for related services. Handout 4.3 provides a sample Menu of Options form.

> Providing people with more than one option for how a goal might be met makes it more likely they will follow through on a plan.

## Action Planning and Goal Setting

After generating a list of several options, help the parent become more specific about his or her goal and the plan for achieving it. The parents may have only discussed broad goals to this point in the discussion (e.g., "helping my son do better at school," "learn new parenting skills," "become more involved at school"). During the planning process it is helpful to start to narrow down these broad goals into concrete steps of action the parent can take in line with a broad goal. Handout 4.4 provides a goal-setting sheet that helps facilitate this discussion and planning of the most immediate actions the parent will take. Be sure to emphasize the strengths of the parent and child as you initiate the planning process.

> Now, let's talk about next steps. On this form, let's first think back to what is going really well or is a strength of the family. Whatever plan we come up with should be sure to use this strength to ensure its success.

Ask the parent to reflect on the most important areas to work on: "We just talked about some ideas for areas to improve. Which do you think are the most important to target at this time?" Next, elicit specific, observable goals from the parent.

One way to do this is to ask clarifying questions, including who, what, where, when, and how often. For instance, if the parent says "better coping skills," ask him or her what that would look like. For example, you could ask, "How would you know?" "What would be different that you could see?" or "How often would you see him doing it?" Lastly, discuss potential barriers to meeting or working on the goal, and brainstorm ways to overcome these barriers.

## Promoting a Systems Approach to Problem Solutions

As you work with parents in developing effective behavior-management skills, many will experience a transformation in their way of thinking about their child's problems. They may initially seek support from others to "fix" their child; to the extent school-based professionals comply and deliver only individual interventions to the child, they reinforce the perception that the problem is within the child. However, by taking a systems approach and delivering feedback to the family about the family environment and not just the child's symptoms they send the implicit message that the solution lies within the system, not the child. At some point, parents experience a fundamental insight, "I have some influence over my child's behavior. It's about me as much as my child."

As parents learn new skills, they also often develop awareness of how they used to be versus how they see their parenting behaviors now. One parent expressed this eloquently. She was talking about how things have changed in her home for the positive and how she was trying to get her child's father on board with some of the things she learned: "So he started giving him directions and I had to tell him that he was doing it wrong because he is how I *used to be*...you know, before I started this program." She went on to talk about how her interactions with her children are completely different, especially in the way she speaks to her children.

We have noted the physical change in parents as they become empowered. Their growing confidence and sense of self-efficacy begins to show in their posture and tone of voice. These are signs that your work is making a difference.

---

### EVERYDAY CONVERSATIONS ABOUT CHANGE

At a parent/teacher conference, Mr. Davies, a second-grade teacher, broaches the topic of Dixon's off-task, disruptive behaviors with his mother, Donna, at the end of the meeting, after first discussing several positive things about Dixon and his progress.

**Teacher (T):** In addition to all the things that are going well for Dixon, I wanted to bring up one area of growth I see for him.

**Parent (P):** Okay.

**T:** Dixon is having trouble staying on task and completing his work. Sometimes he gets into trouble for talking out of turn or getting his classmates to laugh at him.

*(continued)*

---

### EVERYDAY CONVERSATIONS ABOUT CHANGE (*continued*)

P: That's surprising because I don't have any problems with him at home.

T: Well, that's not too unusual. Classrooms are unique places and require a separate set of skills to be successful.

P: Well at home I tell him what to do and it's fine, he does it.

T: So this is really surprising to you. It's hard to imagine him having any troubles at school.

P: I guess all kids have some troubles sometimes; it just seems like a bigger problem the way you are talking about it.

T: So you can see how all kids need some support at school but something about the way I said it made you think this was a problem we couldn't solve.

P: I don't know. So what's he doing?

T: Well I try to keep good records of things so that I can paint a clear picture for parents. In a typical day, Dixon has his ups and downs. It looks like during math and reading, these behaviors are more likely to happen. In a 30-minute block of time during math and reading, he talks out of turn, gets out of his seat, and makes side comments about 10 to 15 times. His peers, on average, do this maybe once or twice during the same period.

P: That is a big difference.

T: What do you make of that?

P: Not sure. Doesn't sound like him. Like I said, he's a good kid at home.

T: Oh, he is a good kid here too. I like him a lot. We just need to find ways to help him be more successful during math and reading times. He can do this.

P: What do you think would help?

---

*Here the teacher reflects the mother's surprise that her child is acting out at school and then provides her with very specific details about the problem behavior in relation to his peers. The teacher expresses confidence that this is a solvable problem and elicits a question from the mother regarding how they can work together to solve it.*

---

## SUMMARY

MI strategies work well with parents. Engaging, focusing, evoking, and planning provide a set of processes to guide every interaction between school professionals and parents. These interactions can take place as brief snippets in a day or as ongoing scheduled visits. Our focus in this chapter was on those brief everyday opportunities to make these interactions more successful. In Chapter 7, we describe a structured MI intervention for integrating work with parents, teachers, and students called the Family Check-Up.

## RESOURCES FOR SUPPORTING PARENT BEHAVIOR-MANAGEMENT SKILLS

### Sample Evidence-Based Parenting Programs

*Preschool and Elementary*

Incredible Years: http://incredibleyears.com
First Step to Success: http://www.firststeptosuccess.org
Triple P: http://www.triplep.net
Non-Compliant Child: http://www.strengtheningfamilies.org/html/
    programs_1999/02_HNCC.html

*Middle and High School*

Strengthening Families: http://www.strengtheningfamiliesprogram.org
Adolescent Transitions Program: http://www.ojjdp.gov/mpg/Adolescent%
    20Transitions%20Program-MPGProgramDetail-289.aspx
Multisystemic Therapy: http://mstservices.com

### Sample Books for Parents

Barkley, R. (1998). *Your defiant child.* New York, NY: Guilford Press.
Barkley, R. (1995). *Taking charge of ADHD.* New York, NY: Guilford Press.
McMahon, R. J., & Forehand, R. L. (2005). *Helping the noncompliant child: Family-based treatment for oppositional behavior* (2nd ed.). New York, NY: Guilford Press.
Rapee, R., et al. (2008). *Helping your anxious child.* Oakland, CA: New Harbinger Publications.

# Handouts and Forms

## HANDOUT 4.1 VALUES CARD SORT EXERCISE

The values card sort exercise is conducted during the initial interview of the Family Check-Up. The activity description was adapted from Frey et al.'s (2013) *Enhancements for the First Step to Success*, and based on the work of Theresa B. Moyers and Steve Martino (2006), *The Personal Goals and Values Card Sorting Task for Individuals with Schizophrenia*. The original card sort activity was developed by W. R. Miller, J. C'de Baca, D. B. Matthews, and P. L. Wilbourne (2001). Parents can complete the card sort on their own, but the final sorted cards should be discussed in person.

### MATERIALS AND SETUP

- Use the value list below to generate a pack of individual cards. You can do this by printing each value on a separate index card or by printing each on a label and then putting each label on an index card.
- Tell the parent you will be using an exercise to help you learn more about what is most important to him or her in life.
- Lay three cards in three side-by-side columns labeled "Not Important," "Important," and "Very Important."
- Give the client the remaining cards and ask the client to sort them into those three piles based on their family values and their goals for their child. (Alternately, you can read the cards with parents, especially those whose literacy skills are challenged, and complete the exercise through an interactive discussion.)
- Once finished, pick up the Very Important pile and ask the client to re-sort, pulling out the top five cards in that stack. Do not be concerned if the client cannot further edit the Very Important stack, or ends up with more than five cards, or fewer.

### DISCUSSION

- The goal is to facilitate a discussion in which the parent's values are affirmed, linked to current versus ideal child behavior, and linked to current versus ideal parenting and family-management practices.
- Discuss at least the top three values in detail.
- Use the cards to ask open-ended questions about why the client picked the card, what it means to him or her personally, how he or she knows that he or she has this value or goal (e.g., what does he or she see in his or her life that convinces him or her this is important), and how this relates to the target behavior (parenting).
- Listen for examples of child behavior and parenting practices that do not fit with the stated values and ideals. Reflect these examples by validating the parent's struggles, affirming his or her commitment to these values, and evoking arguments for change.

- Use an MI approach (like rolling with resistance) if the client provides answers that indicate his or her card choice is consistent with an undesirable behavior (a common one is Having Fun).
- Listen carefully for the presence of change talk that might occur and reinforce it as you hear it.
- After the value sort, the next task (if has not occurred already) is to facilitate a conversation that directly links the identified values to the family's ideals of self and life generally, and experiences and exceptions of school, parenting, and the child's strengths and challenges specifically.
- This exercise will facilitate a discussion of values and goals between you and the parent. It is intended to develop a discrepancy between a deeply held belief and a current behavior so that MI can move forward. That is its only purpose, so please do not be overly concerned or meticulous about procedural details. The content of the cards selected by the client does not really matter either, and can be expected to change from time to time in any case. A word of caution: we do not recommend bypassing the cards in favor of using the values and goals as a list. There is something about the sorting itself that is very powerful in this exercise.

| | |
|---|---|
| Being a Good Parent | Getting an Education |
| Working Hard | Being a Good Friend |
| Being True to My Religion | Being Happy |
| Being Loyal | Being Healthy |
| Being Honest | Being Responsible |
| Being Loved | Having a Good Sense of Humor |
| Being Respected by Others | Doing Something Good in the World |
| Being Part of My Community | Having Nice Things |
| Having a Safe Place to Live | Staying Out of Trouble |
| Being Successful | Gaining Wealth |
| Being Real/Genuine | Being Powerful |
| Being Kind | Helping Others |
| Seeking Justice | Doing the Right Thing |
| Taking Care of My Family | Being a Good Spouse/Partner |
| Staying in Control | Being Patient |
| Having Fun | Looking Good |
| Feeling Good About Myself | Other Value: |
| Other Value: | Not Important |
| Important | Very Important |

# HANDOUT 4.2 FEEDBACK FORM

Profile for:_____  Child's Age:_____  Date:_____

## Youth Adjustment

| Problem Behavior | |
|---|---|
| Attention | |
| Anxiety | |
| Depression | |
| Coping Skills | |
| Friendship/Social Skills | |
| Other:_____ | |

        Strength                                             Needs Attention

## Family Adjustment

| Family Relationship | |
|---|---|
| Use of Encouragement | |
| Clear Rules and Expectations | |
| Limit Setting | |
| Supervision | |
| Academic Supports at Home | |
| Stress Management | |
| Other:_____ | |

        Strength                                             Needs Attention

## School Adjustment

| Attendance | |
|---|---|
| Academic Performance | |
| Study Skills | |
| Attitude about School | |
| Home–School Communication | |
| Disruptive Behavior | |
| Aggressive Behavior | |
| Rule Violations | |
| Other: _____ | |

        Strength                                             Needs Attention

# HANDOUT 4.3 MENU OF OPTIONS

Family :_____          Date: _____

| Target Areas for Improvement: |
|---|
| *Based on the feedback, what areas would you as a family like to focus on?* |
| 1. |
| 2. |
| 3. |

Menu of Options:

| Collaborative Ideas for Child Supports | Menu of Caregiver Supports |
|---|---|
| | Building Academic Supports in the Home |
| | Managing Stress |
| | Parenting Tool Kit: Behavior Management |
| | Family Problem Solving and Communication |
| | Family Schedules and Routines |

*NEXT STEP*: Identify from the menu one or more strategies to put into place. Complete Action Planning Form to identify the specific goal (e.g., meet for 1 hour each week to work on reducing stress).

# HANDOUT 4.4 GOAL-PLANNING FORM

Family :_____          Date: _____

| Those things **going well** in my family: | Areas I would like to **focus on improving** in my family: |
|---|---|
| | |

| Specifically, **my goal** is to: |
|---|
| |

| What steps do I need to take to meet this goal? | | | |
|---|---|---|---|
| What needs to be done? | My plan | Resources I need to do it | Timeline |
| | | | |

| How **important** is it for you to meet this goal in your classroom? | The **most** important reason for making this change and meeting this goal is: |
|---|---|
| 1   2   3   4   5   6   7   8   9   10<br>Not Important At All       Very Important | |

| How **confident** are you that you will meet this goal in your classroom? | Some reasons that **I am confident:** |
|---|---|
| 1   2   3   4   5   6   7   8   9   10<br>Not Confident At All       Very Confident | |

| Is there anything that could get in the way of meeting this goal? | What can I do to help make sure this doesn't get in the way? |
|---|---|
| | |

# 5

# Motivational Interviewing With Teachers

Teaching is a demanding profession. Few other professions require so much responsibility with such high levels of public scrutiny. Consider that teachers serve as the primary care provider during school hours for 20 or more children. Further, the level of accountability has increased significantly over the past decade for teachers. Not only does society expect teachers to keep children safe and provide quality instruction, it also expects them to produce results for each and every child in their classroom. In fact, many teachers leave the profession early in their careers as a result of not feeling supported or capable of meeting the current expectations in their field.

Teachers, after all, are only human and as is true for all of us, change and self-improvement can be difficult. Yet we expect teachers to continue to grow and learn and become better each year. Like most of us working on self-improvement plans, sometimes teachers are highly motivated to do this, and other times they are ambivalent. Teachers really benefit from having a supportive ear, a consultant, who can listen to their concerns and offer gentle guidance over time. Many school professionals can play this role of supportive consultant: a fellow teacher, a principal, a school consultant or psychologist, a special educator, or in some cases, an instructional consultant.

The skills described in this chapter are intended for this range of professionals who find themselves working with, supporting, or consulting with teachers to improve classroom practices. As is true when working with anyone on behavior change, there are strategies that make it more or less likely that these encounters will be helpful and even motivational. All of the motivational interviewing (MI) methods described to this point fit equally well when working with teachers.

In this chapter, we extend these MI methods to teachers. The content will be familiar. But there are some unique challenges and issues that arise when applying these methods to teacher consultation. We structure our discussion around the four processes of MI: engaging, focusing, evoking, and planning. Keep in mind that although these processes can be thought of as sequential stages of an interaction, they are also overlapping and recursive in that they influence one another and may reemerge out of sequence. That is, after proceeding through engaging, focusing, and evoking, you may find a need to reemphasize the focusing process after a teacher identifies a new behavior to target. Or, you may need to give more attention to the engaging process after a teacher has missed several appointments. The key point is that these processes should not be treated as static phases but rather as benchmarks for conceptualizing change conversations and the types of responses that may be most helpful depending on the process.

We conclude the chapter with a brief description of a structured consultation model for supporting teachers, called the Classroom Check-Up (CCU) that adheres to the four processes of MI. As you will note, the skills and strategies used with MI can be applied in any consultation visit with a teacher, with or without the formal structure of the CCU. To highlight the use of MI during even brief visits with teachers, we have included examples in the section called "Everyday Conversations About Change."

## ENGAGING

MI strategies are relevant for every consultation visit. At the beginning, the focus is on establishing the spirit of MI and simply building rapport. In addition, a first meeting with a teacher may include gathering more information about any problems the teacher wants to address in her classroom, as well as her strengths, resources, expectations, and prior experiences in working with a consultant. In an MI approach, it is important to elicit and identify core teacher values. These values will be useful in highlighting any discrepancies between deeply held beliefs and current behaviors. Below we highlight strategies to use during the engaging process.

### MI Spirit Applied to Teacher Consultation

The qualities of effective consultants and aspects of the spirit of MI described in earlier chapters all apply to working with teachers, and help facilitate the engaging process of MI. Effective consultants create a sense of partnership and collaboration in their interactions with teachers. They convey acceptance by affirming the teacher, using accurate empathy, and believing in their absolute worth and autonomy. They have a deep compassion for the teacher's circumstances. Further, they use evocative interactions that draw out of the teacher ideas, solutions, and resources rather than indoctrinating or lecturing them.

> Watching these effective consultants, one gets the sense that their consultation meetings are friendly social encounters rather than stiff, professional conversations.

In addition to these central aspects of the MI spirit, here we highlight two corollary qualities that we have observed as especially influential for effective teacher coaches: personal comfort and confidence. First, effective teacher consultants are comfortable in their own skin. They have an ease about their interpersonal interactions that invites others in. They approach their meetings with teachers as they would any social encounter, without any sense of trepidation or rigidity. Watching these effective consultants, one gets the sense that their consultation meetings are friendly social encounters rather than stiff, professional conversations.

> Most impressive, the best consultants convey an additional sort of confidence—the belief that the teacher will do what the teacher says he or she intends to do.

We have had the opportunity to work with several highly effective teacher consultants over the years. One consultant we work with exemplifies this quality of comfort very well. It is clear when watching her interact with teachers that she genuinely enjoys being with them. She enjoys listening to them and getting to know them. There is nothing forced about her interactions. She is also very much in tune with each teacher's interpersonal style and comfortably matches her style to theirs. We suspect if we compared her conversations with her friends to these interactions with teachers that her nonverbal messages would be the same in each situation.

She sets this tone from the first moments of an interaction. Consider the following example. Prior to the meeting with an elementary-school teacher, the teacher disclosed to the consultant in passing that she will likely need surgery to fix her enduring neck problem. At the start of the meeting, the consultant sets up a video camera (we often ask consultants to videotape their meetings for supervision purposes) and announces (from behind the camera): "Okay. That should do it. We're all set."

> The teacher asks with a smile, "Are you going to be in it?"
> "I HAVE to be in it," the consultant announces twice as she walks back into camera view and smiles at the camera. They both chuckle.
> The consultant sits down, "So were you out yesterday because of your neck?"
> "Just the afternoon," the teacher says, looking down.
> The consultant pauses and tilts her head. She says, "Ahh. I'm sorry. So they are going to put metal in your neck?"
> The teacher quickly interjects, "I already have metal in my neck."
> The consultant whispers, "Oh my gosh." Then says, "I'm sorry they are going to put *more* metal in your neck."
> "That's what we got to do."
> "Okay," the consultant says and pauses. Then in a louder voice, "Fantastic," as she pulls out forms for their discussion.
> "Fantastic!" the teacher says. "What do we got."

In this 30-second interaction, the consultant masterfully displays empathy and genuine concern for the teacher's ailing neck, inviting her to tell her more, and then matches her response style to move the conversation forward. The transition, "Fantastic" works here because the teacher has shown her that she likes to communicate in a playful, humorous tone ("Are you going to be in [the video]?"). It sends the message in a single word, "I'm hearing that you would rather not dwell on your neck problem right now and instead would rather get to work." If she had said this instead, it would not have matched the teacher's communication style.

In addition to comfort, a second key teacher consultation quality is confidence. Teacher consultants need to convey a sense that they know what they are doing. They need to believe it themselves. This confidence often comes with experience. That's why classroom teachers can often be very effective consultants. But confidence also comes with adherence to a good theory of intervention. A guiding theory strengthens a consultant's resolve and confirms his or her belief that he or she can be helpful in solving problems. Most impressive, the best consultants convey an additional sort of confidence—the belief that the teacher will do what the teacher says he or she intends to do. Effective consultants believe, and communicate this belief through their actions, that the plans they develop with teachers are reasonable and doable. The opposite of this is illustrated by consultants who give teachers an excuse for not completing the plan. They do this in subtle ways, by communicating in words or actions that it would be understandable if the teacher were not able to complete the plan: "Do what you can."

Effective and confident consultants get teachers to do things. The metamessage they send is, "You can do this. I expect you to do this." Another consultant we have worked with for a number of years has repeatedly demonstrated the quality of confidence. She has the ability to get teachers on board with very large plan changes. In watching her work, it seems to come from the subtleties of her communication. After she develops plans, she asks what can get in the way of the plan being successful and problem solves potential barriers. But once the plan is set, the language becomes all about success and follow through. "So when I see you again, I can't wait to see the changes in your classroom." Or she might say, "You made a good choice. I've seen many teachers be successful with the plan you created." Inside, we are certain that she believes that teachers will follow through on their plan as well. Thus, an important aspect of being a confident consultant is one's own internal dialogue. Confident consultants say to themselves, "This is reasonable. The plan is good. I'm certain the teacher will do this." This is very different self-talk than a consultant who is thinking, "I hope this works," or even more damaging, "She's not going to do this," or "This is too much to ask." Your own beliefs as a consultant can become self-fulfilling prophecies.

---

### EVERYDAY CONVERSATIONS ABOUT CHANGE

Ms. Sampson and Mr. Lopez are eating lunch when Ms. Sampson starts complaining about students in her class. Mr. Lopez knows that Ms. Sampson struggles with classroom management and wants to support her without telling her what to do.

**Ms. Sampson (S):** I'm just sick and tired of students who couldn't care less about school. I have these three jokers in my class who ruin it for everyone. I mean, they really don't belong in school.

**Mr. Lopez (L):** That is frustrating.

**S:** I just want to teach, not babysit.

**L:** Who knew that teaching would be as much about teaching behaviors as academics?

*(continued)*

---

### EVERYDAY CONVERSATIONS ABOUT CHANGE (*continued*)

S: I didn't. That's not what I signed up for.

L: That's fun to think about. I guess I never asked you. Why did you sign up for this? What made you want to be a teacher?

S: Hmm. I don't know. I guess I really wanted to make a difference. To help kids learn and become more successful. To get through to them. I really thought I'd be good at it, too.

L: So you really got into this because you wanted to be able to reach those kids who needed an extra boost—the ones who wouldn't make it without you.

S: Yeah, it's disappointing.

L: That's part of your frustration that the students who want you to give up on them are the ones you most want to reach.

S: Yeah. But I wish they just wanted to learn…I know that sounds silly because I want to help them to want to learn. Urgh. It's just hard.

L: You don't want to give up on them but that's how their behavior makes you feel.

S: I know, I can't let them win. I need to be stronger.

---

Here Mr. Lopez could have engaged in the typical conversation that occurs every day in teachers' lounges by encouraging Ms. Sampson to simply complain about her students without moving the conversation forward. Venting certainly can serve a function for teachers to help them feel validated and supported by their peers. Having an outlet for frustration is important, especially if the teacher feels empowered and refreshed after such conversations. Unfortunately, often these types of conversations become ruminatory and circular and end with the teacher feeling more pessimistic about her classroom.

Instead of engaging in this type of self-defeating conversation, Mr. Lopez changed the conversation by listening and asking evocative questions. The turning point happened when he asked Ms. Sampson to reflect on why she became a teacher. This question elicited a core value of hers, which was to make a difference in the lives of children. She then drew the connection herself that she was not only feeling frustrated but also disappointed for not being able to reach the very students she most wanted to help.

### Get to Know You Interview

Although consultation visits with teachers can often involve fly-by, brief interactions, we recommend intentionally setting aside 25 to 45 minutes for an extended conversation, when possible. Teachers are usually able to find some time to do this, often over lunch or doing a break. The consultant should tell the teacher the purpose of the meeting ("to learn more about you and your goals for your classroom") and the amount of time to expect the meeting to take.

Consistent with the engaging process of MI, we have found it helpful to focus the first part of the meeting on getting to know more about the teacher's

**Table 5.1 Sample *Get to Know You* Interview Questions**

*Teaching Experiences and Background*

- How long have you been a teacher?
- What made you want to become a teacher?
- What's the best part of being a teacher?
- What is the most difficult part of being a teacher?

*Classroom Atmosphere*

- How would you describe the culture of your classroom?
- What is it like for students to be in your classroom?

*Classroom Management Practices*

- What strategies do you use to manage student behavior in your classroom?
- What areas of classroom management do you do well and less well?
- How do you handle misbehavior in the classroom?
- What strategies work the best for your? What strategies have you found not to work?

*Ideal Classroom*

- What would your ideal classroom look like?
- What do you want children to learn from being in your classroom?
- What do you want children to remember about you and your classroom?

*Past Consultation Experiences*

- Tell me about any prior consultation experiences you have had?
- What worked well and not so well in this past experiences?

experiences. Asking, "What made you want to become a teacher?" is particularly effective at connecting with the teacher's initial passion and usually gives important information about a teacher's personal values. We also routinely ask about what the teacher likes most and least about being a teacher.

Other areas we ask about during a first meeting include the current classroom environment ("How would you describe the culture [or climate] of your classroom?"), the teacher's classroom-management style ("What is your classroom-management plan?" and "How do you handle misbehavior in the classroom?"), their ideal classroom ("What would your ideal classroom look like?"), what they want students to learn from the classroom and apply in their own life, and prior consultation experiences. Table 5.1 presents sample interview questions in each of these categories. Note these are all open-ended questions, consistent with the O of the OARS (open-ended questions, affirmations, reflections, and summaries) skills. The consultant should ask questions like these and then affirm, reflect, and summarize the conversation that ensues.

## Exploring Values: The Teacher Values Card Sort

In addition to gathering information about a teacher's background, skills, and interests, we also recommend engaging in a brief values card sort task during the *Get to Know You* interview (card sorting is described in more detail in Chapter 4 for parents). We usually use this early in the interview, after eliciting information about the teacher's experiences and likes and dislikes. As with the parent card sort, we give teachers a stack of value cards (see Handout 5.1) and ask them to sort them into three piles: Very Important, Important, and Not Important. Next we ask them to identify three to five of the values in the Very Important stack as their most important values. We then ask the teacher to tell us why they selected each of those most important values. The goal is to learn more about the teacher's deeply held convictions. The consultant simply uses OARS to guide this discussion, asking lots of open-ended, clarification questions (or posing statements such as, "Tell me more about that"), affirming the person's values ("I can see why that would be so important to you"), reflecting their comments ("You get energized when you recall what led you to become a teacher in the first place"), and summarizing the discussion ("So making a difference, being trustworthy, and being a strong leader are your most important values. And you are keenly aware of how these values have shaped your life, including how you are as a teacher.").

## Sample First-Meeting Conversation

Here we provide a transcript from a teacher consultation visit to highlight some of the key skills in using MI to facilitate the engaging process. In this first example, the consultant begins the *Get to Know You* interview by asking some simple open-ended questions. As you read through this example, pay attention to a few things. First, notice how little the consultant says compared to the teacher. In traditional clinical settings, good MI practice suggests that clients should be talking more than consultants at a ratio of 10:1. This is an unreasonable expectation in teacher consultation settings, however, where the nature of the relationship is very different and the amount of time is limited. Still, a very basic metric in the early stages of a consultation relationship is that the teacher should be talking more than the consultant. More speech from the teacher provides more opportunity for change talk, and change talk is what we are after.

Second, notice how the MI processes are dynamic and interrelated. Although this is the beginning of a first meeting with a primary focus on the first process of engaging, the interview starts the process of focusing with its selective questions as well as evoking with its open-ended questions. Third, notice how these simple questions elicit deep and meaningful value statements by the teacher. The consultant highlights these value expressions by reflecting and even amplifying them. Connecting to people's values is key, because often we have energy attached to our values. Our values can move us to action, especially when we realize our current behaviors are not aligned with what we truly believe.

> Our values can move us to action, especially when we realize our current behaviors are not aligned with what we truly believe.

| Interview Dialogue | Comments |
|---|---|
| **Consultant (C):** So I'm going to ask background questions. What do you think it was that made you want to become a teacher? | Open-ended question |
| **Teacher (T):** It was my sixth-grade teacher. | |
| **C:** Your sixth-grade teacher? | |
| **T:** Yeah, my sixth-grade teacher, Mrs. Slokowsky. And then I remember getting really annoyed by my mom because my mom went back to school to become a teacher around that time, and I was like, "What are you doing? This is my career." (laughs) Yeah, but sixth grade, she was incredible because she respected—I don't know if you need to know all this—but she really respected who I was as a kid. I was fine academically and socially. I had pretty good relationships but I had this strange quirk that I couldn't part with anything. I was a hoarder, like an unbelievable hoarder. And she just called my mom and set up a regular meeting with her so my mom would come and help me clean out my locker so that I was. . . . It was so funny. I should be embarrassed by it but now it's just to see how she as a teacher just really respected that was a unique part of me and didn't get annoyed that my locker was always overflowing. She just was like, "How can we help, you know, your child?" I come from a really small community so that parent–teacher connection was always really close, it was a respect issue between the two of, you know, the adult, the parent and the teacher agreement: "This is my child and I'm letting you take care of her for 8 hours a day," and "This is your child and I'm teaching her. How can I do that in a respectful way?" She just was an awesome teacher. And she really shaped my desire to be a teacher. If I could teach sixth grade I would. | Values |
| **C:** To be just like her. | Reflection |
| **T:** Oh yeah. And you know sixth grade is an incredible year. You learn so much. | |
| **C:** It's such an opportunity to influence a life. | Complex reflection |
| **T:** Exactly. | |
| **C:** And you had such a good model for how to do it the right way. To make a difference, like Mrs. Slokowsky did for you. | Reflecting a value |

(continued)

| Interview Dialogue | Comments |
|---|---|
| T: Right. | |
| C: So what makes you most excited about teaching or what would you say is the best thing about being a teacher that you found? | Open-ended question |
| T: The best thing about being a teacher would be the bond you form with kids. Like obviously their education is huge but that's any teacher. You know teachers should have the education piece as a priority, but I really love to make that relationship. Like at the end of the day now, I was telling another teacher this, you tell these kids, especially our population that you care about them and that you love them and that you know and they hear that. But when a kid walks out the door and says, "Love you Ms. Kendrick," You know, and you don't say it first. That really shows me they know that I'm not just saying I care about them, that I really do so that they feel comfortable saying it to me knowing it's normal. We're all just a community in here. You start at the beginning of the year as strangers and everybody's kind of like, "Who are you?" And you reach a point where you're just a community. I love watching my kids socialize. I see them as little citizens and I can help them go out into the world and be successful with that. | Values |
| C: It's more than learning numbers and letters for you. The real excitement for you is helping children feel loved and important. | Reflecting values |
| T: That's what it's about. You need that before you do anything else. | |
| C: Your classroom gives students a foundation for everything else. So on the other hand, what would you say is probably the most difficult thing or challenging thing about being a teacher? | Open-ended question |
| T: I would say working with other adults is challenging. I think that the culture you create as adults in a school building really affects the culture that comes out through your teaching and to the kids. And I've come from two very extremes. When I taught students, I was in extreme community culture. I mean, we all did everything together, teaching and brainstorming. Like I had kids from another teacher's classroom in my math group because that's where they were developmentally. And then I came to a very "close your door," "teach by yourself," "only give each other information that's necessary to do the job but not to enhance the job." And so I'm struggling the most with teaching with…getting the help and the…even just the enrichment from working with other really quality teachers just is really lacking. And that I think that would help me to be more successful as a teacher. | Values |
| C: Teaching is really about creating a community for you. So when that community is shut off from you, you feel disconnected and less effective. | Reflection |

*(continued)*

| Interview Dialogue | Comments |
|---|---|
| T: Yeah. I just think we are all better off when we support each other and we realize we're all in this together. | |
| C: That philosophy of building community really extends beyond your classroom to the entire school and really the entire community. | Reflecting a value |
| T: And as the new teacher at this grade level, I got hired late. All the materials were taken out of my room so every time I come across like a new math lesson, it says I need tiles. So I don't have those tiles so I have to go find all the materials. This material shortage is a huge issue. | |
| C: Anything else? What about within your classroom, or just as far as the students are concerned, what would you say is the hardest challenge? | Open-ended question |
| T: The most challenging would be the variation of learners in the classroom, that really big broad spectrum. And in reading, it really lends itself to having reading groups so you can really break it down by levels. But then math is whole-group instruction, and there's a way to differentiate math. I haven't quite figured it out here with this curriculum. I have a solid third of my class going "I need help. I don't get this. I don't know what to do," and I end up having seven kids around the reading table during math that I'm reteaching a lesson to, while my independent kids, work independently, but also need some support. I didn't know where to be and where to go at the beginning of the year. I've worked on it, but that, the differentiation has been a huge challenge for me, especially in math. | |
| C: Meeting the needs of all students and meeting them where they are at is difficult. | Reflection |

As you can see from this dialogue, a series of four open-ended questions with a few complex reflections elicited a deep and meaningful conversation with this teacher. We already know a lot about her, what she wants and what she deeply believes. We have found these conversations to be very powerful and informative. They provide the seeds for supporting teachers in making potential changes. By connecting with their values and getting a sense of what moves and drives them, you are tapping a well spring of energy and passion that can be the resource needed for moving them forward with change in the classroom. Moreover, these meaningful conversations, when conducted skillfully in the spirit of MI, help forge a collaborative bond between the consultant and the teacher in short order that is the foundation for a solid working relationship.

## Responding to Emotions

As a word of caution, be prepared for teachers to become emotional during these engaging conversations. One reason is because the questions we ask tap something very personal and important to them. Sometimes when we awaken our passions, we have strong emotional connections to them. A second reason that you should not be surprised by tears during your first meetings with teachers is simply because many teachers are under a great deal of pressure in this era of accountability and high-stakes testing. Schools and communities place a lot of burden on teachers, and teachers feel it. Often teachers do not have outlets for these tensions, so when given the opportunity to sit quietly with an attentive and supportive listener, they reveal these pressures. Usually they are surprised by it themselves because they are so used to moving forward that they simply have not taken time to reflect on the challenges of the current school environment. If a teacher becomes sad, if he or she cries during your meeting, remember your role is simply to be present and accept where he or she is. You do not need to fix anything. Just acknowledge whatever the person is experiencing, wait a moment, and then proceed.

> If a teacher becomes sad, if he or she cries during your meeting, remember your role is simply to be present and accept where he or she is. You do not need to fix anything. Just acknowledge whatever the person is experiencing, wait a moment, and then proceed.

| Interview Dialogue | Comments |
|---|---|
| **Consultant (C):** So you've been at this school a long time. What's kept you here? | Open-ended question |
| **Teacher (T):** You know, I just really like it. Honestly. I love the school, I love the community. It's cozy. That's how a childhood is supposed to feel. I like my classroom. I like everything about this area. | |
| C: It really does feel cozy in here. | Simple reflection |
| T: Thank you. Yeah I really want it to feel that way. | |
| C: What made you want to become a teacher? | Open-ended question |
| T: Um, I had a rough childhood and I didn't feel protected. And so I guess that's it… | |
| C: You want to protect kids. | Reflection |
| T: Um, hum (nods head with tears in her eyes) | |
| C: (Pauses) I can see how important that is to you. | Reflection |
| T: Yeah. I'm sorry, I'm just not a morning person. | |
| C: No need to apologize. We feel strongly about things that are important to us. (Pause.) Tell me about some things that you most like about teaching. | Affirmation |

Responding to emotions in teacher consultation contexts can be tricky. The appropriate response can be more straightforward in clinical settings where clients seek services with the implicit understanding that some of the topics discussed may be emotional. Teachers do not usually expect their consultation relationships to elicit an emotional response and thus may be uncomfortable revealing themselves in this way. The skillful consultant acknowledges and validates the feelings that are expressed but keeps the meeting focused on the larger task at hand: solving the problem that led to the consultation meeting in the first place. Notice that the consultant here had many options. She could have given an emotion reflection about the tears ("It makes you sad to remember how you were not protected as a child") and invited more disclosure ("Tell me more about what is making you sad right now"). Both of these responses, however, would have steered the conversation to focus on the more personal revelations from the teacher, and very early in the relationship at that. Instead, the consultant simply acknowledged the tears ("I can see how important this is to you"), validated them ("we feel strongly about things that are important to us"), and then shifted the focus ("tell me about what you like about being a teacher"). In the limited time we have teachers, we need to maximize our impact and also minimize their sense of vulnerability.

## FOCUSING

### Agenda Setting and Structuring

Often the focus of a teacher consultation visit is predetermined by the request of the teacher (e.g., wanting support with classroom management) or the role of the consultant (e.g., a principal doing performance evaluations). Other times, the focus will be unclear. In either case, at some point in a consultation visit, be it for 5 minutes or an hour, it is up to the participants to decide whether their conversation will continue beyond engaging toward a goal. In formal scheduled meetings it is best to set this expectation early by providing an overview and rationale of the visit.

> So my role is to support you in any way that you find helpful in building your classroom-management skills. Today, I'm going to ask you some questions about your background and your current practices and ask you to fill out some forms. I'll do some observations in the classroom and then we will find a time to meet so I can share with you what I have learned. At that time you can decide what, if anything, you would like to work on together.

In less formal meetings, the agenda may emerge later in the conversation. The consultant can structure these conversations using OARS. He or she might summarize the current conversation and then end with an open-ended question inviting participation in creating the agenda.

> You seem really frustrated with a lot of things going on that feel out of your control; the behavior problems in the classroom, some challenges with administrators, and

some worries about whether this is the best career for you. What would make sense for us to work on together?

## Ecological Assessments

Assessment information can provide some level of focus to a conversation. The nature and type of assessments gathered depend on the goal of the consultation. These assessments can be predetermined by the consultant based on his or her expertise and the nature of the consultation visit, or they can be decided on together with the teacher if the visit is not tied to a specific intervention or plan. Given the focus of existing MI teacher consultation models, such as the CCU model, on improving classroom and instructional management skills, the sample assessments here focus on that domain.

In general, you will want to gather direct observations of critical teaching behaviors in addition to teacher self-perceptions. These behaviors include opportunities to respond, correct student responses, praise (general and specific), reprimands (harsh and explicit), disruptions, and time on task. Additional teacher behaviors to observe include supervision and monitoring (does the teacher move about the room). Critical aspects of the teaching environment include the design of the classroom (does it allow ease of movement and transitions).

To gather important information about the teacher's use of classroom management, you can use observation forms provided in *Coaching Classroom Management* (Sprick, Knight, Reinke, Skyles, & Barnes, 2010) or *Motivational Interviewing for Effective Classrooms* (Reinke, Herman, & Sprick, 2011). Both books provide forms for conducting frequency counts of classroom behaviors and assessing on-task student behaviors. Another option is to create your own observation forms.

An important note about conducting observations, your presence in the classroom is part of the intervention. Be aware that your visits can be perceived as an intrusion. Conducting unobtrusive observation is a skill. Skillful consultants do the following to ensure their observations are not intrusive: (a) ask the teacher the best time to observe, (b) assess the climate of the room when you visit (if it's bad time for any reason, be flexible enough to do it another time), (c) stand in an area of the room in which you can observe teacher and student behaviors without interfering with instruction, (d) offer a reason for your visit to the students to make it seem like an everyday activity (e.g., "I am just here to see what fifth graders are learning at your school"), and (e) avoid interacting with the students during the observation. However, if the teacher is comfortable with you in the classroom, interacting in a supportive manner with the students (e.g., walking around the classroom helping students during independent work) outside of these observations can give you additional information while building rapport with the teacher and students.

Compiling data across two or three 10-minute observations of teacher use of praise, reprimands, opportunities to respond, and classroom disruptions during the time the teacher finds most challenging provides important indicators of the level of disruption and current use of classroom strategies. These can then be used to provide the teacher with feedback specific to his or her classroom and students. When providing feedback it is good to have a frame of reference for what is considered effective practice, an area of some concern, or an area in need of immediate attention. For instance, an appropriate praise-to-reprimand ratio for teachers is about three praise statements to every reprimand. A 1:1 ratio is an area that may be in need of attention, whereas a ratio of less than 1:1 or no positive interactions at all is considered ineffective and in need of immediate attention. For other behavioral benchmarks refer to the resources at the end of the chapter.

Assessments can also include rating scales and questionnaires the teacher completes about the targeted domain. These include questions about the teachers' self-reported use of all the critical teaching behaviors that you observe.

## EVOKING

Evoking can occur during any MI process or stage, although change talk toward a specific direction is much more likely to lead to behavior change. As Miller and Rollnick (2013) described, evoking refers to the process whereby the consultant draws out the consultee's arguments for change. A primary tool during the evoking process is open-ended questions. Sometimes the questions that invite focus can also evoke the very arguments in favor of the focusing direction. Thus, focusing and evoking often go hand-in-hand.

### Evoking Change Talk With Open-Ended Questions

As before, good open-ended questions can evoke change talk in teachers. Questions should ask about how the teacher wants things to be different, advantages of changing, reasons for changing, and optimism about being successful (see Table 4.1 in Chapter 4 for sample evocative questions). In the examples below, the consultant has already established a broad focus for the discussions: improving classroom-management skills. The questions serve to narrow that focus a bit and evoke change talk. Consider the following exchanges between consultants and teachers:

| Dialogue | Comments |
|---|---|
| **Consultant:** What do you want support with? | Open-ended question |
| **Teacher:** I would love support with disrespectful behaviors in the class. The calling out, the yelling at teachers. I mean just constant lack of regard for the rules. I hate the talking while you're teaching, the out-of-seat behaviors. I just want help getting them to do anything that they are supposed to be doing. | Change talk: desire and reasons for change |

Notice here, the answer to the question, "What do you want support with?" provides focus for the conversation and an opportunity for change talk. The teacher describes her desire for change ("I want help") and reasons for wanting change. In line with the logic of MI, these self-motivational statements expressed publicly make it much more likely that the teacher will begin to enact a change plan.

| Dialogue | Comments |
| --- | --- |
| **Consultant:** What would you like to be different? | Open-ended question |
| **Teacher:** I talk too much. I know I do. I want to fix that but I don't know how to fix it. | Change talk: desire for change |

Here again, an open-ended question (what she would like to be different) invites the teacher to talk about her desire for changing and a specific behavior she would like help changing. This type of language is associated with increasing levels of motivation, and in turn, the intention to change the desired behavior.

In the next example, the teacher begins with a statement against change (praising will take too long to quiet down a class), and the consultant responds with an open-ended question. The question shifts the conversation and elicits change talk. The consultant asks first about the disadvantages of not changing and then the advantages of changing. The teacher responds with a list of reasons for moving forward.

| Dialogue | Comments |
| --- | --- |
| **Teacher (T):** For me it's a time thing. It takes longer to quiet people down by praising the students who are on task and waiting for the others to get on task than to just tell them. | Status quo talk |
| **Consultant (C):** What are the disadvantages of doing that? | Open-ended question |
| **T:** Well it doesn't always work, especially for the kids who like to talk out. | Change talk: reasons for change |
| **C:** What would be the advantage of doing both, stating your expectation, "Sit quietly," and then praising those who meet the expectation? | Open-ended question |
| **T:** Well, it helps clean up the mess. It gives me another tool for getting everyone on task. So most kids will sit quietly when I ask and then the praise for those kids might draw the others in. Plus, it's also nice giving attention to the kids who always do the right thing. It's easy to overlook them, but this way I'll be giving them the attention they deserve. | Change talk: reasons for change |

### Keeping It Going: Elaborating Change Talk

When you hear change talk, the goal is to keep it flowing. The other elements of OARS are especially useful for inviting a teacher to continue to talk about change. You could respond to change talk, for instance, with an affirmation ("It's great to hear how motivated you are to do this"), a reflection ("You are really committed to making this happen"), or a summary ("The reasons that you really want to do this are because you are feeling worn down this year, you want to make a positive difference in the lives of students, and because you have had success making changes in the past"). Any of these responses would invite a teacher to continue talking about her desires, ability, reasons, needs, or commitment to change. Alternately, a basic strategy for inviting more change talk is simply to say, "tell me more," or some variant of an invitation to continue talking.

Continuing the dialogue from above after an open-ended statement elicited change talk, the consultant kept the conservation going as below:

| Dialogue | Comments |
| --- | --- |
| **Consultant (C):** What would you like to be different? | Open-ended question |
| **Teacher (T):** I talk too much. I know I do. I want to fix that but I don't know how to fix it. | Change talk: desire for change |
| C: You feel very strongly that you are talking too much and this interferes with your classroom. | Reflection |
| T: Yes. I know my message gets lost on students if I say too much. I know they hear me better and are more likely to respond positively if I can be concise. | |
| C: So you want to learn how to give effective commands. That makes a lot of sense to me. | Reflection and affirmation |

### Using Feedback to Focus and Evoke

In structured teacher consultation visits in which there is opportunity to gather assessment information and share with the teacher, personalized feedback can be used to further structure and evoke. Ideally, this feedback is delivered in a scheduled meeting in a private location. Although it is not required, we strongly recommend delivering feedback using a structured form with all the feedback details summarized on a single page. The best way we have found to do this, to lower the threat of delivering and receiving what may be uncomfortable feedback, is to use a form

> We strongly recommend delivering feedback using a structured form with all the feedback details summarized on a single page.

like the one depicted in Handout 5.2. This form is a sample used in working with a teacher on classroom and instructional management but can easily be adapted to deliver feedback on any domains you choose by typing in the categories of interest into the blank version. Examples of feedback forms can be found in the resources at the end of the chapter, and a color version is available online at http://prevention.missouri.edu/downloads.

### Reflection Question ("What I Have Learned" Question)

It is a good idea to start a feedback meeting by asking the teacher what thoughts he or she has had about teaching since your last meeting. Often completing an engaging and evocative interview and rating forms can spark teachers to reflect about their profession and their classroom. So simply asking, "I just wanted to start by asking where you are. I'm wondering if you have any new thoughts or ideas since our last talk." It is fine if the teacher says that nothing new has happened. Teachers tend to be very busy so sometimes they literally will not have had another moment to reflect on your conversation. On the other hand, some teachers will have had new insights and ideas for directions they want to take. It is good to get this on the table at the outset so that you can keep it in mind for the remainder of the conversation.

### Overview and Introducing the Feedback Form

Next, it is a good idea to give an overview for the feedback meeting. A brief introduction like the following works well:

> So today I want to share with you the information that I have been gathering. I really want to hear your thoughts about the information I give you. Based on the information and what you want to do, we will then come up with a plan for next steps that you want to take. Sound good?

| Feedback Dialogue | Comments |
| --- | --- |
| **Consultant (C):** The purpose of today is to go over your feedback. I'm going to start by showing the form I use to go over the feedback. Obviously, as we go further down there are things you may want to pay attention to here. As we do this, I'm going to write down things on a menu of options that you may want to work on. If we put it down it doesn't mean we have to work on it, just that we may want to. At the end we'll look over the menu and decide what next steps to take. And as we do this I want feedback from you about this, any questions you have and especially your reactions to what I say. | Overview |

Invite the teacher to ask any questions about the process or agenda for the meeting. Next, introduce the feedback form. One strategy that we use is to first show a blank feedback form to explain how to interpret the data as it is presented.

> I have compiled all this information onto a single sheet. On this side, you notice different aspects of your classroom, some related to student behavior, some teacher behaviors, and some concern the overall classroom environment. For each of these areas, you will see a mark from green to red indicating where your classroom falls. Marks in the green indicate those are strong points for your classroom, yellows are warning/ pay attention areas, and reds are ones we'll really want to think about changing.

### Giving Constructive Feedback

The feedback form and MI style provide an optimal way of giving constructive feedback. Teachers will only learn to improve targeted skills if they have accurate information about their current performance levels. The task of the consultant is to provide positive and negative feedback in a way that is nonthreatening and about behaviors than can be changed. The feedback form helps in this regard. By marking the teacher's performance on a form, it takes the focus off the consultant as the bearer of bad news and instead becomes about the "report." The best way to deliver this information is in a matter-of-fact approach without explaining it away or apologizing for it. The other key skill here is to ask the check-in questions to assess how the teacher is responding to the feedback ("What do you make of that?" "Does that seem right to you?" and "What are you thinking right now?").

> The best way to deliver this information is in a matter-of-fact approach without explaining it away or apologizing for it. The other key skill here is to ask the check-in questions to assess how the teacher is responding to the feedback.

Be sure to place the feedback on the table between you and the teacher rather than on a clipboard in your lap. This setup conveys collaboration as opposed to evaluation. Leaning back with the form on your lap may arouse concern and anxiety about being judged.

In the example below, notice how the consultant uses all of these strategies. Notice also how the consultant catches herself from her intuitive response and continues with an MI approach.

| Feedback Dialogue | | Comments |
|---|---|---|
| **Consultant (C):** | So with praise and reprimands they often go together. So you see your rate was 1 praise to 6 reprimands. | Matter-of-fact feedback |
| **Teacher (T):** | It should be more even? | |
| **C:** | Actually, research tells us it should be more like 3:1. | Matter-of-fact information giving |

*(continued)*

| Feedback Dialogue | Comments |
|---|---|
| T: Wow. So almost the opposite. | |
| C: That really surprises you. | Complex reflection |
| T: Yeah, I had no idea. | |
| C: I will say for most teachers, this is a pretty common challenge. | Normalize |
| T: So I'm not so much of a meanie? | Catches her intuitive response to educate. Instead asks open-ended question. |
| C: Not a meanie at all. Part of the reason this is common is...well, why do you think this is common? | |
| T: We're always trying to put out the fires. You saw this when you were in there. There are so many kids who are disruptive that I give all my time to do that. And sometimes I remember to thank the kids who are doing the right thing but then I get caught up in these kiddos up front. And then I get a little angry and then I don't feel like praising anybody. | |
| C: Ah, interesting how you see a chain reaction there. So the disruptions anger you and it keeps your mind away... but what if... so what if... [(to self) Let's keep away from the "what ifs"]. It keeps your mind away from the praise and you go to the reprimands because you are so busy trying to put out fires. | Catches herself from giving advice. Instead stays with a reflection |
| T: That's right. It is just a bad cycle I get sucked into. | |
| C: Then you get annoyed and that makes it hard to even notice anything positive. | Complex reflection |

Here the consultant catches herself twice. The first time, her impulse was to tell the teacher why it is common for teachers to have difficulty praising more than reprimanding. She stopped her statement and shifted to simply asking an open-ended question to invite the teacher to answer this question herself. In the second instance, the consultant found herself wanting to give the teacher advice on how to interrupt the negative cycle of her classroom. If they were in the problem-solving phase and had the teacher's permission to give advice, this may have been fine. But in this instance, the consultant realized that her goal was to give the teacher feedback and understand how this problem was undermining her classroom. She opted to simply reflect the statement to highlight the problems with the status quo.

### Check-In Questions

As you deliver feedback it is especially important to invite the teacher to respond to the feedback. An effective way to do this is to regularly ask check-in questions such as, "What do you think of that?" "How does that fit with what you were thinking?" or "What's your reaction to this information?" If the teacher has visible reactions to the feedback, this is an opportunity to invite conversation about his or her reaction by using reflections. For instance, you might say, "That really surprises you," after a teacher says, "Wow." Or if you notice a teacher furrow her brow as you are talking you might simply comment, "Something about that isn't sitting well with you," or "Tell me what you are thinking about right now."

Below is an example of dialogue invited by a check-in question:

| Dialogue | Comments |
|---|---|
| **Consultant (C):** So disruptions. You're right in the middle about one per minute ... hmm. You had a reaction to that. | Check-in question |
| **Teacher (T):** It's highly unacceptable. Like certain classes I can't get through basic instructions without major disruptions so I just say okay, you're doing bookwork the rest of the period. That really drives me crazy. One per minute. That's just way too often. | Change talk: dissatisfaction with the status quo |

### Correcting a Misperception

Feedback, along with check-in questions, can help clarify misperceptions that teachers have about themselves and/or about the information being shared with them. Sometimes teachers have overly negative perceptions about their teaching behaviors. Providing clarification from an objective standpoint can be empowering and a basis for moving them forward in their professional growth.

| Dialogue | Comments |
|---|---|
| **Consultation (C):** Does this fit with what you're thinking as far as the classroom structure? | Check-in question |
| **Teacher (T):** Hm hm, um, for the most part. I'm surprised about this one though [points to paper and her feedback on Organization and Harsh Reprimands] because I feel like, like if my head weren't attached, I'd lose it in this room. I feel like that. | |
| **C:** Really? | |
| **T:** Yeah | |
| **C:** Wow. | |
| **T:** So it makes me feel better that you don't think that. | |
| **C:** I think your classroom is very well organized and you are very calm. But even your reprimands are not harsh. They're not emotional. I don't know that I've ever counted even one harsh. | Affirmation and feedback |
| **T:** Oh my gosh, that's really good to hear, too, because I feel like I am. | |

## Summarize

Remember to frequently summarize the discussion. At the end of each section, it is a good idea to offer a two- to three-sentence summary to be sure you both are on track and in agreement. For instance, after giving feedback about student behaviors, you might summarize by saying, "So students in your class have pretty highs rates of disruptions and off-task behaviors and that really bothers you.

> At the end of each section, it is a good idea to offer a two- to three-sentence summary to be sure you both are on track and in agreement.

Finding ways to fix that is a high priority for you." It is also a good idea to use a summary of the entire feedback discussion as a transition to the goal-setting part of the meeting. Aside from providing transitions and opportunities to check agreement and understanding, remember summaries can be used strategically to highlight discrepancies, emphasize change talk, and collect a series of ideas into a larger theme.

Also, feel free to invite the teacher to provide summaries of the discussion. This keeps him or her engaged and allows yet another check on shared understandings. Here is an example of inviting a teacher to summarize the discussion.

| Summary Dialogue | | Comments |
|---|---|---|
| **Teacher:** | So tell me how you are making sense of all these. What are the big ideas we've been talking about that are sticking with you? | Open-ended question inviting a summary |
| **Consultant:** | Well, I'm not in the horrible area on anything. Yes, my praise ratio can be improved and I want to improve. I want to be good teacher. I'm learning about myself. I learned about follow through, I need to do better at follow through. We talked about rewarding them and the reprimands to the praises. And I'm going to work harder on that. | |

Below, we provide an example of an introductory dialogue about feedback with a teacher. Notice how the consultant describes the feedback process and uses check-in questions to gain a deeper discussion of areas on which to focus.

| Sample Feedback Dialogue | | Comments |
|---|---|---|
| **Consultant (C):** | The purpose of today is to go over your feedback. I'm going to start by showing the form I use to pull together all the information gathered from my visits and the forms you completed. | Overview |

*(continued)*

| Sample Feedback Dialogue | Comments |
|---|---|
| **Teacher (T):** Okay. Sounds good. | |
| **C:** [shows blank form] So the form I use looks like this. It has the areas that I collected information about on this side [points to the left]. I use red, green, and yellow to indicate where you were on each of these areas. So things that are marked toward the green are things that you do very well, things in the yellow are areas that could be improved, and things in the red are ones where we want to stop and look at closely in terms of thinking about what to do. Does this make sense? | Describing the feedback form |
| **T:** Yep. | |
| **C:** As we do this, I'm going to write down things on a menu of options that you may want to work on. If we put it down it doesn't mean we have to work on it just that we may want to. At the end we'll look over the menu and decide what next steps to take. Okay? | Check-in question |
| **T:** Yes, that sounds good. | |
| **C:** [turns over feedback form] So let's start with the classroom structure. Overall this was an area of real strength for you. Notice most of these were in the green zone. The first one is the layout of your classroom. Here, you are in the green zone because your room is well organized, there are clear walking paths that give you access to all the students and them access to materials and resources without any problems. How does that fit with your views? | Explicit feedback and examples<br><br>Check-in question |

## PLANNING: GOAL SETTING

After delivering the feedback, the teacher is now in a position to better select goals to work on and to develop a plan for achieving the goals. Below we provide strategies for facilitating the planning process.

### Summary, Transition, and Menu of Options

A good way to transition to goal setting is to first summarize the feedback and the teacher's reaction to it. For instance, a consultant may say, "So you have a lot of areas in the green zone, things that are going well. You have great relationships with students and your classroom is very organized. The one area that stood out to you, and that we included on the menu of options,

> A good way to transition to goal setting is to first summarize the feedback and the teacher's reaction to it.

was the ratio of praise to reprimands in your classroom. That's something that surprised you and that you want to be different." The summary allows the consultant to check in regarding shared understanding about the feedback, gives the teacher a chance to hear the important parts of the feedback again, and helps confirm any change talk elicited during the feedback. Also by way of summarizing, the consultant can review the menu of options generated during the feedback discussion: "You came up with three things that you wanted to put on our menu for further discussion: developing clear expectations, improving transitions, and improving your positive-to-negative ratio. Anything else you want to add to the list?" Again, the summary confirms what was said and gives the teacher an opportunity to elaborate or expand on the menu.

### Create an Action Plan/Goal Setting

The remaining discussion focuses on establishing next steps. A basic way to do this is to ask the "what's next?" question and follow the teacher's lead in setting goals. A more structured discussion can occur with the use of a goal-setting form that includes the following questions (see Handout 5.2 for a sample goal-setting form):

- What's going well in the classroom?
- What goals does the teacher want to set?
- What steps or resources are needed to achieve the goal?
- How confident is the teacher in reaching the goal (using rulers)?
- How important is the goal to the teacher (using rulers)?
- What obstacles might get in the way and how can these be overcome?

Below, we present an extended dialogue of a consultant helping a teacher generate a concrete action plan. One important skill to notice in this dialogue is how the consultant pushes the teacher to get more and more specific by using focusing questions. At the end of the conversation the teacher has a concrete goal and plan.

| Action Plan Dialogue | Comments |
| --- | --- |
| **Consultant (C):** So this is the point where we come up with an action plan. | |
| **Teacher (T):** Okay. | |
| **C:** And we start with all the things that are going well. So what are the things going well in your classroom? | Open-ended question |
| **T:** Definitely the relationships and a lot of kids who started the year off the wrong way are back on track. | |

*(continued)*

| Action Plan Dialogue | Comments |
|---|---|
| C: That's rewarding to see kids moving in positive directions. | |
| T: Yes. I'm getting used to this population because these kids are unique and have unique needs. At first I thought, they had no social skills and no interest, and I thought they were so rude. But then I realized, well of course they don't have these things. No one ever forced them to do things I was expecting of them, so I just said okay, I will teach them. | |
| C: So you turned it around yourself and decided rather than being disappointed in them you would do what you could to teach them what you expected. | Reflection |
| T: Yeah, it was a real eye opener. | |
| C: So you end up feeling empowered because you now see the difference it has made for many kids rather than feeling annoyed or even helpless like you did at first. | Reflection |
| T: Right. | |
| C: So what do you want to focus on improving now? | Open-ended question |
| T: Definitely the amount of disruptions. | |
| C: Okay. What specifically would you like to see happen? | Focusing question |
| T: My specific goal. I want to find more constructive ways to deal with disruptions when they happen. | Change talk: desire |
| C: So you want to decrease disruptions by… | Focusing |
| T: By…[pause]…helping students meet expectations by using praise and reprimands more effectively. | Change talk |
| C: Okay…[writing pause]…using praise and reprimands more effectively. So what would that look like? | Focusing question |
| T: I definitely want to work on improving my ratio of praise to reprimands. | Change talk |
| C: So improve the ratio. How will that help? | Evocative question |
| T: I just know that when I give positive behaviors more attention it can only help reduce the negative behaviors. | Change talk |
| C: Okay, so your goal is to reduce disruptions by increasing your positive responses and reducing negatives. What's a good starting goal for you? | Focusing |

*(continued)*

| Action Plan Dialogue | Comments |
|---|---|
| T: I'm going to start with 2:1 because I can't go from a 1:6 ratio to a 3:1 ratio overnight. | Change talk: mobilizing |
| C: I like how you're thinking about setting realistic goals, because that way you set yourself up for stepping up instead of leaping. So what do we need to get this done [next step]? | Affirmation<br><br>Focusing |
| T: [Pauses] Wait. Is a stare, a teacher stare considered a reprimand? | |
| C: Mmhmm. A reprimand is anytime you give your attention to a misbehavior, to a behavior that violates one of your expectations. | |
| T: Oh goodness. I might have to start at 1:1 as a first step then! It could be hard. I'm from an English background and we don't praise people a lot. Even if they are doing something exceptional. Like I would do really well in school, and my mom would say yeah I expected that. I don't feel like I should praise someone unless they're really deserving of it. Like in my mind, I shouldn't praise someone for doing what is expected. But now I see I need to shift that to be, "Well what I think doesn't necessarily work for everyone, does it?" | Value clues |
| C: What do you think of shifting that? Why is that important to you? | Evocative question |
| T: I just think remembering that kids act out for attention and if I can give it to them in another way that's more positive, it will be more productive for both of us. Because whether I react negatively or positively they're still getting the attention, so I have to figure out how to give them positive attention rather than negative. | Change talk: mobilizing |
| C: Okay. So reminding yourself that you are giving kids attention one way or the other so you might as well focus on giving it to them when they are meeting your expectations rather than when they are not. | Reflection |
| T: I do like effective praise. I mean I want to make my praise more specific. The other reason is I know that the more I do this, the fewer disruptive behaviors I will see. | Change talk: desire and reasons |
| C: I've heard you give specific praise. You say, "I love how this side of the room is quiet." It's part of what you do already, so it is just a matter of increasing it, not inventing it. | Feedback and affirmation |

*(continued)*

| Action Plan Dialogue | Comments |
|---|---|
| **T:** Yeah I can do this. | Change talk: ability |
| **C:** So what do we need to do to meet this goal? | What next question |
| **T:** So I need to work on coming up with things that I can praise them for. Like following class procedures. To counter a bad behavior, let's say certain people are turning around having conversations, I can say, I really like how so and so and so and so are focused on me without having conversations. | Change talk: mobilizing |
| **C:** So coming up with a specific list of things you can praise. You talked about expectations. So maybe doing them one at a time focusing on each one on a given day. | Reflection |
| **T:** Right, so like calling out. I really like how so and so is raising her hand. | |
| **C:** Yes. So what do you need to get that done? | Focusing |
| **T:** I can talk to colleagues to see what they say. I can just start writing a list based on my classroom expectations. | Mobilizing |
| **C:** So, when do you want to come up with this list? | Focusing |
| **T:** By the end of the week. | Mobilizing |
| **C:** Okay, so thinking about this goal, decreasing disruptions by increasing praise. How important is it to you, from 1 to 10? | Ruler |
| **T:** It's a 10. | |
| **C:** Whoa, a 10. Why a 10 and not a 5? | |
| **T:** I just think the class will run that much smoother. If I'm able to work out my praise and reprimands and the disruptions slow down, I don't expect them to stop. One per minute [the current rate] is completely unacceptable to me though. That's like 10 seconds out of each minute, and if it's a 60-minute class that's like many minutes of it is filled with disruptions. I don't even know how many minutes that is, but that is too many minutes. | Change talk: reasons |
| **C:** So it sounds like you are really committed to getting some of that time back for you and your students. I mean this is as important as it gets for you. | Reflection |
| **T:** Yes. It has been a stressful year and I want to get this under control. | Change talk |

*(continued)*

| Action Plan Dialogue | Comments |
|---|---|
| C: What about in terms of confidence level, same scale. | Ruler |
| T: A 6. | |
| C: Okay. So you could have said a 3. So why a 6 and not a 3? | |
| T: Because I'm usually confident. If I want to do something I can do it. | Change talk |
| C: So when you put your mind to things you get them done. When you want something, and you already said you want this. | Reflection |
| T: Hmm. Hmm. | |
| C: What would it take to get 6 to 7? | |
| T: I think I just need to see some success. | Change talk |
| C: So with each step you see yourself getting more confident. | Reflection |
| T: That's right. | |
| C: What do you see that could get in the way? | Open-ended question |
| T: Just if I lose sight of it. If it gets lost in the pile of things to do. | |
| C: So what can we do to prevent that? | Open-ended question |
| T: Just keeping reminders. Maybe even making myself a little sign and putting it on my desk. Oh I got to do that. That's a good idea. | |
| C: So the plan is you are going to increase your use of praise in the classroom and reduce reprimands. Your first step is to flip it to at least 1:1. You are going to write a list of things you want to praise by the end of the week. You are also going to put a sign on your desk. When are you going to start this? | Summary<br><br>Eliciting commitment |
| T: On Monday. | |
| C: So on Monday, when I visit, I will see your sign and I will notice you paying more attention to positives than negatives. And I will be hearing lots of specific praise. | Summary and affirmation |
| T: That's right. | |
| C: After that, sky's the limit because your confidence will just keep blossoming with each step you take. | Affirmation |

## Ending Each Consultation Visit With Rulers

We recommend that you use rulers at the end of each meeting. This provides another opportunity to assess the motivation of the teacher and any barriers to change. Here is an example of the effective use of rulers to end a visit:

| Rulers Dialogue | | Comments |
|---|---|---|
| Consultant (C): | So talking about importance. Here's a scale with 1 being not important at all to 10 being very important. This goal of yours how important is it for you in the classroom? | Ruler |
| Teacher (T): | I'd say 8. Only because I really want to get better. | Change talk: desire for change |
| C: | Okay, great. Clearly important to you. Why an 8 and not a 7? | Open-ended question |
| T: | Because it gives us order in the classroom and it helps the kids. Because I go home happy. Our families are happy. And it's stability for everyone. | Change talk: reasons for change |
| C: | That's awesome. I'm running out of space to write these. | Affirmation |
| T: | This is it. I mean I need to make a change. I'm going to make this change. | Change talk: commitment |
| C: | So you're saying by improving your praise rate and your follow through, you can see how this will make the classroom a better place to be but also how this will make everyone happier, including your family. | Reflection |
| T: | Yeah, I mean it all flows together. If I'm not happy at school, it oozes over into the rest of my life. | Change talk: reasons |
| C: | Wow, that's powerful. I can see why this is so important to you. | Affirmation |
| C: | And in terms of confidence now, same scale, 1 being not very confident to 10 being very confident, how confident are you that you can achieve this goal? | Ruler |
| T: | Okay, I'm going to give a double answer. I'm confident I can do it, I'm less confident that I can document it. It's just the reality of my day. Like I have to think about content and praise and a lot of stuff. This sitting to the side gets forgotten. We don't have time between classes. So in reality this will get done at the end of the day, so I think it is very likely I will forget many days. | Barriers |

*(continued)*

| Rulers Dialogue | Comments |
|---|---|
| C: So let's take the first part first. So you're confident you can do it, you can increase your praise rate, 1 to10? | Focusing |
| T: An 8. | |
| C: An 8 again. Very confident. What makes you so confident? | Open-ended question |
| T: Because I'm committed to doing this. Because it's best for the kids. Because it's my job. I want to prepare children to be leaders. If I'm not doing my job here that won't happen. And we are going to have anarchy if I don't step in the right direction. | Change talk: ability |
| C: Great. So you are going to make this happen. Your only concern is the documenting. Why is it important to document? | Open-ended question |
| T: Well, I know it is good to keep track so that I can show that I am changing. I think it reminds me to do it. It can be a good tool. | |
| C: So you want to keep track of it because you see it can help. The key seems to be finding a way to keep track without added burden to your day. Should we spend some time coming up with an easy tracking system that doesn't get in your way? | Reflection<br><br>Question to resolve barriers |
| T: Yes. That would be great. | |

The teacher responds to the confidence ruler by saying she felt confident, but then shifts to talking about what might get in the way of her achieving her goal. If the consultant had simply followed her lead, she would have missed an opportunity to draw out specific ability talk and likely would have elicited more sustain talk. Instead, she focused the teacher and prompted her to tell her reasons why she was confident about the plan. This ensured that the teacher would end the meeting expressing her reasons for being confident. Then the teacher could focus on one of the potential barriers to change and solutions to overcome it.

## EVERYDAY CONVERSATIONS ABOUT CHANGE

Ms. Frederich stops by to chat with the school counselor about a student.

| | |
|---|---|
| **Ms. Frederich (F):** | I'm at the end of my rope with Zach. |
| **School Consultant (SC):** | What's going on? |
| F: | He's just not making any progress. |
| SC: | That is frustrating. |
| F: | I've tried everything with him and nothing works. It's like he doesn't even care. |

*(continued)*

---

**EVERYDAY CONVERSATIONS ABOUT CHANGE (*continued*)**

SC:   You've really stuck with him.

F:   I just wish I understood how to get through to him.

SC:   Finding that spark in him.

F:   I think he has it. That's the frustrating part. He can do it. He's a smart kid.

SC:   He's worth fighting for.

F:   Urgh! Yes. I just wish I could see some progress.

SC:   So what are you gonna do?

F:   Keep fighting, I guess. I just need an outlet and a reminder why it's worth the effort.

SC:   I wonder if I can help with that.

---

*In this example, the consultant simply listened to the teacher's frustrations, reflecting her feelings and the underlying gem: her persistence and commitment to helping connect to this student. The teacher came to her own conclusion, that it was worth the effort, and the consultant offered to help.*

---

## THE CCU

The CCU was developed as a consultation model that addresses the need for classroom-level support while minimizing treatment integrity problems common to school-based consultation. The purpose of the CCU is to (a) target teachers' motivation to maintain current practices that are important for student success, (b) reduce teacher–student interactions that are likely to exacerbate problem behaviors, and (c) increase teacher behaviors that promote student competence and success. The CCU is described in an extensive manual (see Reinke et al., 2011).

The CCU was patterned after an assessment intervention designed for and effectively implemented with families of children with problem behaviors, the Family Check-up (FCU). The FCU will be described in Chapter 7 (Dishion & Kavanaugh, 2003). Like the FCU, the CCU was developed from empirically driven theory, with an emphasis on the important relationships among assessment, intervention, and triggering behavior-change theory (see Miller & Rollnick, 2002; Stormshak & Dishion, 2002). Also like the FCU, the CCU involves an initial interview, direct observations, and a feedback/planning session.

The CCU includes two meetings, an interview and a feedback/planning session, and follows a series of steps: (a) interviewing the teacher and assessing the classroom, (b) providing the teacher with personalized feedback, (c) developing a menu of possible interventions, (d) choosing the intervention, (e) having the teacher self-monitor implementation of the intervention, and when appropriate (f) providing performance feedback (see Reinke, Herman, & Sprick, 2011, for details).

The structure of the CCU is designed to intentionally prompt the four processes of MI: engagement, focusing, evoking, and planning. The interview is crafted to facilitate engagement and focus through a series of open-ended questions and values exploration. Personalized feedback delivered at the second meeting is intended to be affirmative and evocative, eliciting concern or desire for change in the teacher. The feedback sets the stage for the development of a menu of options, very much in line with what Miller and Rollnick (2013) describe as agenda planning. The menu of options provides the transition to planning. From the menu, the teacher selects one or more areas of focus and proceeds through a series of goal-setting and action-planning steps. The meeting culminates with more evoking as the consultant asks the teacher about the importance and confidence rulers related to his or her plan.

## SUMMARY

The MI processes and strategies and the CCU framework position consultants to help teachers move toward positive change. Rather than waiting and hoping for teachers to want to change, the process meets teachers where they are. Some teachers will be very ready to make needed changes in their classrooms. If so, you can move swiftly with them to start creating a plan of action. Spending too much time trying to build the motivation of someone who is already motivated can backfire. Still, even with these teachers, be sure to monitor the re-emergence of ambivalence. If you start hearing pessimistic language or a desire to return to the status quo, that

> Some teachers will be highly ambivalent about changing and may even be not considering change at all. For these teachers it would be a mistake to rush into creating a change plan. It won't work. Teachers will not change until they are ready.

is a sign that their motivation is waning and you will want to return to strategies to build their readiness for change again. Other teachers will be highly ambivalent about changing and may even be not considering change at all. For these teachers it would be a mistake to rush into creating a change plan. It won't work. Teachers will not change until they are ready. In these cases, it makes much more sense to spend your time as a consultant using the strategies described to explore the teacher's ambivalence, highlight discrepancy, and evoke change talk. Only after getting agreement from a teacher to proceed, will your best-laid plans manifest.

## RESOURCES TO SUPPORT TEACHER DEVELOPMENT OF CLASSROOM-MANAGEMENT SKILLS

Reinke, W. M., Herman, K. C., & Sprick, R. (2011). *Motivational interviewing for effective classroom management: The Classroom Check-Up.* New York, NY: Guilford Press.

Sprick, R. (2008). *Discipline in the secondary classroom: A positive approach to behavior management* (2nd ed.). Eugene, OR: Pacific Northwest.

Sprick, R., et al. (2010). *Coaching classroom management: Strategies and tools for administrators and coaches* (2nd ed.). Eugene, OR: Pacific Northwest.

Sprick, R., Garrison, M., & Howard, L. (1998). *CHAMPS: A proactive and positive approach to classroom management.* Longmont, CO: Sopris West.

Stormshak, E., & Dishion, T. J. (2002). An ecological approach to child and family clinical and counseling psychology. *Clinical Child and Family Psychology Review, 5,* 197–215.

# Handouts and Forms

## HANDOUT 5.1 TEACHER VALUES CARD SORT CARDS

| | |
|---|---|
| Accepting Differences in People | Being a Good Teacher |
| Working Hard | Taking Time for Myself |
| Being Organized | Being Happy |
| Not Giving Up | Being Healthy |
| Being Honest | Being Responsible |
| Being Liked by Everyone | Being a Leader |
| Being Respected by Others | Doing the Right Thing |
| Being a Lifelong Learner | Being a Role Model |
| Having Fun | Having a Safe Classroom |
| Feeling Good About Myself | Being a Good Colleague |
| Other: | Communicating Effectively |
| Being Aware of Personal Biases | Being Self-Reflective |
| Relating to Students | Understanding Others |
| Being a Good Listener | Being Fair |
| Taking Care of My Family | Helping Others |
| Staying in Control | Making a Difference in the World |
| Being Real/Genuine | Being Patient |
| Being Kind | Being Flexible |
| Important | Very Important |
| Not Important | |

# HANDOUT 5.2 SAMPLE GOAL-PLANNING FORM

Teacher:_____  Grade:_____  Date:_____

| Those things **going well** in my classroom: | Areas I would like to **focus on improving** in my classroom: |
|---|---|
| Specifically, **my goal** is to: | |

| What steps do I need to take to meet this goal? | | | |
|---|---|---|---|
| What needs to be done? | My Plan | Resources I need to do it | Timeline |
| | | | |

| How **important** is it for you to meet this goal in your classroom? | The **most** important reasons for making this change and meeting this goal is: |
|---|---|
| 1  2  3  4  5  6  7  8  9  10<br>Not Important At All  Very Important | |
| How **confident** are you that you will meet this goal in your classroom? | Some reasons that **I am confident:** |
| 1  2  3  4  5  6  7  8  9  10<br>Not Confident At All  Very Confident | |

| Is there anything that could get in the way of meeting this goal? | What can I do to help make sure this doesn't get in the way? |
|---|---|
| | |

# 6

# Motivational Interviewing With Students

Although the vast majority of the motivational interviewing (MI) literature has been focused on applications with adults, recent efforts have extended the MI principles to working with youth. Most research-based applications to date have focused on working with adolescents regarding their use of substances and other addictive behaviors. More recently, efforts have expanded to include motivating youth on a range of other behaviors, including academic-related problems.

In this chapter, we review appropriate applications of MI with youth, emphasizing developmental adaptations that are needed to be successful. We provide an extended example of using MI to decrease substance use given that this topic has the strongest support in the literature. We then extend the principles derived from this example to other applications within schools.

## DEVELOPMENTAL CONSIDERATIONS

### Language and Cognitive Development

Given that MI is primarily a language-based intervention intended to highlight discrepant cognitions, it is important to consider the developmental implications of this method. First, language skills are a prerequisite for applications of MI in its traditional format. Obviously, it would be difficult to apply MI change talk principles to preverbal children. Extending this

> Children, like adults, prefer to experience consistency between their actions and their beliefs or values.

logic, one would expect any language delay or barrier to interfere with the typical MI approach. Second, a primary tenet of MI is that people are motivated to change their behavior when they become aware of discrepancies between their

**139**

current behaviors and their values or desired behaviors. Presumably, this type of awareness requires one to have values and some level of cognitive sophistication to be able to reflect on one's behavior and consider it in relation to self-perceptions or beliefs or to an alternative, ideal behavior.

How old does someone need to be to engage in this sort of metacognitive reflection? This is open to debate. On the one hand, developmental literature suggests that cognitions in young children through the age of 9 or 10 are less crystallized and more fluid than they are in older children and adolescents (see Herman, Lambert, Reinke, & Ialongo, 2008). The primary influences on behavior, mood, and decisions prior to this age appear to be contextual and environmental. For instance, if a 6-year-old is sad, there is probably something objectively wrong in his or her life. For adolescents and adults, however, we can be sad simply because of how we are thinking about things. In this sense, the level of cognitive maturity that occurs around the beginning of middle school may be a good marker for when children may benefit from a more conversational intervention like MI.

However, some research does suggest that even young children experience cognitive dissonance that can influence their beliefs and actions. Strait et al. (2012) reviewed literature showing that many of the same underlying mechanisms of MI may apply to children. For instance, children may experience attitude change when external incentives are not sufficient to warrant actions that violate a social norm. The classic adult study on this topic showed that when adults were paid money to lie (e.g., telling someone else that a boring task was actually fun), they were more likely to change their beliefs to match the lie (e.g., to later remember the original boring task as fun) when the payment for the lie was low (Festinger, 1957). In other words, we as adults prefer that our actions and values align. If we are given a strong external reward, in this case, a lot of money, it allows us to justify why we violated a social norm. If the external reward is insufficient to justify violating the norm, this causes cognitive dissonance and forces us to change our attitude or belief. In this case, participants came to believe the task was not boring, which meant they really did not tell a lie at all.

Through his cognitive dissonance theory, Festinger (1957) explains this phenomenon by suggesting that humans are motivated to maintain consistency between their actions and their beliefs. When we are given strong external incentives to change our behavior (e.g., get paid a lot of money) we can justify the behavior and experience low dissonance. However, when the incentive is low and we still engage in the behavior, it encourages us to reconcile the discrepancy by changing our beliefs.

Studies have shown this effect to occur in young children as well (see Strait et al., 2012). Children, like adults, prefer to experience consistency between their actions and their beliefs or values. Inconsistency leads both children and adults to change their behaviors or attitudes so that they are congruent.

In light of these developmental considerations, what are some good rules of thumb for the application of MI with youth? First, MI is likely to be more useful and influential as youth grow older. You are probably safe using many of the basic MI principles and strategies with adolescents. Many youth in middle school likely would be responsive. Consistent with this recommendation, several studies have found that MI-style interventions may produce meaningful change in youth. Second, for younger children, any use of MI likely will require developmental adaptations. Although the goals may be similar (e.g., to evoke cognitive dissonance), the strategies for accomplishing them may be less verbal and more activity based. In sum, at this point, it is safe to say that an MI approach likely can be adapted to work well with adolescents, as there are several examples of this with solid research. The verdict is still out on how well these methods will work with younger children, but with reasonable modifications, it is likely we will continue to see extensions of MI to younger populations.

## Social Development: Autonomy Support

A key developmental push experienced during adolescence through early adulthood is striving for autonomy and independence. Effective motivational strategies need to be aware of and capitalize on the energy associated with this push. Try to push against it by blocking it or denying it and you get a strong sense of the energy attached to this developmental demand. For instance, when you

> Emphasizing autonomy support when working with adolescents appears to be a promising adaptation to the application of this approach with youth.

tell an adolescent that he or she cannot or should not do something that he or she wants to do, most will respond with strong, visceral arguments about why he or she can or should. Sometimes when you tell him or her not to do something, he or she will argue about why he or she should, even though initially he or she may not have been particularly interested in it. Simply blocking something can arouse energy to get it. Therefore, emphasizing autonomy support when working with adolescents appears to be a promising adaptation of the application of this approach with youth.

## Ecological Dependence: A Word of Caution

We believe it is important for children who require mental health services to be served within the context of an ecological perspective, which demands symptoms be viewed as being influenced by the child's daily interactions with teachers, caregivers, and peers as well as community dynamics and resources (Dishion & Stormshak, 2007). Individual counseling has been consistently shown to be less effective than behaviorally based intervention strategies in school settings. Thus, it is with caution that we recommend MI as a strategy for children—particularly those with challenging behavior and mental health concerns. Focusing on individual counseling alone abdicates adult responsibilities. We believe changing youths' environments is likely to be the most beneficial way to affect their behavior. That being said, using MI with adolescents is likely to improve relationships, which are associated with a number of positive outcomes. Additionally, counseling is sometimes an important component of a multifaceted treatment plan.

## ENGAGING STRATEGIES FOR YOUTH

### Responsibility

Given the push toward autonomy, the emphasis on responsibility becomes even a stronger MI message with youth. Clearly communicating to youth that it is

> Clearly communicating to youth that it is ultimately their decision about any changes they might make is an important element of engaging them in any conversation about change.

ultimately their decision about any changes they might make is an important element of engaging them in any conversation about change. It is common for adults who work with youth to occasionally find themselves pushing or even demanding behavior change from youth. If and when you find yourself sensing that you are pushing for change harder than you wish, this is usually a good prompt for you to give an explicit response. "Look, this is up to you. If you want to work on this, I'm happy to help and support you. It's your choice."

### Decisional Balance

Engaging in conversations about the decisional balance can be disarming for youth who are prepared to have arguments with adults about their behav-

> Engaging in conversations about the decisional balance can be disarming for youth who are prepared to have arguments with adults about their behaviors.

iors. The typical conversations some adults have with youth about problem behaviors can be very didactic, pedantic, and authoritative—exactly the opposite types of behaviors MI would suggest as helpful. Thus, many youth expect all conversations with adults about their behavior to be in that mode. Changing the nature of the conversation oftentimes catches youth by surprise and allows them to reposition themselves in relation to the behavior and the conversation.

Recall from Chapter 3 that decisional balance conversations ask about the pros and cons of the current behavior as well as the pros and cons of adopting a new behavior. If the conversation is about doing homework, the consultant would first ask the teen what the advantages and disadvantages are of not doing homework. Next, the consultant would ask about the advantages and disadvantages of doing homework. This conversation would provide valuable information about the student's perspective on the problem and also likely elicit some change talk, especially the questions about disadvantages of not doing homework and advantages of doing it. Handout 6.1 depicts a decisional balance worksheet that can be used to guide these conversations.

### Values Exploration

Much like the values-exploration activities used with parents and teachers, asking students about their values and core beliefs can yield a great deal of information and promote a positive relationship. Doing a values card sort activity or even simply just asking open-ended questions about values can be helpful.

Even very simple and brief value manipulations have been shown to create lasting behavior changes in adolescents and adults. For instance, researchers found that getting middle school students simply to reflect on their values in a specific way led to improvements in grades at the end of the year compared to a group of students who did not do the values reflection exercise. In one study, students were asked to indicate their most important value and write a brief paragraph about why the value was important to them. In a separate study, students were asked to do the same activity with two or three values. To reinforce their selection, students indicated their level of agreement with statements concerning their chosen value(s) (e.g., care about these values). In both studies, the effects on grades persisted over the academic year (Cohen, Garcia, Apfel, & Master, 2006).

Other types of successful brief manipulations of self-affirmations have created lasting changes in adolescents and may be beneficial for younger students as well. These self-affirmation manipulations (Armitage, Harris, Hepton, & Napper, 2008; Reed & Aspinwall, 1998) encourage participants to elaborate on their past acts of kindness, "a highly important personal value," according to Reed and Aspinwall (1998, p. 107). The manipulations consist of a series of questions designed to encourage participants to recall and give examples of past acts of kindness. Sample questions include: "Have you ever forgiven another person when he or she has hurt you?" and "Have you ever been considerate of another person's feelings?" If participants answer "yes" they are then prompted to provide a specific example. These could be used in a classroom writing and reflecting exercise or in activities that are completed in smaller groups with a school consultant.

---

### EVERYDAY CONVERSATIONS ABOUT CHANGE

Mrs. Sanchez is frustrated with Caesar, a student in her seventh-grade math class. He is bright but he doesn't seem to put any effort into his work and instead spends much of the class period making silly comments or doing nothing. She wants to have a productive conversation with him about his concerns, so she asks him to stay after class one day for a brief visit.

**Teacher (T):** So, Caesar, I'm concerned about you and wanted to talk with you to see how I can help you be more successful in my class.

**Caesar (C):** Okay.

T: Does it surprise you to hear that I'm concerned about you?

C: Not really. I know I'm not doing my work.

T: How do you feel about not doing your work?

C: I don't know. It's probably not good.

T: "Probably"…so somewhat good, somewhat not good.

C: No, it's not good. I should be doing more work.

T: Why's that?

*(continued)*

---

### EVERYDAY CONVERSATIONS ABOUT CHANGE (*continued*)

C:   Well, it's hard to get a good grade if I don't do my work.

T:   You would like to get a good grade.

C:   Sure. Good grades are better than bad grades.

T:   How do good grades make your life better?

C:   Lots of ways, I guess. It feels better to get a good grade. My parents don't hassle me if I get good grades.

T:   Makes things easier and you like the feeling that goes with getting good grades.

C:   Yeah.

T:   Give me a better sense of how this fits into your life, things that you value. Where does doing well in school fit into things that are important to you?

C:   It's important. I want to do well in school. I don't want to fail.

T:   So sticking with school and being successful is one of your values.

C:   Sure. Of course. Everyone knows it's hard to do anything in life without graduating.

T:   Finishing school will help you do even bigger things.

C:   Yeah. I'm going to get a good job.

T:   What are the steps you need to take to get there?

C:   I know. I know. I need to be better in school now.

T:   Is that something you want to do?

C:   I have to. I know it.

T:   You are pretty certain of that.

C:   Yes.

T:   What's the first step to doing better in school?

---

## SPECIFIC EXAMPLES OF FOCUSING, EVOKING, AND PLANNING STRATEGIES WITH YOUTH

The methods for focusing, evoking, and planning conversations described in earlier chapters all fit well for working with youth. As before, focusing is facilitated with directed questions about the goals and purpose of the conversation and can be structured around an interview guide.

Feedback and rulers can be used as part of evoking change talk from the youth. Note that given the growing influence of peer relationship during early adolescence, personalized feedback about peer perceptions can be especially evocative for youth. For instance, collecting social norm data in your school or district can provide valuable information in this regard.

> Providing accurate social norm feedback can serve as a tool for eliciting discrepancies for the youth.

This data might include anonymous surveys from students about how often they engage in specific behaviors (e.g., academic behaviors such as study habits, attendance, grades; social behaviors such as friendships, extracurricular activities, and interactions with adults; and risk behaviors such as substance use or sexual activity). This social norm data can then be shared with students who you consult with about those targeted behaviors. A useful format is to first ask students to estimate the percentage of their peers who engage in the targeted behavior (e.g., study every night) and what percentage have a favorable attitude about others who engage in the targeted behavior. Youth commonly misperceive social norms and base their estimates on their observations of their closest peer group. Thus, providing accurate social norm feedback can serve as a tool for eliciting discrepancies for the youth.

Importance and confidence rulers work the same with youth as they do with adults. One reaction to be aware of that we commonly see in adolescents is the tendency to give sarcastic or exaggerated responses on the ruler questions. For instance, whereas we rarely if ever hear an adult answer the ruler questions with a lowest possible response (i.e., 0), some youth will give this response. One way to respond to a very low rating is to give an amplified reflection such as, "So changing your study habits is the absolutely least important thing you have ever considered doing." The youth may agree with this (which would provide important information) or they may lower their sustain talk a bit (e.g., "Well, not the least important thing ever."). Another strategy we have found that can engage the student in these situations, especially when we get a sense that the response was intended as sarcasm, is to play along in a similar mode: "A 0, huh. I was sure you were going to say a negative 10." Such responses can lighten the mood and engage the youth in subsequent conversation.

## Substance Abuse: An Example With Smoking Cessation

Talking with adolescents about their substance use provides an excellent illustration of how the MI processes occur in this context. The same principles apply: collaboration, autonomy, support, evocation, and compassion. When beginning such conversations, we find it helpful early in the conversation to clarify our biases and lay them on the table. For instance, we might say, "As an educational professional, I think it is a good idea for you to quit smoking." We find that such a brief statement is often disarming for an adolescent. Sometimes the biggest struggle in connecting with an adolescent is getting him or her to trust you. By explicitly stating any hidden agendas, the conversation can move forward. Note also that the statement includes an explicit recommendation, advice on what to do. Recall that advice giving can sometimes produce change in others when it occurs in the context of the other elements of MI or when the person giving advice is deemed a credible informant on the topic. For community consultants or psychologists, you might tweak your language, for example, "As a health care professional..." to make a more explicit link between your expertise and your advice.

Next, perhaps even in the next sentence, it is important to emphasize autonomy and personal responsibility. For instance, we might say, "I also realize it

> Such frank discussion usually puts adolescents at ease knowing that professionals will be direct and not try to coerce them to make decisions against their will.

is completely your decision to make. No one can change your smoking but you." This statement is true. It states the obvious, very clearly supports the autonomy of the adolescent, and helps to further reduce concerns about hidden agendas. Such frank discussion usually puts adolescents at ease knowing that professionals will be direct and not try to coerce them to make decisions against their will.

Structured approaches to these conversations using MI guiding principles have been developed (e.g., Brown, Ramsey, & Sales, 1998; Miller, Zweben, DiClemente, & Rychtarik, 1992). The 50-minute conversation includes seven components: (a) rationale, (b) decisional balance, (c) nicotine dependence, (d) smoking norms, (e) financial costs of smoking, (f) carbon monoxide (CO) feedback, and (g) future plans regarding the participant's smoking behavior. First, because the manual was designed for use with students regardless of their intention to quit, sessions begin with a 5-minute discussion about the rationale for the meeting ("to learn more about smoking on campus" and "to help [the student] think about [his or her] own smoking"). Consultants clearly state their biases and offer advice while simultaneously supporting the client's responsibility for change ("It is up to you how you want to proceed"). It also helps to communicate that the consultant does not intend to coerce the client to change. Such frank discussion usually puts clients at ease knowing that the consultant will be direct and not try to persuade them to make decisions that they do not want to make. These steps are also consistent with the motivation-enhancement philosophy and strategies (e.g., advice giving and responsibility are components of effective brief interventions; see Miller, 1993).

A good place to start in evoking reflective language from the adolescent is to use the decisional balance. In this case, we invite a discussion about the advantages and disadvantages of smoking and of changing, beginning with the positive aspects of smoking: "What are some good things about smoking?" Again, this type of question usually catches the adolescent off-guard. Adults rarely if ever ask adolescents such questions. The question implies empathy for the adolescent's decision making and again recognizes the obvious: people smoke for a reason. They get something out of smoking, so putting this on the table for discussion is helpful for understanding the behavior and ultimately how it can be changed.

After the adolescent gives reasons for smoking, remember to invite additional positives with verbal prompts ("Anything else?"). You can then shift to asking about any negative aspects of smoking. The final two aspects of the decisional balance invite the adolescent to reflect on a hypothetical: the good and bad aspects of quitting. So, we ask, "If someday you were to quit smoking, what might be some good things that would come of that?" and then "And what might be some challenges that would go along with quitting?"

We find adolescents easily engage in this activity and are able to contribute many examples for each side. It can be helpful to write down the pros and cons on paper for further reflection. The decisional balance helps highlight any ambivalence, making it explicit, and opens the topic for further exploration. It is important to rely on listening skills to gather more information, affirming, reflecting, and summarizing what is said.

Capitalizing on adolescents' attention to peer influences and perceptions can be very helpful in providing some normative feedback to the adolescent. Providing accurate norm data promotes motivation to change (Schroeder & Prentice, 1998). Research has shown that adolescents greatly overestimate the percentage of peers who engage in the same behaviors they do. When asked to guess what percentage of other adolescents regularly smoke cigarettes, adolescent smokers routinely guess 80% or higher than the actual rate, which is closer to 20%. Some examples of norm data that we have given to adolescent smokers include the national and local percentage of students who smoke; percentage of teen smokers who expect to be smoking 5 years after graduation (5%) versus the actual percentage of teen smokers who are still smoking 5 years after graduation (75%); percentage of smokers who want to quit (70%); and percentage of smokers who are able to quit successfully for 1 year. We present all of this information in the elicit/provide/elicit approach during which we first ask adolescents to estimate a response, then provide data, and finally elicit their reaction about the data.

It can also be helpful to explore the negative impact or expenses associated with smoking. For instance, we ask adolescents to calculate the costs of smoking, that is, how much money they spend on smoking each year. After calculating yearly expenditures, reactions are elicited and we ask them to consider how else they might spend that money. We ask for specific examples of what they would buy and encourage them to "spend" all of their yearly smoking expenses on other things. We might also explore how smoking affects appearance (e.g., wrinkles, tooth color, smell, etc.) and the relationship between smoking and their smoking network (e.g., who in their life smokes and how friends and family respond to their smoking).

With the adolescent's permission, it can also be helpful to gather assessment information from them, both through conversation and standardized measures. We can ask them to complete a brief measure of nicotine dependence (i.e., the Fagerstrom Tolerance Questionnaire: Adolescent Version [FTQ]; Prokhorov, Pallonen, Fava, Ding, & Niaura, 1996) and calculate their score during the meeting. We provide them with information about the meaning of nicotine dependence, and note that quitting becomes more difficult as dependence grows more severe and persists.

In a more structured approach to smoking-cessation conversations, we have used physiological measures of dependence. For instance, when discussing drinking behavior, clinicians in health care settings might collect liver function tests. Recall that this is a very effective application of personalized feedback. With regard to smoking, we have used smokerlyzers, handheld devices that measure the amount of CO in the lungs. When using this type of feedback, we first ask adolescents what they know about CO and provide missing information about its properties (e.g., "a tasteless, colorless, odorless, and toxic gas") and how it is harmful to the human body (e.g., it interferes with the transport of oxygen to vital organs). Providing adolescents with their CO level compared to normative data (e.g., nonsmokers tend to score 10 parts per million [ppm] or lower, light to moderate smokers 10 to 20 ppm, and heavy smokers 20 to 80 ppm). Smokerlyzers can be purchased from medical supply companies or borrowed from local agencies such as the American Lung Association. In health care settings, spirometers provide a more comprehensive measure of lung function and allow the computation of lung age (e.g., "Your lungs are functioning like those of a 76-year-old").

With or without physiological measures, we conclude the conversation by asking structured questions about the client's future plans. Rulers are used to assess their perceived importance of change ("On a scale of 0 to 10, 0 being not important at all, 10 being the most important thing in your life, how important is it for you to change your smoking?") and confidence ("How confident are you that you could change your smoking?"). Regardless of clients' responses, consultants next ask how they chose their ratings ("Why did you rate it a _____ and not one lower?") and what it would take to get them to move one or two points higher on each scale. Importance and confidence rulers evoke change talk and statements that support client self-efficacy (see Miller & Rollnick, 2002).

If the adolescent is willing, we invite him or her to develop a change plan by first setting a goal related to smoking and identifying steps toward the goal, resources, and potential barriers. Finally, we ask him or her to re-rate his or her confidence levels to see if the plan promoted confidence in the adolescent's ability to change.

## Talking With Students About Academic Performance

Extending the logic of MI substance-use applications to academics is a promising idea (Strait et al., 2012). The content of the conversation may be different, but the same principles apply. The structure of these conversations would include the following: (a) a rationale for the conversation, (b) self-reflection and exploration of values, (c) personalized feedback, and (d) planning.

### Rationale

Consider how you might start a conversation with an adolescent about his or her academic performance. You might first provide a rationale for the discussion: "I would like to talk with you about how I can support you in doing well in school." You might also get any hidden agendas on the table: "It may not surprise you, but I really want you to get better grades in my class." Early on, be sure to support students' autonomy with an explicit statement about responsibility: "It's up to you. As much as I want to help you, ultimately it's your choice what you want to do."

### Self-Reflection and Values Exploration

A decisional balance conversation about academics would invite reflection about some of the good and bad things about doing well in school, and the good and bad things about adopting a new behavior (e.g., studying more, attending classes more). As noted with the substance-use check-ups, these conversations tend to lower resistance because it is unexpected for adults to engage adolescents in conversations about the status quo ("What are the advantages to doing nothing?"). The decisional balance could be augmented with open-ended questions to prompt further self-reflection about their current behavior:

- How important academic performance (getting good grades, attending class) is to them.
- How confident they are that they could improve their academic performance.
- How satisfied they are with their current academic performance.
- Concerns they have about their academic performance.

OARS (open-ended questions, affirmations, reflections, and summaries) are used to elicit and elaborate change talk that emerges from the decisional balance and self-reflection conversations.

It is important to listen for value expressions that occur during these conversations as well. Alternately, it is likely it would be beneficial to engage in a specific value-exploration exercise such as the values card sort described in prior chapters. Spending 10 minutes inviting the adolescent to sort the cards and identify his or her three to five most important values and then telling you why provides an engaging activity and a rich source of personal information. Asking directly about discrepancies between the adolescent's values or beliefs and his or her current behaviors can provide the foundation for creating cognitive dissonance. Open-ended questions about how his or her academic performance compares to the student's preferred performance would invite some conversation about this. Even more specific questions could probe the following dimensions:

- How many hours the student studies versus how many hours the student wishes he or she studied
- His or her current grade point average versus his or her preferred grade point average
- Current attendance rate versus his or her desired attendance rate
- Current number of credits passed versus his or her desired number of credits passed

*Feedback*

Personalized feedback in these conversations involves providing the adolescent with normative information about how his or her test scores, grades, attendance, office discipline referrals, and other academic behaviors compare to peers in his or her class, at his or her school, in his or her district, and even across the nation. This feedback is best provided in a matter-of-fact approach: "So you have missed 22 classes so far this year. That puts you at the 99th percentile in this school, meaning you have missed more classes than 99% of students here." Remember, feedback is designed to evoke reflection and further conversation so be sure to check in about the adolescent's reaction to the feedback ("What do you make of that?").

You also provide the student with social norms about adolescent perceptions of school performance. By conducting regular surveys about student attitudes and self-reported behaviors, schools can use this information to establish norms that can be used as part of feedback. Questions on surveys might include:

- How many hours a night do students study (separated by student grade point average [GPA])?
- What percentage of teens think it's important to get good grades?
- What percentage of teens have a favorable attitude about students who fail classes or drop out?
- What percentage of teens have a favorable attitude about students who get good grades?
- What percentage of students would date someone who got good grades? What percentage would date someone who dropped out?

Rapid advances are being made related to the development, dissemination, and use of school- and district-wide progress-monitoring systems. These systems will increase the ease with which school personnel can collect data that can be used to provide individualized feedback.

### Planning

After providing feedback and a summary of the highlights, it is important to transition to develop a plan of action. One effective way to begin conversations about planning for change with youth is to ask hypothetical questions: "If you decided to (get better grades, attend more classes), what might be some reasons you would do that?" or "If you decided to make this change, how confident are you that you could do it?

After you have engaged the youth and elicited his or her self-reflection on the possibility of change, it is helpful then to ask more specifically, "What's next?" Versions of this question include

- So what do you think are you going to do?
- What's the next step?
- Where do you go from here?
- What are you going to do now?
- What are you thinking of doing next?
- What changes, if any, are you considering making?

How the youth answers the question provides you with information about what he or she is considering regarding making changes and how to structure the rest of the conversation. Some youth will reveal that they want to make a change and express strong commitment to do so. For these youth, creating a plan with clear goals and needed supports is the logical next step. Other youth may still be in the contemplative stage of change, which may mean eliciting agreement to continue the conversation and meeting again as a next step.

For those who decide to create a plan, the following elements make it more likely the plan will be successful:

- Specify a clear, measureable goal
- Discuss reasons why the goal is important
- Develop a plan for accomplishing the goal that includes a timeline and supports

When developing a plan, it is helpful to ask the youth for ideas for accomplishing the goals. It is also fine for you to collaborate in coming up with ideas after asking for and getting permission to do so. Ask youth what supports they might need in accomplishing the goal and what role others (including you) can play in helping them be successful. The plan should specify when each step will occur and who will be responsible for each element. It should also have a plan for monitoring progress and checking back in to ensure the plan is working.

The final step after creating a detailed plan, or simply agreeing to meet again, is to ask the ruler questions: How important is it for you to achieve this goal (or attend our next meeting) on a scale from 1 to 10? How confident are you that you can achieve this goal on a scale from 1 to 10? As before, with each ruler question get the student to elaborate on the importance of change and his or her confidence by asking, "Why that number and not one lower?" to elicit change talk. Finally, it is a good idea to ask about any barriers that might get in the way of the plan being successful and problem solve any that are brought up.

---

### EVERYDAY CONVERSATIONS ABOUT CHANGE

A school consultant sets up a time to talk with Kaipo, a ninth grader who meets the district profile for being at risk for dropping out. Kaipo was a strong student in middle school, but in his first semester of high school, he has started skipping classes and is receiving several failing grades.

**Consultant (C):** Hey Kaipo, thanks for meeting with me today. I wanted to talk about how things are going in school for you.

**Kaipo (K):** No worries. It's all good.

C: Doing well in school is not that big a deal to you.

K: Nah. It is. I'll do it. I'm fine.

C: So you want to do well in school.

K: Yeah, sure.

C: Why's that?

K: Ah man. It just is. I don't know.

C: Just looking at your record, you did really well in middle school.

K: Yeah. School is easy. Like I said, it's no big deal.

C: You're really confident that you can get good grades, which is great, you clearly can. So what's getting in the way of your grades at this school?

*(continued)*

---

### EVERYDAY CONVERSATIONS ABOUT CHANGE (*continued*)

K:  I don't know. It just hasn't been at the top of my list. I got other things going on.
C:  Other things are getting in the way.
K:  It's hard. I don't think about it much, I guess.
C:  Not as much as you would like.
K:  Nah, I'm having fun and it's like I forget about it.
C:  Where do you want to be at the end of the year with your grades?
K:  Back on track. You know, the same grades I got before.
C:  So you want to be getting A's and B's.
K:  Yeah, I will.
C:  I'm impressed with your commitment. What's it gonna take for that to happen?
K:  I need to get serious again. I've been distracted. I know what I need to do.
C:  Because you've done it before.
K:  That's right.
C:  So give me some sense of the things you were doing in middle school that helped you get the grades you wanted.

---

*Here the consultant invited a conversation about change with a student who initially did not want to talk. The consultant slowly drew the student into the conversation by focusing on his past success and paying particular attention to the language he was using about intended changes. She reflected and affirmed this and supported his self-efficacy. Finally, she invited him to get more specific about a plan for making positive changes by reflecting on what he did before to be successful.*

## ENCOURAGING ADULTS TO INTERACT WITH YOUTH IN THE MI SPIRIT

Using the spirit of MI to encourage more positive relationships between adults and students would be a productive application of MI in schools. Most evidence-based practices for addressing youth behavior or emotional problems begin with the importance of establishing positive environments at home and school. Both school-based programs such as Positive Behavior Supports and Interventions (PBIS) and the Safe and Civil School series and home-based programs such as the Incredible Years and Noncompliant Child parenting programs emphasize the importance of high rates of positive attention and noncontingent reinforcement as a prerequisite for supporting youth. Adults provide the foundation for establishing these positive environments by how they interact with youth. The MI spirit is aligned with these goals.

Recall from Chapter 3 that the MI spirit is comprised of four interrelated aspects of a relationship: partnership, acceptance, compassion, and evocation. On a school-wide level, adults can communicate messages of partnership to youth by encouraging them to be active participants in the creation of positive school environments. For instance, youth-led surveys and committees tasked with understanding and improving the school environment are consistent with a partnership value. Acceptance is conveyed through empathy, affirmations, and respect. Thus, training school personnel to use

OARS effectively in their interactions with youth makes it more likely that the school climate will set the tone of acceptance. An additional component of acceptance that is especially salient for youth is supporting their autonomy. Schools that provide options to youth and encourage their participation in decision making about relevant matters support autonomy. Compassion is focusing on the welfare of others. This aspect of the MI spirit is grounded in the perceptions and intentions of adults at school and requires self-reflection. Encouraging school staff to reflect on their intentions and reminding them of their shared goal in supporting youth to reach their full potential can evoke compassion.

These first three aspects of the MI spirit are likely familiar and easily fit within existing approaches and ideas to creating positive school environments. Evocation, the fourth aspect of the MI spirit, is unique and may often be overlooked as a critical component of positive environments. Recall that evocation is the idea of "calling forth" the strengths and positive intentions from within the individual. School environments that are focused on helping students identify their own strengths and preferences and that create interventions and supports that attend to these resources are consistent with the evoking aspect of MI. As is clear in earlier chapters, evoking is also established through conversation. Open-ended questions that invite youth to reflect on solutions and participate in problem-solving support the evoking aspect of the MI spirit.

### SUMMARY

Using MI with youth involves adapting the MI strategies to their developmental level. Most, if not all, of the same principles apply to working with youth. Moreover, the spirit of MI fits well with most well-established interventions for youth in terms of providing a positive foundation for behavior supports.

### RESOURCES: SAMPLE EVIDENCE-BASED INTERVENTIONS FOR STUDENT EMOTIONAL AND BEHAVIOR PROBLEMS

Barrett, P. (2004). *FRIENDS for Life program: Group leader's workbook for children* (4th ed.). Brisbane, Queensland: Australian Academic Press.

Clarke, G. (n.d.). *Coping with depression course for adolescents.* Free download. Retrieved from http://www.kpchr.org/research/public/acwd/acwd.html

Hawken, L. S., Pettersson, H., Mootz, J., & Anderson, C. (2005). *The behavior education program: A check-in, check-out intervention for students at risk.* New York, NY: Guilford Press.

Kendall, P. C., & Hedtke, K. A. (2006). *Cognitive behavior therapy for anxious children: Therapist manual* (3rd ed.). Ardmore, PA: Workbook.

Lochman, J., Wells, K., & Lenhart, S. (2008). *Coping power: Child facilitators guide.* New York, NY: Oxford Press.

Merrell, K. W., Carrizales, D., Feuerborn, L., Gueldner, B. A., & Tran, O. K. (2007). *Strong Kids—3–5: A social and emotional learning curriculum*. Baltimore, MD: Paul H. Brookes Publishing.

Merrell, K. W., Carrizales, D., Feuerborn, L., Gueldner, B. A., & Tran, O. K. (2007). *Strong Teens: A social and emotional learning curriculum*. Baltimore, MD: Paul H. Brookes Publishing.

Merrell, K. W., Parisi, D., & Whitcomb, S. A. (2007). *Strong start—Grades K-2: A social and emotional learning curriculum*. Baltimore, MD: Paul H. Brookes Publishing.

Merrell, K. W., Whitcomb, S. A., & Parisi, D. A. (2009). *Strong start—Pre-K: A social and emotional learning curriculum*. Baltimore, MD: Paul H. Brookes Publishing.

Stark, K., Simpson, J., Schnoebelen, S. Hargrave, J., Glenn, R., & Molnar, J. (2006). *Therapists' manual for ACTION*. Broadmore, PA: Workbook.

Walker, H., et al. (1997). *First step to success*. Longmont, CO: Sopris West.

Webster-Stratton, C. (2005). *Dina dinosaur child training program*. Seattle, WA: Incredible Years.

# Handout

**HANDOUT 6.1 DECISIONAL BALANCE WORKSHEET**

| Decisional Balance | |
|---|---|
| Good things about _____ <br>    (current behavior): | Bad things about _____ <br>    (current behavior): |
| New behavior: _____ <br> If you were to try it, what might be some <br>    benefits? | If you were to try it, what might be some <br>    challenges? |

Handout

## HANDOUT 6.1 DECISIONAL BALANCE WORKSHEET

| Decisional Balance | |
| --- | --- |
| Good things about (current behavior) | Bad things about (current behavior) |
| New behavior: If you were to try it, what might be some benefits? | If you were to try it, what might be some challenges? |

# An Example of a Structured Motivational Intervention for Families, Students, and Schools: The Family Check-Up

MI can be practiced as a stand-alone intervention without any formal structure. As noted in the first chapter, our intention in writing this book is to make school professionals more aware of effective ways to have everyday conversations about change. In this sense, the spirit and principles of MI can be applied in 30-second "drive by" consultation visits that occur in schools every day. These brief encounters set the stage for change,

> Delivering feedback using a Family Check-Up approach facilitates the sorts of interactions with parents that promote more collaborative, open, optimistic, and productive encounters.

for either cementing commitment to change, or when done poorly, discouraging motivation. All the strategies discussed up to this point can be used to make these interactions more effective.

For longer interactions, when teachers, parents, or students are willing and able to set aside time to meet on one or more occasions, the added structure provided by Check-Ups can provide the framework for applying MI in successful ways. Check-Ups align with the stages of MI described by Miller and Rollnick (2013): engaging, focusing, evoking, and planning. Typically, they involve two or three meetings ranging from 20 minutes to an hour each. The first meeting involves a structured interview and an ecological assessment involving self and other reports of strengths and areas of concern related to the target problem; and the second involves delivering personalized feedback that is used to develop goals and an action plan. MI is the foundation for each meeting—MI principles guide the structure of the interview and feedback meetings.

In this chapter, we describe the rationale for using structured Check-Ups and for delivering effective feedback in an MI style. We focus on the Family Check-Up (FCU) given that it involves all three groups targeted in prior chapters: parents, teachers, and students. Before you read forward, take a minute to reflect on your preferences for working with parents. Do you prefer working with parents who are angry, defensive, and not interested in meeting with you? Or, do you prefer working with parents who are collaborative, interested in talking with you, and who feel hopeful and energized to address concerns? Delivering feedback using an FCU approach facilitates the sorts of interactions with parents that promote more collaborative, open, optimistic, and productive encounters.

## CHECK-UPS: AN OVERVIEW

The concept of Check-Ups is borrowed from medical terminology where individuals are encouraged to visit physicians for routine exams. In this model, the physician conducts a battery of physical examinations and laboratory tests to determine the health of the person and then provides the results to the patient. The original adaptation of the Check-Up concept was the Drinker's Check-Up (see Miller & Rollnick, 2013). Much like the medical version, the Drinker's Check-Up involved a visit with a health care provider who gathered a range of assessments, some through self-report and others through laboratory tests (including liver function tests), and then met again with the patient to provide personalized feedback about the results. The rationale for these adaptations grew from the FRAMES (Feedback, Responsibility, Advice, Menu, Empathy, and Support Self-Efficacy) model.

### FRAMES

As a precursor to the development of MI, Miller reviewed literature regarding the essential ingredients of brief interventions. He found that brief interventions had many common elements. He summarized his findings with the acronym FRAMES. We introduced these concepts in Chapter 1 and describe them in more detail here as they provide the foundation for MI Check-Ups.

*Feedback* is a tool used to promote motivation. To be effective, feedback must be tailored or personalized for the individual or community. For instance, 400,000 people die in the United States from smoking-related illness. Although that statement is true, it is not likely to motivate smokers to change, that is, to stop smoking. A general statistic is easy to dismiss. A smoker could easily counter this statistic in his or her mind by thinking, "I know many people who smoked their entire lives and never got cancer." Instead, if we gathered specific, personalized assessments about the impact of smoking on the person's life, this

> The keys to effective advice giving are that it is used sparingly, is not provided prematurely, and is best offered only after it is invited.

would be much more effective. For example, gathering spirometry data, which might show a 30-year-old smoker that his or her lungs are functioning like an 80-year-old's, would be very personalized and likely to be effective. Or, for alcohol, a liver function test that revealed a concerning liver profile would be specific to the person and more likely to get him or her to consider drinking less or not at all.

*Responsibility* emphasizes the role of personal autonomy in making decisions about change. Miller found that brief interventions were more effective if they consistently communicated to the person that responsibility for changing his or her behavior rested with the individual. For instance, saying the following sends a message of responsibility: "It's ultimately up to you to decide whether you want to do anything about this problem."

Giving direct *advice* can also be motivational when it is given by a credible person and in the context of a caring relationship. The keys to effective advice giving are that it is used sparingly, is not provided prematurely, and is best offered only after it is invited. Consider asking for permission before giving advice: "If it is okay with you, I'd like to share with you some thoughts I have about where to go from here."

If individuals express an interest in changing a behavior, giving them a *menu* of options for next steps can make it more likely they will continue to be motivated to change. For instance, "There are several ways that other teachers have been successful in reducing disruptions. Would it be okay if I tell you about a couple? Then, you can let me know which one sounds best to you."

Expressing *empathy* throughout these discussions is essential to promote an individual's likelihood of moving forward. Empathy here refers both to identifying with the individual's current situation and feelings, as well as to empathizing with his or her ambivalence about change. It is important to communicate that ambivalence is normal and at the same time to use reflective listening to get at the nature of that ambivalence, to gain an understanding of what is keeping the person stuck and making change difficult.

Supporting each person's *self-efficacy* (his or her belief that he or she can follow through with next steps and make the intended changes, if he or she chooses to do so) is another element of effective consultation and brief interventions. One way to help the individual see that change is within his or her reach is to draw attention to his or her current successes in changing ("How did you make that happen?") and to ask about times in the past that he or she has successfully managed challenging situations ("Tell me about the last time you had a disruptive class and how you were able to get control of it").

## SCHOOL-ENHANCED FAMILY CHECK-UP

Parent engagement strategies and motivational interviewing (MI) principles provide a flexible set of strategies for promoting family engagement and removing common barriers to help seeking. These strategies can be applied across intervention contexts and can be implemented as part of any treatment program. In this section, we describe a structured intervention that integrates parent, student, and teacher involvement called the School-Enhanced Family Check-Up

(SE-FCU; Herman et al., 2012). The SE-FCU provides a comprehensive framework for working with families in schools.

The FCU was developed as a structured, brief intervention that uses many of the engagement strategies described earlier for providing effective family interventions for youth with mild to serious emotional and behavioral concerns (Dishion & Kavanagh, 2003). Dishion developed the FCU in part because of the complexity of intervening with families and the need for brief approaches that could be easily adopted and implemented in school settings. Although the efforts of strategic or structural family therapy are elegant, they require much more training and supervision to become proficient. Dishion hoped to develop a model that simplified the work of the interventionists to target the critical variables. Typical targets of the FCU include parenting behaviors (e.g., discipline practices, monitoring) and child externalizing behaviors. A wealth of research supports its efficacy in reducing disruptive behavior in young children in families with multiple risk factors; increasing parent involvement; use of positive behavior supports and decreased family conflict; improving middle schoolers self-regulation, which in turn resulted in higher school engagement and lower adolescent antisocial behavior and substance use (Connell, Dishion, Yasui, & Kavanagh, 2007; Lunkenheimer et al., 2008; Shaw, Dishion, Supplee, Gardner, & Arnds, 2006).

The FCU attempts to build parent motivation and capacity to effectively manage his or her child's behavior by gathering data about these contextual environments, sharing this data with parents, and helping them make informed decisions about how to best support their child's behavior. The FCU includes as many as three sessions (see Figure 7.1). The first session involves building a relationship with the family, learning about parent concerns, preparing the family for change, and motivating families to be engaged in intervention. Assessments (parent and, when appropriate, child responses to questionnaires) are collected before or after the first meeting (sometimes a second meeting is arranged for this purpose) and, in the original FCU model, families participate in structured interaction tasks that are videotaped and coded. The child's teacher(s) also are asked to complete questionnaires about child functioning at school as part of the ecological assessment. During the final session, the family receives feedback based on these assessments and is encouraged to set goals and establish an action plan by selecting from a menu of next steps.

In our adapted version of the FCU model, the SE-FCU, we have strengthened data-collection elements focused on the school environment and collapsed the first and second session into a single assessment session followed by a feedback

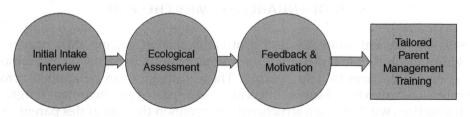

**Figure 7.1** Phases of the FCU.

session (Reinke, Splett, Robeson, & Offutt, 2009). We also eliminated the video-based feedback component to make FCU delivery more feasible to adopt and deliver in the school context. Instead, we included brief observations of the child in his or her classroom and other school settings. A key element of a successful SE-FCU is to involve teachers and the student in the assessment process.

MI is the interaction style that permeates the FCU interaction. The FCU structure is intended to make the foundational MI processes explicit for the individual working with the family. The interview and assessment experiences are intended to be engaging and to assist in developing a case conceptualization focused on child and family strengths and areas of growth that impact the presenting concern. The feedback session, with its personalized information about family relationships and child and functioning, is intended to evoke the change process by making parents aware of patterns, encouraging self-reflection, and drawing out their reactions to this information (i.e., eliciting change talk). The menu of options and action-planning steps are in line with the planning process of MI. As with any encounter, the four MI processes—engaging, focusing, evoking, and planning—may occur within any of these phases of the FCU.

## INTERVIEW AND ASSESSMENTS

### Session 1: "Get to Know You" Meeting

During the initial meeting, the consultant meets with the whole family as a group to discuss logistics and to provide a roadmap of what is to come.

*Sample Overview*

> Thank you for meeting with me. Our goal is to work with families and schools to help kids be more successful at school. We will meet two times. This first meeting is just a chance for me to get to know more about you, your values, and any concerns you might have. In the second meeting, I will share all the information that I have collected from you, your child, and his or her teacher about how things are going at school and home. Parents usually find this information very helpful in thinking about what is going well for their children and what they would like to be different. At the end of the second meeting you can decide what else, if anything, you want to do.
>
> Today I'm going to ask you some questions and ask you to complete some forms. I'll also ask your child some questions and have him or her complete forms about his or her behavior, his or her friends, and his or her feelings about school. Later this week, I'll meet with your child's teacher to collect information and have him or her also complete a few forms as well. I'll also visit your child's classroom to observe. The purpose of collecting all of this information is to get as much information as I can about what's going well and what can be improved. I find it's helpful to get many people's views of these questions.

One of the common goals of FCU meetings is to help the parent adopt more effective behavior-management strategies. If this is one of your goals in working with a particular family, it is a good idea to let them know this in advance: "One reason many families have asked to be part of the FCU is to learn more about their parenting skills and to get support or suggestions for improvement." Additionally, if this is one of your goals, it is important to gather assessment-and-intervention information about parenting skills that you can use to deliver as part of the feedback session.

Finally, prepare parents for future meetings. You might say, for example, "After I collect this information, I will pull it all together. Then I'll set up another time to meet with you here. I'll tell you everything that I find and then come up with a plan for next steps. It's totally up to you how you want to proceed after that meeting. Together we will look at all the information and come up with a list of possible next steps, a menu of sorts. Then, if you want, you will work with me to determine what from the menu fits the best for your family. That will help us come up with a plan for what to do next."

After this overview and review of logistics, the parents and the child should meet with a consultant separately. It is good practice to have two consultants meet with the family, so that each can concurrently meet with the parents and the child. If there is only one consultant available, meeting with the parents first is recommended. It is important to first prepare the child for separation, either working with the other consultant or going into a different location. Depending on the age of the child, having another adult sit and interact with the child may be appropriate, even if not the consultant. You may want to ask the child's permission to separate: "So we can get to know all of you, I'm going to sit and talk with your family and [other consultant] is going to spend some time with you. Sound okay?"

### Assessments

One of the goals of the first meeting is to gather assessment data that can be used to inform and guide the feedback session. The assessment is meant to gain multiple perspectives on the child, family, and school needs; symptoms; and resources (see Figure 7.2). We recommend that standardized, paper-and-pencil data are collected prior to administering the more detailed interview.

When considering areas to assess and specific measures to use, it is important to ensure that all areas selected connect directly to the intervention options that are available. We recommend that you avoid assessing areas that it will not be possible to address within available intervention options or for which community resources are not available if concerns are raised. Standardized broadband behavior rating scales such as the Behavior Assessment Scale for Children-2 (BASC-2; Reynolds & Kamphaus, 2004) or the Child Behavior Checklist (CBCL; Achenbach & Edelbrock, 1983) can be useful given that they are well-established, norm-based measures that include a range of internalizing and externalizing symptoms. The BASC-2 has the advantage of including several adaptive behavior scales, which can also provide useful information as part of a feedback session. Often these scales are used by school psychologists or special educators in a school district, so these may be available for use. Ultimately, whatever measures or forms are used to gather data, it is important that the consultant has the

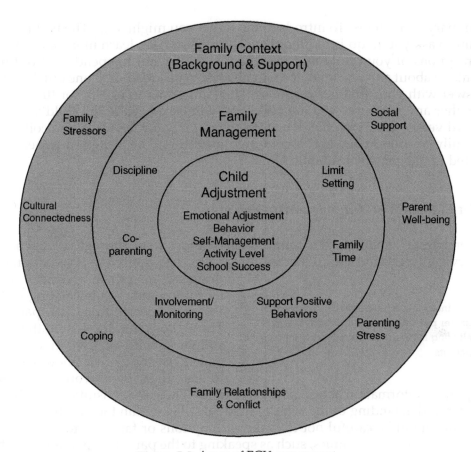

**Figure 7.2** Areas of FCU assessment.

needed knowledge to score and interpret these data appropriately. If not, there are some free behavior rating scales that do not involve complicated scoring or interpretation procedures that could be used instead.

In addition to child symptoms and school functioning, it is helpful to collect information about self-perceived parenting behaviors. The Alabama Parenting Questionnaire (Elgar, Waschbusch, Dadds, & Sigvaldason, 2007) and its nine-item short version is an excellent choice because of its brevity and cost (it is publically available at no cost). Parent stress scales can also be helpful in establishing how stressful the parenting role is (Berry, 1995). The Parent Stress Inventory (Abidin, 1995) is commonly used, but it is not free and it can be time-consuming. We have used the Daily Hassles (Crnic & Greenberg, 1990) questionnaire as well. Measures of the child–parent relationship from both the child and parent's perspective can also provide meaningful data. Consider using the free Child–Parent Relationship Scale (Driscoll & Pianta, 2011). Additionally, a measure of family relationships and communication can be informative (see Corcoran & Fischer, 2000).

Don't spend a lot of time explaining the forms. Just ask parents to read each item and go with their first gut response. If they express concerns about the accuracy of some items, reassure them that no single response will tilt the scores in a wrong direction. The scales ask a lot of questions, so offer a summary of all items. To introduce the forms you might say, "The first thing I want to ask you to do is to fill out some forms so I can learn more about your perceptions of your child and your home life. Try not to spend a lot of time thinking about any one item. It's usually best to just read each one quickly and answer with your first gut response." It is important to clarify for the parent whether any measures you are collecting will be placed in the child's school record versus your own file. We recommend that new data that you collect as a family consultant be kept in your own records and be protected rather than stored in the general academic file.

### "Get to Know You" Interview With Parents

After parents complete the rating forms, guide them through a structured interview (see Handout 7.1 Parent Interview). The interview is intentionally designed to gather pertinent family information while eliciting motivational speech from the parents. Throughout the discussion, the consultant should ask evocative, open-ended questions that allow parents to use their own words to share

> The interview is intentionally designed to gather pertinent family information while eliciting motivational speech from the parents.

important information about family dynamics. Thus, the consultant can obtain a clear understanding of the roles individuals play within the family. The consultant should be careful not to make assumptions or fall prey to supporting ineffective family dynamics, such as speaking to the parent who dominates the conversation while leaving out the other. Additionally, every effort should be made to involve all central caregivers, even when it seems easier to work with the one "more involved" caregiver.

Start by providing parents with a detailed overview of the interview. "To begin, let me ask you some questions about your family and child." Be sure to use lots of reflective listening, affirmations, and summarizing as parents respond to your open-ended questions. Remember the mantra—talk less, listen more. In particular, listen for their values and file these away for future reference. Knowing the parents' hopes and dreams for their child, for example, will be useful during the feedback session for engaging parents in reflection about the ways in which their child's and their family's current status will support or get in the way of meeting their goals for their child. Listen for reasons the parent might want to change and successful changes they have made in the past. Some of the open-ended questions embedded in the parent interview were designed specifically to elicit change talk. Listen for change talk and invite parents to elaborate on it, either with statements like "tell me more about that" or by simply reflecting back what you hear: "The way things are going right now isn't working for you." It is useful to get a sense of where they are in the change process; use the information from the interview to help you assess whether they are even considering making a change, whether they are ambivalent about making a change, or whether they are already planning on making a change.

| Intake Dialogue | Comments |
|---|---|
| **Consultant (C):** So what have you told John about our work together? Or John, what do you know about our work together? | |
| **John (Dad):** She (the mom) said you would be here at 4 o'clock today. She gave me a little breakdown. You want to study Drexel (the son) and, um, help him at school. | |
| **Mom:** To help families coordinate with schools to make sure we're on the same page. | |
| **C:** Exactly. So we're going to meet with you two times. This time we're just gathering information. Next time we're going to summarize the information you give us and tell you about what we found. What you are doing well and what areas you might be able to improve on. We're going to do the same thing at school, talk to the teacher and observe Drexel. Then we'll talk about coming up with a plan of what you want to do. Your choices, whatever you want to do, to help Drexel be more successful at school. Sound okay? | Summary and preview |
| **Dad:** Every little bit helps. How about that? | |

During the interview, it is important to get some sense of parents' perceptions of parenting practices and how commonly they implement them by directly asking about these practices. Handout 7.2 provides some common questions used for getting parents to reflect on parenting behaviors (based on Capaldi & Patterson, 1994). When more than one parent is participating in the FCU meetings, it is common for discrepancies to emerge in each parent's perception of his or her practices and values. Simply acknowledge that everyone has strong feelings about parenting practices and that it's common for people to disagree about some aspects of parenting. If you find that one parent in a meeting is talking more than the other, it can be helpful to invite the other parent to respond. This helps to ensure that both parents' perspectives are represented.

It is important to provide summaries throughout the meeting to check for shared understanding, to highlight themes, and/or to transition to new topics. It is also a good idea to spend time summarizing the entire meeting at the very end. We have created summary questions (see Handout 7.3) to help facilitate these ending conversations and draw out change talk while also helping to prepare them for the second session. The bottom of the form asks parents to rate the importance of attending the second session and their confidence in being able to do so. As noted in prior chapters, these rulers are based on MI and are designed to build commitment to attend the feedback session. Begin by asking, "From 1 to 10, how important is it for you to attend our next meeting, with 1 being not important at all and 10 being extremely important?" Regardless of their response, say something along the lines of, "A 4, so somewhat important. Why would you say a 4 and not a 3?" Be sure to attend to change talk here and reflect it. Next, ask the same question regarding how confident they are. Again, summarize and ask why they said the number they did instead of one number lower.

### Child Meeting

We described MI strategies for working with students in Chapter 6. Here, it is important to note that when conducting an SE-FCU interview with parents, it is important to gather information from the child as well. Your visit with the student is an opportunity not only to gather information but also to build motivation. Using OARS (open-ended questions, affirmations, reflections, and summaries) to elicit information and change talk in ways that have been described throughout this book makes it more likely the child will be an active participant in the creation of a support plan. The age of the child will be highly influential in determining the nature of these visits. For young children, these conversations might not involve many direct questions, but simply include engaging in activities and playing games together to build rapport and observe the child's behavior. With older and more verbal youth, you will be able to ask open-ended questions that can be useful in forming a clear impression of the family environment. We have often found that children have great insights that are helpful in developing a plan toward supporting their success.

> Your visit with the student is an opportunity not only to gather information but also to build motivation.

A sample structured child interview is provided in Handout 7.4. The interview guide asks about the youth's perception of school, the student's strengths and interests, and his or her awareness of any problems. The questions about the problem behavior are intended to understand the antecedents and consequences of the problem. If children are old enough, you might also ask them to complete rating scales such as the BASC-2 and other scales that ask them about their family environment.

It is important to be clear with the parent and child from the outset what information, if any, you will keep private and what information you will share with the parent. This includes obligations to report safety issues to parents, and other required disclosures, including suicidal or homicidal thoughts or instances of abuse.

### Observations or Videotaped Interactions

Your direct observations of family interactions (spouse, parent–child, siblings) provide another important source of information to share with the family. These observations can be informal or structured. In the original FCU model, these interactions are actually videotaped and coded along important dimensions, and whenever possible, consultants prepare video segments for parents to video during the feedback session. However, this practice was eliminated from the SE-FCU to increase the feasibility of conducting the FCU in schools (i.e., reduce time and costs associated with videotaping, coding, and playback).

Parents are often not aware of their parenting patterns. Thus, sometimes the parent interview and rating forms will not accurately portray family interaction patterns. It is important therefore to collect some observational data about these patterns whenever possible. These can be informal observations in which you observe how the parent interacts with the child in different settings, at school or in their home if you conduct a home visit, or at the very least during their visits to participate in the SE-FCU. Ideally, you can set up some problem-solving tasks for parents and observe how the family reacts. For younger kids, this can involve having the parent(s) play a game with the child and then asking the child to clean up, or discuss bedtime routines. You also might set up a frustrating task (e.g., asking parents and children to jointly complete a challenging task such as a maze) to observe how parents help children manage negative emotions and how they cope with their own frustration. For older kids, you can ask the family to plan a fun activity together, talk about goals for school, or discuss a time when they did something without their parent to elicit a conversation about monitoring and supervision, or solving a problem. Dishion and colleagues have developed specific coding procedures for each of these scenarios (see the website to the Child and Family Center: http://cfc.uoregon.edu/intervention .htm). In general, you will want to attend to the quality of the relationship and the communication style and skills of each participant, the amount and type of praise and attention the adults give the children, the extent of monitoring and supervision by the parent, whether adult expectations are clear, whether consequences are predictable and reasonable, whether goals are specific and measureable, and whether problems are discussed and solvable. All of this information will be useful in constructing personalized feedback.

## Teacher Interview and Observations

After obtaining parent consent, the consultant should contact the child's teacher to set up a time to collect teacher data. As before, engage in social conversation with the teacher. Your job is to convey the importance of the assessment and to collect any information the teacher can provide about the child. As with the parent meeting, it is important to provide teachers with an overview of what you intend to speak with them about, and to explain how their perspective is a critical piece of a larger process for helping parents and children address school-related concerns.

> In addition to eliciting change talk from the teacher, it is critical that you convey positive impressions of the child and family in all of your interactions with the teacher and other school personnel.

Ask the teacher to briefly describe any problem behaviors the child is having at school. Encourage the teacher to be specific about the conditions under which those behaviors are most likely to occur—the times of day, settings, and peer composition during which you are most likely to observe those behaviors. Ask permission to observe the child in the classroom during those times and in the settings when each problem is most likely to occur. Finally, ask the teacher about any interventions he or she has tried to help with the problem behavior(s) and anything that has worked or is working.

As with any interaction, your visits with the teacher are also an opportunity to build motivation. In addition to eliciting change talk from the teacher, it is critical that you convey positive impressions of the child and family in all of your interactions with the teacher and other school personnel (e.g., "The family is very excited about working together," "I met with them last night and they are really committed to helping (child) be more successful in school"). If the teacher has negative things to say about the child and/or family, simply acknowledge the teacher's feelings with a reflective statement (e.g., "That's very frustrating for you") without agreeing with the teacher to avoid belittling the child or family.

Then, ask the teacher to complete the BASC-2 or other appropriate rating scales. If possible, ask whether he or she could complete it while you are there. If not, ask when would be a good time for you to pick it up. Also, direct the teacher to simply give his or her gut response for each answer and not spend time thinking too much about any single item.

## Classroom Observation

Observe the child for at least 20 minutes in the setting(s) where the identified problem behavior is most likely to occur and at the time it is most likely to happen. You might use an observation form that allows you to record when the behavior occurs, what it looks like, and what happens just before and immediately following the behavior. As a consultant working with a teacher and family, it is helpful to have some experience in conducting observations and an understanding that behavior serves a purpose or has a function. For instance, a child who has a tantrum can exhibit this behavior to try to get something he or she wants (e.g., to gain attention from an adult) or to avoid something he or she doesn't like. As you observe, simply note any behaviors you see in behavioral terms (observable, measurable) and then write down what happened immediately before the behavior started (antecedent) and then what happened right after (consequence). For antecedents, pay particular attention to the task the child was engaged in (group instruction, individual seatwork, direction giving by teacher, proximity to peers, etc.). For consequences, note the adult and peer response to the behavior and whether the child successfully accessed anything (attention, tangibles) or escaped anything (the task, situation). See Handout 7.5 for an example of a behavior-detective worksheet for answering questions about the antecedents and consequences associated with direct observations of a child's behavior (Handout 7.6 is a blank behavior-detective form for your use).

## PREPARING FOR THE FEEDBACK SESSION

To prepare for feedback, the consultant needs to integrate the multiple perspectives collected about the target concern and consider the ways in which the data collected supports what he or she intends to communicate. An important first step is to spend time integrating findings into a comprehensive case conceptualization (see Figure 7.3). It also is useful to put the data gathered from interviews, measures, and observations onto the feedback form. This will require the integration of norm-based scores with clinical judgment.

### Case Conceptualization

Through the process of integrating findings into a case conceptualization, you are trying to define the problem in a very specific and solvable way and to identify malleable factors that can alleviate and solve the problem. At the same time, you are trying to identify practices that you want to support the child and parents in maintaining because they are strengths that can be brought to bear on the problem. Essentially, you are asking yourself: What are the most pressing needs of the child and family, and what are their most important assets and resources? By first taking time to reflect on these issues and identifying the one or two most pressing issues, you will be better prepared to create the feedback

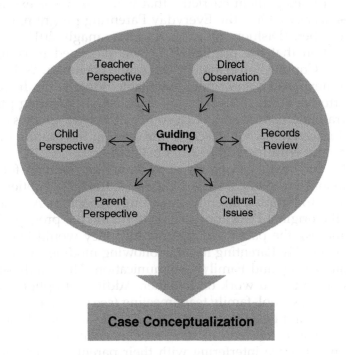

**Figure 7.3** Case conceptualization.

form and deliver the feedback session. The following four questions are helpful in guiding your case conceptualization:

- From what you know, what is the most important thing to communicate to this family?
- How does the data collected support what you need to communicate to the family?
- How will you display this information in a manner that helps communicate it well?
- How does the data connect directly to the intervention options that are available (specific parenting programs, community referrals)?

### Connecting Ecological Assessment to a Menu of Options

Recall that the primary objectives of the feedback session are to narrow the focus and increase commitment toward changing a specific behavior(s). If this is accomplished parents set goals and select from a menu of intervention options to help them achieve their goals. While planning for the feedback session, the consultant should develop options to put on the menu that are determined by the types of interventions and services that are available in your school and community, and are directly linked to the assessment areas to be reviewed. Quite often, the goal is to connect parents with services to improve their family and parent behavior-management practices. There are many evidence-based parent behavior-management curricula that would serve as excellent options for a menu of services. One, the Everyday Parenting program, is inexpensive and well researched (Dishion, Stormshak, & Kavanagh, 2011). This program is the intervention that the original FCU was designed to connect parents to. Another, the Coping Power parent program (Lochman, Wells, & Lenhart, 2008), is also inexpensive and widely available. Finally, the Incredible Years (Webster-Stratton & Reid, 2010) is a well-established parenting program with an excellent training manual and a rich source of video vignettes of actual parent-and-child interactions. We describe our work at integrating the FCU with Coping Power and with Incredible Years in Chapter 9.

Ultimately, the menu of options should include options for services to improve behavior-management skills. One way to frame this option would be to invite the parents to complete an entire parenting curriculum. Another way, more aligned with the original FCU approach, is to divide the program into a series of modules and ask the parents which modules they would like to complete. For instance, Everyday Parenting has the following modules: Positive Behavior Support, Limit Setting, and Family Communication. The family selects one or more of these modules to work on together. Additional options on the menu include arranging a school–family team meeting (see Chapter 8 for more details on how to arrange and lead these meetings), seeking additional community services (including psychiatric consultation or community counseling to support parent problems that are interfering with their parenting such as depression, substance abuse, or marital conflict), or less intensive approaches to skill development such as bibliotherapy or other independent-learning strategies.

# UNDERSTANDING STANDARDIZED SCORES
## (*T*-SCORES AND PERCENTILES)

Many rating scales are reported as *T*-scores or percentiles. It is important to understand what these scores mean in terms of need for support. A general rule for placing *T*-scores on the feedback form is scores on clinical scales that are above 69 are placed in the red zone, scores of 60 to 69 are in the yellow, and scores below 59 are in the green. These scores should also be placed on a continuum to capture their redness or yellowness. For instance, a 69 should be placed very near the red zone, whereas a 60 should be closer to the green zone. For adaptive behavior scales (social skills, communication) where higher scores indicate higher levels of adaptive behaviors, the interpretation is flipped.

## BASC (Standardized Scores)

- *T*-Scores (Mean = 50; Standard Deviation = 10)
- BASC *Clinical Scales*
  - Less than 60 = Green
  - 60–69 = Yellow
  - 70 or greater = Red
- BASC *Adaptive Scales*
  - Greater than 60 = Very Green (Strength)
  - Greater than 40 = Green
  - 31–40 = Yellow
- 30 or lower = Red

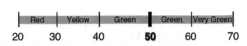

## Discrepancies Among Informants

One challenge, even with norm-based scores, is how to combine discrepant data from multiple informants. For instance, a teacher may report a very high score for conduct problems, whereas the parents may not report elevations on this behavior. These should be noted in the different settings on the feedback form. Keep in mind, your job is not to capture the "truth" about these areas but only to highlight them for conversation so that parents can come to an understanding about why the discrepancies exist (e.g., Does their child act differently under the conditions present in the different settings?). Thus, in the feedback session, your role is merely to highlight these discrepancies and allow parents to interpret them ("What do you make of that?").

For case conceptualization purposes, consider that some informants are better reporters of certain symptoms or behaviors. Teacher ratings of attention problems and hyperactivity, for instance, are considered the gold standard for normative comparisons on these symptoms because they are exposed to a large number of children with varying ranges of activity level. Teachers tend to be less reliable reporters of internalizing symptoms. Instead, child self-reports of internalizing symptoms (including depression, anxiety, and self-perceptions) are considered the most important indicators of these symptoms. On the other hand, children tend not to be reliable reporters of their attention problems or externalizing symptoms. Parents tend to provide adequate ratings of most symptoms.

These are only general rules, though, and should not be rigidly applied. For instance, a given 6-year-old may have difficulty understanding some of the items on the questionnaires and may not provide a great estimate of his or her own anxiety symptoms even though, typically, child reports of internalizing symptoms are considered reliable. Also, discrepancies between parent and teacher observations may reflect two accurate perceptions and indicate setting-specific problems at home or school.

## Preparing Specific Examples

After scoring the measures, examine the items of significant scales carefully for specific examples. This will be helpful to you during the feedback session to give concrete examples of the most important areas of concern. For instance, if the child scores high on an attention scale by teacher report, examine the items from that subscale to determine which items the teacher endorsed in the scored direction. When you visit with the parent, you can then elaborate on the score (e.g., "He scored at the 99th percentile for attention problems at school. In particular, his teacher rated him as having a lot of problems with following directions, completing assignments, and remembering things").

In a similar vein, it is important to examine the critical items section of measures, if available. This list includes items that are uncommonly endorsed, or, when endorsed, highlight problems that may require clinical attention. In particular, examine items about thoughts of self-harm (although these should have been checked before leaving the first family meeting). Additionally, the item "sleeps in parents' bed" is a correlate of child anxiety problems that may require further investigation.

## Attend to Strengths and Resources

As you organize the feedback that you will deliver to parents, you will be thinking about the main areas of concern. However, also be sure that the feedback form reflects both strengths and areas in need of attention. Every form should contain indicators in the green. If this is not reflected in the existing categories, identify an area and write it into the "other" category. Similarly, if an area of concern was identified that does not fall under the feedback categories, write the area of concern into the "other" category. This is particularly important if you think the concern is a major contributor to the problems exhibited by the child. For instance, marital discord or poor family communication are not listed on the form but may be areas that need to be targeted for intervention.

## Remember: Parents Choose

All of this preparation can lead to a common error in which consultants get overly attached to a direction for the parents prior to the feedback session. Keep in mind that the whole process of preparing feedback is intended only to determine possible tailoring options for the family. You always need to be open to what the parents ultimately decide to do. It would be a mistake to come to the feedback session with a rigid goal of what you expect the

> Trust that parents will make the best decision for themselves and their family. Your role is simply to be prepared with options so that parents can make informed choices.

parents to select. Trust that parents will make the best decision for themselves and their family. Your role is simply to be prepared with options so that parents can make informed choices.

## Summary and Guiding Principles of Preparing for Feedback

- Do not spend a lot of time fretting over the precise placement of Xs on the feedback form. The form is intended to be delivered as part of a conversation, not as a laboratory report. Use it to stimulate discussion and evoke change talk.
- Plan what message you want to send to the family based on your case conceptualization and strategically place Xs where you want the family to focus their attention/efforts.
- In general, any scores greater than 1 standard deviation (*SD*) above the mean on any scale (e.g., a *T*-score of 60 or higher) should be noted somewhere in the yellow zone or higher (regardless of discrepancies between informants); scores greater than 2 *SD*s above the mean (e.g., *T*-score of 70 or higher) should be noted somewhere in the red.
- Come prepared with specific examples of the most important areas you want to highlight. Use percentiles when possible ("He is in the 99th percentile for low self-esteem compared to other kids his age. This means..."). Give specific examples from the critical items on measures, or from interview data or observations ("He shared that he does not feel good about himself") but do not share confidential information ("He says he does not like his stepfather because he yells at him all the time").

## Session 2: Feedback and Action Planning

The feedback session should be with caregivers only. Prepare the parents for this during the first session so they can plan to leave the child or children at home. If this won't be possible, arrange to have someone available to spend time with the child elsewhere during the feedback meeting.

*Social Conversation*

As before, take time at the beginning of your visit to engage in social conversation. Pay attention to your pacing; that is, don't rush the social conversation or push to get started on the feedback immediately. Allow time for you and the family to get settled into the conversation before transitioning to the feedback. Do not bring out the feedback form until you are ready to begin sharing that information. Just like in the first session, it also is important to give the parent a clear expectation for what is going to happen during the feedback session. For example,

> What I would like to do first, if it is okay with you, is to talk with you about Kennedy and how she is doing in school. We will also talk about how things are going at home for you and your family. I asked both you and Kennedy to fill out some forms, and I talked with her teacher and observed her at school. The forms I had everyone complete actually illustrate how Kennedy compares to other kids her age from around the country. I want to share all this information with you. Our work today is all about how to make sure things are going the way you want them to in your family, and if they are not going the way you want, to consider ways in which you would want them to be different. Then, if you are interested, we can talk a bit about what would need to happen for things to be different, including the different options you have for next steps. Of course, I am not here to tell you or your family how things should be and what you should do. Only you can decide what is right for you and for your family and what you need or want to do.

*What Did You Learn?*

Begin by asking caregivers to reflect on what they learned from the assessment process. Often, the interview and assessment questions will have created new insights for family members that they had not previously considered. Asking them about any learning they experienced will provide the interventionist valuable knowledge about where the family is in the change process and any specific ideas they may have already developed for changing. These ideas may appear later during the menu-of-options phase. If the family members say they have not learned anything yet, this may tell the interventionist that the family is in an early stage of change. This might be introduced by saying, "I would like to hear a little bit more about your experience filling out those questionnaires and the time you spent with Kennedy playing games last time. Many parents tell us that they learned something about their child and their family. What did you notice about Kennedy? Was there anything that she did that surprised you or stood out for you? What did you notice about yourself? Did anything stand out for you when you were completing information about your family that you might not have thought about before?"

Next, we provide an extended transcript of a feedback session to highlight the key MI skills that are the foundation for the FCU. In this case, 8-year-old Tyquan was referred to the school consultant for repeated aggressive behaviors at school. His mother was involved with school, but felt the school was not fully supportive of Tyquan's needs. In the first meeting, she disclosed her history of depression and low self-esteem and her concern that Tyquan was at risk for the same types of problems. The school consultant collected a series of assessments from the parent, teacher, and child as well as from school records. Here is the discussion that ensued during their second meeting.

| What-Did-You-Learn Dialogue | Comments |
|---|---|
| **Consultant (C):** Usually after that first meeting, parents come back having had some insights or questions, or it made them think about some other things. So what did you think about after that last meeting? | What-did-you-learn question |
| **Mother (M):** Yeah, I've been thinking about a whole lot of stuff. | |
| **C:** So what kind of things? | Open-ended question |
| **M:** I guess the things that I went through as a kid. I was just thinking about how alike we are and how I don't want him to go down the same path as I did. | |
| **C:** You want Tyquan to be happy. | Reflection |
| **M:** Yeah. I'd like him to be like me. I just want him to be better than me. | |
| **C:** To take all of your good qualities… | Reflection |
| **M:** And use them better. Yeah, I want him to be happy. | |
| **C:** So the things we talked about last time really got you thinking about how you want things to be for him. | Reflection |
| **M:** That's right. | |

## Introduce the Feedback Form

Prior to using the feedback form, tell the parents what red, yellow, and green signify. Tell them that you will take notes of areas that they may want to focus on and determine next steps. "One way to do this that we've found helpful is using a form like this [show family a blank feedback form]. As you can see on this form, areas in green are areas of strength—things that we want to keep going. Yellow areas are ones that are in the warning zone and we may want to consider as areas to work on. Those things in the red are areas we want to stop and think about. These are things we should pay attention to when we think about ideas for what we want to work on and better support Tyquan. As we look over the feedback form, please let me know if certain areas jump out to you as things you want to work on, and I will jot them down. We will come back to these at the end when we decide next steps."

---

**Introducing the Feedback Form**                                        **Comments**

**Consultant (C):** Today I wanted to share with you all the information I have collected from you and Tyquan and his teacher. The format we have is a report that looks like this. It has Tyquan's name on it and we have these three categories: youth adjustment, home adjustment, and school adjustment. Youth adjustment is how he's doing in general, and for himself, what might be internal to him that we might not see. Family adjustment is how he's doing at home, how he is seeing things at home, and how things are going for you as a parent. And school. This is how he is doing at school. So, we can see where he's at and then talk about any options you want to pursue.

**Mother:** Sounds good.

**C:** I'm going to go down one section at a time. If you have any questions let me know. The first section. This would be the green area, things he's doing really well, his strengths. Things in the yellow are things we want to keep our eyes on. They may not be a problem yet but could become one. And in the red area are areas we really want to focus on as areas of concern.

---

## Deliver the Feedback

We'll look at three general areas. The first is titled "youth adjustment." This is basically how Tyquan is doing in different areas that are important for being successful at school, getting along with others, and doing well at home. Then, we will look at family functioning and school functioning. Do you have any questions?

Place the form with feedback on the table so that family members can see it. We suggest using a separate sheet of paper to isolate each area as you talk about it and to cover other areas that might distract the parent from the focused discussion of a particular area.

### Approach 1: Start With the Positives

Let's begin by looking at what is going well. Here you can see that Tyquan has great interpersonal relationships. He is really well liked at school by his peers and his teacher.

### Approach 2: Start at the Top and Move Down the Page in Order

The first thing on the list is whether there are any concerns about defiant behavior. You can see that Tyquan is kind of orange-ish in this domain, so between yellow and red. This is because across all of you, including his teacher, rated Tyquan as exhibiting some defiant behaviors. For instance, you mentioned in our last meeting that Tyquan doesn't always follow rules and he sometimes will argue with adults.

### Showcase Relative Strengths of Child and Family

Some key elements of an effective discussion of strengths include being specific and sincere. Note that your comments are based on both your observations as well as objective data. Look for relative or unexpected strengths (e.g., inattention but good academic skills) and use reframes (e.g., persistent, affectionate, sensitive).

It is important that you are genuine in describing the child's strengths. Some critical aspects of being perceived as genuine include spending enough time on a strength and giving specific examples of strengths you have observed. For instance, "Let me begin by noting many of Jake's positive qualities. First, he's very likeable. He has a gorgeous smile. Second, he's doing well in reading. Quite often boys who are having behavior problems at school struggle with reading. This is not the

> Some critical aspects of being perceived as genuine include spending enough time on a strength and giving specific examples of strengths you have observed.

case for Jake. This is a strength we will want to capitalize on as he progresses in school." Especially note and highlight relative or unexpected strengths (e.g., inattention but good academic skills) and reframe behaviors that can be viewed in two lights (e.g., "stubborn" becomes "persistent"). Some common strengths to consider for a child include well-liked, affectionate, sensitive, endearing, fun loving, problem-solver, good with his hands, and so on. Also be sure to comment on strengths of the family. "It is clear how committed you are to helping Jake be successful. Even meeting with us is a sign of your commitment and love for him."

### Check in to Create Dialogue

The point of the feedback is to engage the family in dialogue about topics that may be difficult or that they had not really thought about before. Therefore, it is important to summarize each section of the feedback form and then to check in with them for their reactions to what they are seeing and hearing. After important feedback points, ask the parents for their reactions ("What do you make of that?" "Does that fit with how you see Nick?" "I can tell by your reaction that that surprises you.").

> A common mistake to avoid during the feedback session is to allow the conversation to shift prematurely to focus on solutions.

Give parents plenty of opportunity for reflection about what the feedback means and how they are interpreting the findings. When possible, give specific numbers and reference points. For instance, standardized measures such as the BASC-2 give specific percentiles and compare the child to other children the same age. Tell the parent the percentile and be sure he or she understands what that means. For instance, "Nick scored in the 99th percentile with regard to inattention. That means that when compared to other kids his age, he scored higher than 99% of his peers for inattention. In fact, he scored high on this domain across all reports. When I spoke with Nick, he even stated that he has trouble paying attention and that he often gets into trouble for not paying attention." Be prepared to describe exactly what each scale means and to provide specific items from each scale (the BASC-2 breaks down each item in the summary report).

Finally, take note of topics that the parents express the most concern about and write these topics on the form or on another sheet of paper. Likewise, if the parents make comments about things they want to change or strategies they would like to try to improve particular situations, write these ideas down as well. You might simply comment as you write, "I'm going to write down some of these ideas so that we can come back to them after we finish discussing the feedback."

*A common mistake to avoid during the feedback session* is to allow the conversation to shift prematurely to focus on solutions. It is very important to keep the attention focused on the feedback before discussing solutions. You want to give parents the full picture offered by the feedback so that they can make informed decisions about how best to proceed and which problem(s) to target first. If the parents start asking for or offering solutions during the feedback phase, you can briefly summarize their thoughts, validate them, and then say that you will write down their ideas so that you can remember to discuss them later. For instance, "Those are great ideas. I'm glad you are thinking about how you might go about solving that problem. I'm going to start a list of things that you might try so we can come back to them when we start coming up with a plan of change."

### About the School

In addition to commenting on the assets of the child and family, be sure to spend time talking about the strengths of the school and the child's teacher(s) and principal. Never speak negatively about the school or school personnel with the family. Of course, you should spend time listening and reflecting frustrations the parents may have experienced in their interactions with the school, but try hard not to convey judgments about the school or its personnel. Instead, note any positive aspects of the school or teacher, especially the teacher's concern for the child and his or her willingness to help the child succeed.

### Sample Feedback Session

Below is the remainder of the feedback session with Tyquan's mother. Notice how the consultant uses all of the strategies to deliver feedback, evoke change talk, and highlight discrepancies.

| Feedback Dialogue | Comments |
|---|---|
| **Consultant (C):** The first are problem behaviors and these are in the red. Mostly, these apply to behaviors at school. The running away from school, being out of the classroom a lot, fighting, issues with peers. His teacher reports he is out of the classroom a lot. Does that make sense? | Feedback<br><br>Check-in |
| **Mother (M):** Yes (laughing) | |
| **C:** So that is not a surprise to you. | Reflection |
| **M:** Not at all. | |
| **C:** So attention. I know you told me he was diagnosed with ADHD and what we see here is the hyperactivity was not coming out a lot but the inattention still is. He has a hard time focusing, and paying attention. | Feedback |
| **M:** Yes (laughing) | |
| **C:** He reports that himself. People tell him he should pay attention more. He says he forgets things. Has trouble paying attention to what he does. He also says he gives up when learning something new. So why be in the classroom? So that leads him to lose interest. It's a real struggle for him. He seems upset about it. He says, "You don't understand how hard it is for me." | Detailed examples |
| **M:** I know. He says the same to me. | |
| **C:** Then we come to anxiety, his worries. He often worries about bad things that could happen. What could happen next? He says he worries about small things. He's bothered about not getting enough sleep. | Feedback |
| **M:** Since he's been on the medicine, his sleeping patterns have been so different. He has trouble falling asleep. Sometimes he's the last one to fall asleep: 10:30 to 2 in the morning. I tell him come lay down and take a nap. Then he is bummed out the whole day. Why don't he take a nap? | |
| **C:** You really see his lack of sleep putting him in a bad mood. | Reflection |
| **M:** Especially when he goes to bed at 2. | |
| **C:** That's late. What's he doing when he's awake? | Clarification |

*(continued)*

| Feedback Dialogue | Comments |
|---|---|
| **M:** Playing in the bed. Just laying in bed playing with a toy. He'll make noise. Ma, do I got a bump right here? Ma, did you hear that? Ma, ma, ma…I say "go to bed." | |
| **C:** Does he tell you that he's worrying at night? | Clarification |
| **M:** Sometimes. About burglars. Because there's been break-ins on our block, that kind of scares him. | |
| **C:** How often? | |
| **M:** Often. At least a couple of times a week. | |
| **C:** So he has worries about break-ins that may or may not be a reality that might happen. One of the things he said is that sometimes he gets so worried he can't breathe. Have you ever experienced that before? | Reflection and feedback |
| **M:** He never told me that. | |
| **C:** He says it happens frequently. | Feedback |
| **M:** Hmm. | |
| **C:** What's that like to hear? | Evocative question |
| **M:** Just the breathing part. I didn't know that. Just like me. He's too much like me. | |
| **C:** You have these same problems. | Reflection |
| **M:** Yeah. I worry a lot. Sometimes I can't breathe. I didn't know he did too. | |
| **C:** You don't want him to worry so much. | Complex reflection |
| **M:** No. It's hard to be happy when you get so upset about things. | |
| **C:** That brings us to the next one, depression. Depression is one of the highest areas: 90%. So that means if there were 100 friends in a room, his level of depression would be higher than 90 of them. Does that surprise you? | Feedback

Check in |
| **M:** Not really. | |
| **C:** Okay. So you're seeing the depression. Tell me more about that. | Reflection and elaboration |
| **M:** When he's depressed. He'll go sit by himself. He rocks back and forth. He starts hitting himself on the head. And I say why are you doing that? Not necessarily hurt himself. Just hit his head but not too hard. Why you doing that? He's like, no reason. He won't say nothing. Like he hear you but he don't hear you. Like he's in another world. He's spaced out. | |

*(continued)*

| Feedback Dialogue | Comments |
|---|---|
| C: One of the things he did report was that he sometimes wants to hurt himself. We'll continue to explore that with him. Have you put anything in place to address his sadness? | Feedback |
| M: I took him to a therapist about that. They said they were going to work on some things. | |
| C: So that doesn't seem surprising to you **at all.** | Amplified reflection |
| M: A little bit. How high it is. | |
| C: You don't like it that he is so depressed. | Complex reflection |
| M: No. I want him to be happy. | Change talk: desire |
| C: You want him to be happy. | Simple reflection |

In this example, the consultant provides explicit feedback to the mother about concerning symptoms the child is reporting. So far, the mother's reaction to the feedback was muted. The consultant tested how unsurprised the parent was by the feedback by giving an amplified reflection (it is not surprising to you "at all"), which elicited some change talk by focusing on a parent desire (wanting the child to be happy). Notice also that the parent provided hints about a major theme and potential discrepancy about how she views her child parallel to herself. On the one hand, she implies she likes their level of similarity and closeness and, on the other hand, she worries that he will follow the same path as she. As the feedback continues, notice how the consultant returns to this theme.

| Feedback Dialogue | Comments |
|---|---|
| Consultant (C): Next, is his coping skills. How he handles things. If things go wrong how quickly he recovers from it. That was in the yellow zone. He's bright, he knows the answers when you ask him a question. Like when you ask what can you do when you get sad? He can tell you, but he has trouble putting it into action. He still has some coping strategies. His friendship and social skills. This is going to be interesting. His friendship skills are in the red but making friends is in the green. So he's very outgoing, he's so enjoyable but he has trouble keeping friends. | Feedback |

(continued)

| Feedback Dialogue | Comments |
|---|---|
| **Mother (M):** Yeah, that's one thing for sure. He's very friendly but as far as it lasting, he's very up and down. He has trouble keeping people liking him. That's something I had a problem with. | Theme |
| **C:** Another similarity. | Reflection |
| **M:** Me growing up. I was friendly, I still am. I make a lot of friends. But to keep them is an issue sometime. Everyone doesn't think the same. And I feel if I'm in the right and you are in the wrong, I'm going to stray off and we are not going to be friends no more. | |
| **C:** So there's this black and white, you either agree or don't agree but if you don't then we are just not going to be friends. No middle ground. | Reflection |
| **M:** Not at all. Either we friends or we're not. | |
| **C:** And with Tyquan we're seeing the same thing. Two extremes. | Connecting to theme |
| **M:** That's not good. | Change talk |
| **C:** You want him to keep friends. | Elaborating |
| **M:** I do. I don't want him to be lonely. *I need him to be better than me.* | Change talk: need |
| **C:** Part of you likes how similar he is to you and another part really needs him to be different. | Double-sided reflection highlighting discrepancy |
| **M:** He can't do the same as me. I want him to be happy. | Change talk: desire |
| **C:** And part of being happy is having friends. | Reflection |

The consultant picked up on the theme of the mother's desire for similarity and difference with her child and reflected it with a double-sided reflection. The reflection elicited change talk and a connection to ways the mother could help her son be different and "better" (developing friendship skills).

Next, the consultant provides a summary of the student-adjustment feedback and introduces the feedback about family adjustment. Notice how she returns to the theme of the mother wanting closeness and distance. She highlights a key issue for the mother, her decision of whether or not to disclose personal information to her child.

| Feedback Dialogue | Comments |
|---|---|
| **Consultant (C):** In summary, all these things go together. When students worry a lot, when they have trouble keeping friends and doing well at school, in time they come to feel sad, even helpless to make things better. Tyquan is telling us he's started to feel these ways. Did I miss anything? | Summary<br><br><br><br><br><br>Check in |
| **Mother (M):** Sounds right. | |
| **C:** Okay. The next section is family adjustment. You can see he is in the greener areas here, which is a testament to your good work with him and your relationship with him. The first one is the relationship. He is very bonded to you and you seem very bonded to him. You do a lot of fun things together. You both reported that; he reported that. He's very happy with you. You use a lot of encouragement. Sounds like there is a lot of encouragement at home, telling him he's doing a good job and wanting him to do well. So that was another area in the green. Clear rules/expectation moved a little to the yellow. That mostly came up, when children are young, they can have difficulty working out mixed rules. So is hitting okay at school and at home? Sometimes he's not clear about the rules at home. Does that make sense? | Feedback and affirmations<br><br><br><br><br><br><br><br><br><br><br><br><br><br><br><br>Check in |
| **M:** Yes. I could do better at that. | Change talk |
| **C:** And with consequences, he wasn't always clear about what sort of punishment he'll get. | Feedback |
| **M:** Sounds about right. | |
| **C:** Same with limits. He has limits, he knows that he has limits but the line can be blurry. | Feedback |
| **M:** Hmm. I can see that. | |
| **C:** Supervision, he's never alone, there's always an adult around. Academic support at home. Sounds like you are doing a great job. There's homework and a routine. You're talking to teachers. So that's not an area of concern. Stress management starts creeping to the red. This is for you. Things can get overwhelming. Sounds like you have a lot going on right now. Is that surprising? | Feedback<br><br><br><br><br><br><br><br>Check in |
| **M:** It's a concern but not that big of a concern. | Change talk & sustain talk |

*(continued)*

| Feedback Dialogue | Comments |
|---|---|
| **C:** So a concern. Is that something you want to be different? | Responds to change talk |
| **M:** For both of us. I would like him to be able to tell me what's bothering him. | Change talk |
| **C:** Kind of like how you are with him. | Complex reflection |
| **M:** I don't know. I don't know if it's good to tell him everything like I've been doing. | Change talk |
| **C:** On the one hand, you share everything with him, on the other, you want to keep some adult conversations from him. | Double-sided reflection ending with change talk elaboration |
| **M:** I've thought about that lately. I've caught myself and I say, "I'll save it for another time." And he lets it go. In the past, he would say, "Ma, you said you were going to tell me something, "Ma you going to tell me now?" I tell him, "Go sit down." | Change talk |
| **C:** So you have made a decision to not burden him with some of your worries. | Reflection |
| **M:** Some things he don't need to know. | Change talk |
| **C:** What do you think that's about when he keeps coming back to it? | Clarification |
| **M:** He's impatient like me. We don't like waiting. I have to tell him, "I'm your mother right?" and he says, "Yeah, but…" and I'll say, "But. What you mean But?" and he'll say, "I am the man of the house." And I say, "Okay you are." Then he'll be back in, "Mom, you gonna tell me?" | |
| **C:** So he checks in with you a lot. I wonder how that relates to his anxiety and worries. | Open-ended question connecting back to theme |
| **M:** That's a possibility. He'll say, "Let's talk." He be thinking he's my therapist sometime. I say, "Hold up." | |
| **C:** There's this whole "man of the house" thing, but he's only 8. Does he feel that responsibility? | |
| **M:** When it first happened. | |
| **C:** What do you mean, "when it first happened?" | Open-ended question |
| **M:** When his father left. | |
| **C:** Where did he get that message "being the man of the house?" | Open-ended question |

*(continued)*

| Feedback Dialogue | Comments |
|---|---|
| **M:** From the other men in the family. My brother told him he needed to take it on to look after his sister and mom. I think he took it a little far. | |
| **C:** You wish he could enjoy being a kid too. | Complex reflection |
| **M:** Yeah. It's hard for me too. He's not an adult. It's hard enough being a kid these days. | |
| **C:** So you made a decision to let him be a kid, to keep your adult worries from him. | Reflection connecting to theme |
| **M:** I'm trying. I think that will be better. | Change talk |
| **C:** To help with his stress and worry. | Reflection |
| **M:** Hmm. Hmm. | |
| **C:** The other part of this is your stress. You are in the yellow for your own stress. | Feedback |
| **M:** Yeah. It's hard right now. I worry a lot. | |
| **C:** You want to feel less stress. | Reflection |
| **M:** I do. I do. | Change talk |
| **C:** So with the family section. You got a lot going right. You and he are very connected and close. And you are trying to figure out ways for you to stay bonded while also letting him be a kid and not carry adult burdens. You also see how it could be helpful to you and him to feel less stress. | Summary highlighting theme |
| **M:** That's right. | |

The consultant strategically highlighted the mother's growing awareness of her desire for her son to be better than her, to be happy. The mother arrived at her own conclusion that one way she can support her son's happiness was by withholding adult conversations from him. The consultant affirmed this decision and also connected it to her son's worries and fears.

### Transition to Planning

After working through all of the feedback, the next step is to provide a summary of the feedback, and then transition to begin talking about next steps. It is helpful to ask the family to summarize their "take home points." For instance, you might ask, "Based on all the information we've covered tonight, what stands out to you the most?" or "What do you see as the most important thing we've discussed tonight?"

As you start moving toward discussing next steps, ask the parents to identify their greatest area of concern or the topical area they want to work on first. "Where do you want to start?" "What is your biggest concern right now?" or "What do you think is the most important thing to focus on first?" Spend some time reflecting back their comments to them, as all of these questions will yield some form of change talk.

### Menu of Options

As you provide feedback, it is important that you also take notes. Using these notes, you can then generate a list that can serve as a menu of options for how to proceed. One way to start generating this list of options is to say, "Given that Tyquan is struggling at school and showing some signs of being inattentive and disruptive at school and home, and given that this is the area of most concern to you right now, let's spend some time generating a list of ideas about how to help address this concern. What ideas have you considered, if any, for taking action in addressing this concern?"

Use a menu of options form (see Chapter 4 for an example) to help with the process. The top of the form begins by asking the family what areas they would like to work on. Additionally, it has a column in which you write down the ideas you develop together. It also has a general list of strategies and ongoing supports that can be useful. Complete the form with the family, and then transition to the action-planning form. A fluid way to transition might be to state something like the following: "Great, we identified several ideas for next steps. Let's take a moment to identify one or two of these ideas that we want to put into action. We are going to use this action-planning form to come up with the next steps. I will leave a copy for you and take one with me so that we know what we have planned to do before our next meeting."

Here, the process is very collaborative and should focus on brainstorming to identify potential solutions. Invite the parents to offer suggestions for addressing the problem. You should also actively contribute to constructing the menu. You should write all the ideas down on the menu of options form and share your own ideas as well. Standard options include (a) continuing to meet with the family intervention team, (b) setting up a time to meet with the school, and (c) providing a referral for related services in the community.

### Action Planning/Goal Setting

After generating a list of several options, present the action-planning form to the parents (see Handout 7.7; we have provided several versions of this form throughout the book to allow you to choose a style that best suits your needs). We recommend that *you* complete the form. This helps keep the discussion moving and gets the important information written down on the page. You can also guide the process to make the plan concrete and ensure that it is doable. Try to come up with a plan that is specific, feasible, and likely to work. For example, if the child is struggling to complete homework and is failing classes, an overarching goal might be to work with the child and make sure he or she completes all his or her homework to pass his or her classes. Then start with the first step toward reaching this overarching goal. For example, identify a place and materials needed for the child to complete his or her homework each night. Determine the time he or she will do the homework, how often to check in with him or her, and a plan to ensure that completed homework is returned to school.

## SAMPLE DIALOGUE FOR SUPPORTING THE ACTION-PLANNING PROCESS

> Now, let's talk about next steps. On this form, let's first think back to what is going really well or is a strength of the family. Whatever plan we come up with should involve using this strength so you can ensure the plan is a success.
> Next, we just talked about some ideas for areas to improve. Which areas do you think are the most important to target at this time?
> Now let's come up with a specific goal to work on this week.

Be sure to elicit specific, observable goals from the family. One way to do this is to ask clarifying questions, including who, what, where, when, and how often. For instance, if the family says "better coping skills," ask them what that would look like. For example, "How would you know?" "What would be different that you could see?" or "How often would you see him doing it?"

### Importance and Confidence Rulers

When you reach the end of the form, ask the parents to complete the importance and confidence rulers; if both parents are present, ask them to give separate responses to each ruler. Recall that these are key MI strategies. We place these questions at the end of the meeting because research has shown that the most important type of change talk (that best predicts whether people actually follow through on change) is the type that occurs during the final minutes of a session. In particular, the more committed the language (e.g., "I'm going to do this"), the more likely people are to actually do what they say.

Complete the importance ruler. Regardless of the number the parent selects, ask him or her why that number and not one less. For instance, if a parent says a six, you might respond with, "Great. That's pretty important. Why a 6 and not, say, a 5?" You could also go lower ("say a 3"). Be sure to reflect the parent's responses here, as this will almost certainly elicit change talk. If a parent says 0, you can amplify and exaggerate by saying, "So this is the least important thing in the world right now to you." This is also a sign that you need to start over and select a new goal.

Next, ask, "What would it take to go from a 6 to a 7? What would have to happen?" You can then walk the parent up to a 10. Write down things the parent says above the numbers he or she gives. So, if a parent says, "If he got another failing grade in school" to get a 7, write "failing grade" above the number 7 on the form. Continue to use active listening and reflection throughout the conversation.

Repeat this process with the confidence ruler. "How confident are you that you can make this change?" Follow up with the "one less" question and then with the "one more" question.

The final step is to discuss potential barriers to meeting or working on the goal and brainstorm ways to avoid or overcome these barriers. It is helpful to give the parents a copy of the action-planning form, and you keep one for review at future meetings.

Before you finish, arrange the next meeting together and review what each person will do before then. For instance, if you decided to hold a joint meeting with the school and you are the person to arrange the meeting, state that you will let the parents know when the meeting is scheduled.

Let's revisit the conversation with Tyquan's mother. The consultant summarizes the feedback and introduces next steps.

| Action Planning | Comments |
| --- | --- |
| **Consultant (C):** So you said the areas you were most concerned about were his depression and worries, his success in school, and your own level of stress. Which of these stands out to you as most important right now? | Open-ended question<br><br>Focusing on goal |
| **Parent (P):** I think his worries and his behaviors at school. | |
| **C:** And what would you like to be different? | |
| **P:** Just to have him be happier and do better in school. | |
| **C:** What do you want to do to help him? | Focusing on parents' role |
| **P:** I want to find ways to be a better parent, to figure out how to help him be happier and do better. | Change talk |
| **C:** Great. That makes a lot of sense. So what plan do we need and what steps are you going to take to accomplish this goal? | What next question |
| **P:** I'm not sure. | |
| **C:** Would you like me to help come up with some ideas? | Asking permission |
| **P:** Yes, please. | |
| **C:** Well, I've worked with a lot of parents on similar issues using this program that has five parts: a parenting tool kit, family communication, parent stress, home–school communication, and problem solving. We can work on all five together or you could choose which ones make most sense to you. | Menu of options |

*(continued)*

| Action Planning | Comments |
|---|---|
| **P:** The tool kit sounds interesting. What is that? | |
| **C:** I was thinking the same thing. It covers effective parenting strategies for promoting positive behaviors and feelings at home and reducing negative behaviors and feelings. | Affirmation |
| **P:** Yeah, I want to do that one. | |
| **C:** Okay, great. So we'll set up a time to meet and start that. So how important is this to you, to work on ways to help Tyquan become happier, from 1 to 10? | Ruler |

The consultant ended the feedback session with the parent by developing a plan for next steps. She encouraged the parent to set a goal by asking focusing questions, and then invited the parent to come up with a plan for accomplishing the goal. When the parent was not sure what a good plan would be, the consultant then asked for permission to participate in coming up with solutions. She presented a menu of options and allowed the parent to choose. She ended the meeting by asking the mother the ruler questions.

## SUMMARY

This chapter builds off and integrates the key ideas from prior chapters. The SE-FCU is a fairly structured version of MI that illustrates how the method can be applied in a systematic way for working with families, students, and teachers. We provided a step-by-step approach to illustrate how the SE-FCU is implemented in schools. Additionally, Check-Ups can be applied more widely as a strategy for building engagement and motivation around virtually any behavior.

## RESOURCES: SAMPLE BRIEF MEASURES TO ASSESS FAMILY FUNCTIONING

Abidin, R. (1985). *Parenting stress index*. Lutz, FL: PAR.

Berry, J. O., & Jones, W. H. (1995). The parental stress scale: Initial psychometric evidence. *Journal of Social and Personal Relationships, 12,* 463–472. Retrieved from http://www.personal.utulsa.edu/~judy-berry/parent2.htm

Cochoran, K., & Fischer, J. (2000). *Measures for clinical practice: Couples, families and children*. New York, NY: Free Press.

Crnic, K. A., & Greenberg, M. T. (1990). Minor parenting stresses with young children. *Child Development, 61,* 1628–1637.

Driscoll, K., & Pianta, R. C. (2011). Mothers' and fathers' perceptions of conflict and closeness in parent–child relationships during early childhood. *Journal of Early Childhood and Infant Psychology, 7,* 1–24. Retrieved from http://curry.virginia.edu/academics/directory/robert-c.-pianta/measures

Elgar, F. J., Waschbusch, D. A., Dadds, M. R., & Sivaldason, N. (2007). Development and validation of a short form of the Alabama parenting questionnaire. *Journal of Child and Family Studies, 16,* 243–259.

# Handouts and Forms

**HANDOUT 7.1 PARENT INTERVIEW**

Date: ____/____/

ID#: _____

Family Consultant: _____

**Introductory Questions:**
I am going to start out by asking some general questions about who lives in your household and about how (name) is doing at home, in school, and with friends.

Names and age of everyone currently living in the home:
_____
_____
_____
_____
_____
_____

How has (name) been doing in terms of getting along with family and others?

Generally, how would you say (name) has been doing at school?

**{If concerns}** What have you tried to help (name) do better at school?

Does (name) have any special needs or receive any special services at school?

Does (name) have an individualized education program (IEP)? **{If yes, what services does he or she receive?}**

Does (name) take any medications? **{if yes}** what is the name of the medication and what is it for?

What hobbies/special activities does (name) have?

What has been (name)'s greatest accomplishment or achievement this year?

What has been most difficult for (name) this year? Why?

What do you most like about your child? What does he or she do particularly well?

What are your greatest dreams for your child? What do you most want for him or her?

What do you most like about being a parent? What do you do particularly well as a parent?

What is the hardest part about being a parent? Is there something you would like to do better as a parent?

Is there anything else that you think is important for me to know about before we complete the rest of the interview?

# HANDOUT 7.2 PARENT MANAGEMENT SKILLS AND PRACTICES

Family _____          Date of Interview: _____

**Home Learning Environment:**

1. How important do you think your involvement is to your child's success in school?


2. How important do you think your child's education is to his/her success in life?


3. How often do you get a chance to go over your child's homework?


4. How often do you discuss schoolwork with your child?


5. How much education would you like your child to complete?


6. How much education do you think he or she will actually complete?


**Parent–Teacher Interaction:**

7. How often do you meet with your child's teacher?


8. How easy is it for you to become involved at your child's school?


9. How often does your child's teacher keep you informed about what he or she is learning in school?


10. How often does your child's teacher keep you informed about your child's progress in school?


**Parent Discipline:**

11. How often do you get the chance to talk with your child about what he or she has done during the day?


12. How often do you get the chance to talk to your child about what he or she is going to do tomorrow?


13. How often does your child spend time at home without anyone over the age of 16 years?


14. How often do you have fun with your child?

15. When you decide to punish your child, how often can he or she talks you out of it?

16. If you tell your child that he or she will get punished if he or she doesn't stop doing something, how often will you punish him or her?

17. How often does your child get away with things that you feel should have been punished?

18. How often do you let your child go unpunished if he or she cries?

19. When your child has done something wrong, how often does he or she know what kind of punishment to expect?

20. What is the likelihood that you would know in a day or two if your child did poorly on a test or assignment at school?

21. What is the likelihood that you would know in a day or two if your child was in a fight?

22. What is the likelihood that you would know if your child brought something home that didn't belong to him/her?

23. How frequently do you feel pleased with your child?

24. How difficult do you find it to be patient with your child's behavior?

25. How pleasant is your child to raise?

26. How well do you get along with your child?

27. How often does your child choose the activity when you play together?

28. When you praise your child, how often do you explain the behavior that you are praising him or her for?

29. How often do you praise your child when he or she does what he or she is told?

30. How do you handle your child if he or she talks back to you or another adult?

31. How do you handle your child if he or she has been fighting?

32. How do you handle your child if he or she does not listen/comply?

# HANDOUT 7.3 SUMMARY SESSION 1

➤ Summarize Session
  • The purpose of our meeting today was for me to learn more about you and your child, including your values and concerns.
    ◦ Some of your most important values are_____.
    ◦ Some things that you would like to be different are _____.
  • Does that sound about right? Is there anything else I should know?
➤ Prepare for Next Meeting
  • We will meet one more time, so that I can give you information from all the forms you completed today and from your child and his or her teacher.
  • Most parents find this information very helpful to support their child.
  • After our next meeting, you can decide what to do next. That may be our last meeting. Or you may decide that you want to meet again. Whatever you think is best. It is up to you.
  • Do you have any questions?
➤ Schedule Next Meeting
  • Would you like to schedule our next meeting?
  • What day and time works best for you?
➤ Rulers

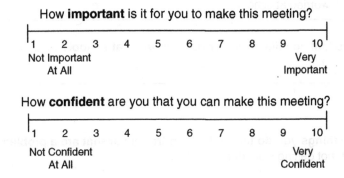

How **important** is it for you to make this meeting?

| 1 | 2 | 3 | 4 | 5 | 6 | 7 | 8 | 9 | 10 |

Not Important At All — Very Important

How **confident** are you that you can make this meeting?

| 1 | 2 | 3 | 4 | 5 | 6 | 7 | 8 | 9 | 10 |

Not Confident At All — Very Confident

Is there anything that could get in the way of attending the meeting?

What can I do to help make sure this doesn't get in the way?

# HANDOUT 7.4 SAMPLE CHILD INTERVIEW

ID#:_____                                    Date: ____/____/____

Family Consultant: _____

**Introductory Questions:**
I am going to start out by asking some general questions about how you are doing at home, in school, and with friends.

**Tell me a bit about how school is going for you this year.**

| | | | |
|---|---|---|---|
| Grades compared to others in class: | not as good | as good | better |
| Teacher relationship: | poor | average | good |
| Gets along with other kids: | OK | problems | |
| Frequently in trouble at school | yes | no | |
| Likes school | yes | no | |
| Anxious, fearful, worried at school | yes | no | |

**What are things that you like to do, or do well, while at school?** (e.g., activities, classes, helping others, etc.) _____
_____


**What are some things you do that get you in trouble or that are a problem at school?** (e.g., talking out, not getting work done, fighting, etc.)


**How often do you _____ ?** ( Insert the behavior listed by the student)


**When does _____ happen?**


**Where does _____ happen?**


**With whom does _____happen?**


**How serious is the _____? (Does anyone get hurt, do you get behind in your work?)**

What usually happens after _____? (What does your teacher do? How do other students react? Do you get out of doing something? Do you go to the office?)


How are things going with other kids?


Do you have friends? (If yes, what are their names?)


| | | |
|---|---|---|
| Has minimum acceptable number of friends | yes | no |
| Neglected or rejected by other kids | yes | no |
| Teased or bullied | yes | no |
| Teases or bullies others | yes | no |
| Frequently in fights | yes | no |


How are things going for you at home with your family?


| | | |
|---|---|---|
| Problems with parents | yes | no |
| Problems with other family members | yes | no |
| Family conflict is prominent | yes | no |
| Anxious, fearful, worried at home | yes | no |


What kinds of fun things do you and your family like to do together?


What kinds of fun things do you like to do with your friends or by yourself?

# Be a BEHAVIOR DETECTIVE!!

## Getting to the bottom of a
# mysterious behavior:

**What?**
- What exactly is the behavior?
- How often does it occur?
- How long does it last?

**Who?**
- What is the child's temperament like?
- Does the child have any medical or developmental difficulties?
- Is this behavior a change from the usual in amount (more of the same)?
- Is this behavior a change from the usual in quality (this is a different child)?

**Where?**
- Does this happen at school/daycare/playground/classroom/lunchroom?
- Does this happen at home?

**When?**
- What happens before the behavior?
- Does the behavior tend to happen at a certain time of day?
- Does the behavior tend to happen during certain events or transitions?

**What happens then?**
- How do parents respond to the behavior?
- How do teachers respond to the behavior?
- How do peers respond to the behavior?

**Why now?**
- Has the child's schedule changed?
- Has something happened in the home/family?
- Has something happened to the child (e.g., medical)?

# Child:
# Presenting Concern:

**What?**

**Who?**

**Where?**

**When?**

**What happens then?**

**Why now?**

# HANDOUT 7.7 SAMPLE ACTION PLAN WORKSHEET

| Things I'd like to continue:<br>For my child…<br><br>For me… | Things I'd like to improve:<br>In my child (e.g., decrease tantrums) ….<br><br>In me (learn/use new parenting tools, stay calm with my child)… |
|---|---|

| How important is it to make these changes?<br><br>1  2  3  4  5  6  7  8  9  10<br>Not at all        Kind of              Extremely<br><br>**How confident are you that your family can make these changes?**<br><br>1  2  3  4  5  6  7  8  9  10<br>Not at all        Kind of              Extremely | The most important reasons for these changes are: |
|---|---|

**Menu of topics for our visits together:**

- Building children's social skills
- Teaching children about emotions and how to cope with feelings
- Teaching strategies for school success
- Encouraging positive behaviors: How to get children to do what we want them to do

- Setting and following rules, routines, and responsibilities
- Setting limits and dealing with limit testing and disrespectful behavior
- Time out to calm down and reduce dangerous behaviors
- Other consequences for misbehavior

**Things that can interfere with the plan:**

| How concerned are you that _____ could make it hard to do? 1 2 3 4 5 6 7 | How concerned are you that _____ could make it hard to do? 1 2 3 4 5 6 7 |
|---|---|
| 1. Things I have done in the past when this has come up: | 1. Things I have done in the past when this has come up: |
| 2. Things I can do to overcome this: | 2. Things I can do to overcome this: |
| Circle the solution you wrote for 1 and 2 that is most likely to help. | Circle the solution you wrote for 1 and 2 that is most likely to help. |
| Who can help me with this? | Who can help me with this? |

# Motivational Interviewing With School-Based Problem-Solving Teams

Most schools are composed of various problem-solving teams to support student learning. Common teams include behavior support teams, response-to-intervention teams, academic support teams, grade-level teams, and teams for individualized education programs. Often these teams bring together a range of professionals and caregivers whose task it is to work together to solve problems. The success of these teams often hinges on the competence of the individual members to solve problems and their willingness and ability to work together.

> Not only are parent and student motivation important, but also school personnel's attitudes about the family and their pessimism about the likely outcome can contribute to unsuccessful plans, or worse, the lack of initiating any plan at all.

The focus of these teams tends to orient to academic or behavioral challenges faced by students. However, it is important to note that a proportion of students with one problem often exhibit the other (i.e., both academic and behavior problems; Reinke, Lewis-Palmer, & Merrell, 2008). Therefore, we recommend having members with expertise in both behavioral intervention planning and academic intervention planning on the team. In addition, students facing challenges at school may also experience challenges outside of the school as well. Thus, it is important for teams to design technically adequate and feasible plans that incorporate caregivers and can be implemented across settings.

Many of the engagement strategies and motivational interviewing (MI) techniques that have been discussed throughout this book can be integrated into the work of school-based problem-solving teams. Thus, in this chapter, we discuss strategies that problem-solving teams can use to support students, particularly those facing significant academic and/or behavioral challenges. We focus on this population because the challenges in supporting students with complex presentation are well known. For instance, students with emotional and behavioral disorders (EBDs) have many experiences at school that often lead to academic failure, expulsion, and drop out (Reid, Patterson, & Snyder, 2002; Wagner, Kutash, Duchnowski, Epstein, & Sumi, 2005, 2006). Further, although many effective prevention and intervention approaches have been developed for students with EBDs, many schools struggle to provide these services. Therefore, schools need new strategies to support these students.

Finally, motivational and perceptual challenges can interfere with the effectiveness of behavior support plans. Not only are parent and student motivation important, but also school personnel's attitudes about the family and their pessimism about the likely outcome can contribute to unsuccessful plans, or worse, the lack of initiating any plan at all. School-based teams can (and often do) ignore these motivational aspects of behavior support planning. Doing so, however, often leads to frustration, blaming, and ultimately plan failure.

## YOUR OWN EXPERIENCES ON AN ACADEMIC OR BEHAVIOR SUPPORT TEAM

Most school professionals have participated on school-based teams at some point in their careers. In many schools, these experiences occur regularly for most school personnel. The structure, spirit, and success of these teams can vary building to building. Take a moment to reflect on your own experiences participating on a school-based team. What was the format of the team? How successful was the team in solving some of the most difficult problems? What were things the team did well? What could have made the team more successful?

> We also guess that like us you have sensed that no matter how well planned and organized the structure of a team is, the success ultimately depends on how interested, motivated, and involved each of the team members was in the process.

Quite often people reflect on the nuts and bolts of these teams. Who is the team leader, and who is invited? Who sets the agenda and keeps the meeting focused? Who has particular expertise to address specific questions about academics or behavior? What gets written down? What plan gets developed, and how is it enacted? All of these are important details and much has been written in other books on the structural aspects of these teams. These aspects of teams set the stage for whether or not they will be successful.

Less considered, but no less important, are the interpersonal aspects of these teams. We suspect that as you reflect on your own experiences, not only do you think about the format of these teams but also the personalities and the attitudes of the people on the team, including parents, students, and community members, when they are involved. We also guess that like us you have sensed that no matter how well planned and organized the structure of a team is, the success ultimately depends on how interested, motivated, and involved each of the team members was in the process.

If you have ever participated in a problem-solving team, take a moment to reflect on how often you heard others say or how often you experienced any of the following thoughts:

- This is a waste of time
- This is never going to work
- These parents just don't care
- This student just doesn't care
- This teacher just doesn't care
- I don't like this family/parent/student/colleague
- This is hopeless

Although not commonly discussed, these beliefs and expressions are frequently experienced by school professionals when working with challenging families, students, and colleagues. If they are persistently experienced by one or more critical team members, there is virtually no chance for the plan developed by the team to work. These types of beliefs and attitudes become self-fulfilling prophesies.

It is in this aspect of team functioning that the application of MI becomes obvious. Much as we discussed individual conversations about change, team conversations about change involve ambivalence. This is normal and expected. Team planning and implementation of change plans will only happen when people are motivated. The strategies for fostering motivation that we have discussed throughout this book apply equally well to teams. In other words, effective teams need one or more members who can facilitate an atmosphere of trust, listening, and support while moving the team through the MI processes: engaging, focusing, evoking, and planning.

In this chapter, we discuss the structural aspects of building a team that will have both the technical and interpersonal skills to be successful. We present a model, based on MI, that we have found successful in bridging the gap between schools and family supports and forging positive relationships that are needed for teams to be successful. We describe an optimal model. Your school may only be able to replicate aspects of the model. If you have a well-functioning team or if the thought of restructuring your entire team is too daunting, focus your attention on the motivational aspects of team functioning that you can add to your team rather than the entire model.

## BUILDING AN EFFECTIVE TEAM

We start with building an effective team because every problem-solving team needs a group of individuals with important skill sets needed to build technically adequate and effective plans, gather needed data, interpret and use the data, monitor fidelity of the plan, and know when to revise a plan as needed. Ideally, the core members of a problem-solving team will consist of six to eight school staff members. The members should include someone with behavioral expertise such as the school psychologist, school social worker, or behavioral consultant and someone with academic expertise such as a special educator.

Additionally, the team would include the building administrator, one or more general education teachers, a school consultant, and specialized staff as needed, such as a speech pathologist. Prior work with school-based behavior support teams indicates that schools need a critical mass of trained professionals to be effective (Hershfeldt, Pell, Sechrest, Pas, & Bradshaw, 2012). The building administrator is an essential team member and needs to be an active participant to provide not only administrative leadership and support but also the ability to reallocate existing resources as needed so that the team can be empowered to make decisions (Chaparro, 2011).

### Designated Family Consultants

As a strategy to include family members in the support planning process, a subgroup of the team can be identified as family consultants. Ideally, this subgroup would consist of two members. One family consultant would have the primary responsibility of making contact with parents and leading family meetings, and the other family consultant would have the primary responsibility of meeting with the student. The school psychologist and consultant or social worker may be ideal candidates for these roles, but other staff members who have experience in effective consultation may also be candidates for this subgroup.

Schools often struggle to involve caregivers in services even though most effective practices suggest parent participation is paramount (Herman et al., 2011). Without family involvement, it is unlikely that adequate supports can be developed at school to avert the long-term negative outcomes for students with the most serious and persistent problems in schools. Unfortunately, families are not routinely involved in the planning and implementation of problem-solving teams. In particular, families from low-income backgrounds and those with children with the highest service needs have the lowest level of school participation (Park, Pullis, Reilly, & Townsend, 1994). Using strategies to engage and motivate caregivers to actively participate in the development of student plans will increase the likelihood of success. Therefore, having members on the problem-solving team who focus on this task, using the engagement and MI strategies outlined in this book, may optimize the likelihood of success.

Figure 8.1 depicts the overall process for building effective problem-solving teams with parent involvement. The process includes assessment and planning meetings to increase the likelihood of parent and staff commitment.

### Involving the Family in the Planning

The family consultant subgroup can use the family engagement strategies detailed in Chapter 2. These include being attentive to common social, cultural, and motivational barriers to participation. For instance, the family consultants may offer to meet at flexible times and in locations outside of the school setting, including at the family's home.

It is important to note that parental attitudes and expectations about participating in services are shaped by the interactions they have with other school

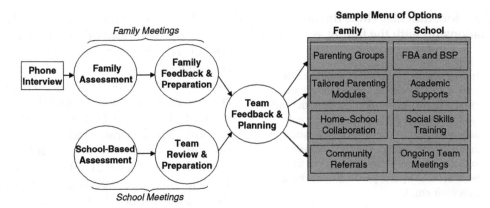

**Figure 8.1** A model for building MI into school-based problem-solving teams. Reprinted from Herman, Reinke, et al. (2012) by permission of Springer SBM.

personnel and social service providers over time. These past experiences that hinder parents intention to participate are often the most hidden and least discussed barriers to participation, but also can be the most important leverage points in facilitating change. Thus, problem-solving team members need to be attentive and discuss these past experiences openly with parents. This is particularly important at the moment of first contact.

> It is important to note that parental attitudes and expectations about participating in services are shaped by the interactions they have with other school personnel and social service providers over time.

Research has shown that relatively simple strategies to foster positive expectations can be used at every point of contact with caregivers and can effectively increase family participation rates over time (McKay et al., 2004; Winslow, Poloskoy, Begay, & Sandler, 2011). For instance, the family consultant in the role of contacting the parents can have an initial phone conversation (or in-person meeting) that begins by identifying the needs and goals of the parents and linking these needs and goals to how the school-based problem-solving team can be helpful and supportive. Additionally, the family consultants should assess any obstacles that might interfere with participation and develop plans to overcome them prior to the first meeting.

## Building Positive Regard Between Families and Schools

Another important role that the family consultants on the problem-solving team play is to build positive regard between families and school personnel. Often, by the time problem-solving teams become involved with students, there has already been a series of interactions between the school and caregivers. In some instances, these interactions become confrontational. Parents feel blamed for their child's school-based challenges. Teachers may feel unsupported by parents. Administrators may feel frustrated with the lack of progress. In our experiences, these past interactions can significantly interfere with building collaborative and effective support plans for students. Thus, the family consultants should work toward entering the relationship with the family as a liaison between the parents and other school personnel. The family consultants should be collaborators working to support the family in building successful experiences at home and school for the student. Thus, the family consultant becomes a collaborator/advocate who presents information to the problem-solving team on behalf of the family. To help mend past conflicts between the school and family, the family consultant identifies and shares family

> To help mend past conflicts between the school and family, the family consultant identifies and shares family strengths with relevant school personnel, sharing only information that is appropriate. In addition, the family consultant brings information to the family about the strengths of the teachers and school personnel working with their child.

strengths with relevant school personnel, sharing only information that is appropriate. In addition, the family consultant brings information to the family about the strengths of the teachers and school personnel working with their child. For instance, during a family meeting the family consultant might disclose that the classroom teacher mentioned that their son is a wonderful artist and enjoys his creativity. The family consultant may share with the teacher or school administrator how willing the family was to meet and work together on supporting their child. Regardless of the situation, both sides always bring strengths to the table. Highlighting these assets across settings can help to repair relationships and build camaraderie toward the mutual goal of supporting the student.

In this model, it becomes clear that the engaging process in MI can occur outside of formal meetings. In fact, in many ways, for families and school personnel who have become disengaged from one another, the first and most important engaging strategies need to occur prior to meetings in everyday conversations about change.

---

### EVERYDAY CONVERSATIONS ABOUT CHANGE

Mr. Thomas Jackson is a school psychologist working with an eighth-grade student, Julio, who has fallen through the cracks. He is failing most of his classes and is disruptive in class when he does attend. Mr. Jackson knows that he needs to organize a team meeting to develop a plan for solving this problem. He also knows Julio's mother has had a difficult history of interacting with school personnel. When Julio was in seventh grade, his mother got into an argument with his math teacher about Julio's grades. She has participated very little in school events during the subsequent year. Julio's mother agreed to meet with Mr. Jackson and the meeting went well. She was very concerned about Julio and wanted help in addressing the situation. At the next problem-solving team meeting, Mr. Jackson put Julio on the agenda and wanted to build team support for working with his mother again:

**Mr. Jackson (J):** Alright, I put Julio on the agenda because as many of you know, he is really struggling at school and we need to come up with a plan for getting him back on track. Today, I just want to get him on

*(continued)*

our radar and find a time in the next week when we can all meet. I want to invite his mother as well.

Teacher (T): Good luck with that.

J: You're skeptical she will come?

T: I haven't had any luck with her this year. She doesn't care. Don't get me wrong. I think it would be great to include her, it's just not going to happen.

J: So why do you think it is important to include her?

T: She has the most influence over him. If she got involved, it might make a difference.

J: I agree. I think we need to do everything we can to get her involved. What do others think?

Principal: Of course, but do you have ideas for getting her involved? We've had a lot of problems in the past.

J: Well, I met with her, and I was really impressed. She was clearly very concerned about Julio and I think she would do anything to support him. I sense that she is feeling like many of us, helpless to fix the problem on her own. She was very interested in being part of the team to see what we can do.

T: That sounds very different than what I would expect. I haven't been able to get her to talk to me all year.

J: It's a surprise. What do you think might have made a difference?

T: Having a different person, you, reach out to her is good. She might just have been expecting me to be calling with bad news about his grades or something.

J: So maybe it wasn't that she doesn't care, just that she doesn't know what to do. I suspect my call gave her some hope that we as a team are going to approach this in a way that can be helpful. I'm optimistic. She's going to be a good partner.

---

*In this example, Mr. Jackson set a goal of trying to re-engage the team members in forming a new attitude about Julio's mother. He invited some conversation about their concerns with open-ended questions, and he reflected their comments to show he was listening. He also quite intentionally planted new thoughts about this parent (e.g., "she cares," "she's trying") that could be used to counter the maladaptive beliefs that some team members had formed about her (e.g., "she doesn't care"). At the end of the meeting, he explicitly reframed the belief that the mother doesn't care as simply not knowing what to do or how to be helpful. These two beliefs carry very different social judgments and if successfully replaced could allow teachers and the principal to form a new more productive relationship with Julio's mother (e.g., if they believe she simply is not sure how to be helpful it is more likely they will treat her with respect and encouragement).*

## Gathering Information

Information needs to be gathered on two fronts: at school and at home. The problem-solving team may want to divide the task. Two groups can be formed: (a) the family consultants gathering information from the parents and student, and (b) the school-based team gathering information from the teacher and other relevant school personnel. In our experiences, having the family consultants meet with families without other problem-solving team members helps facilitate the process and likelihood of success. The family consultants should plan two meetings with the family, one to gather information and a second to provide feedback and form an action plan. During the first meeting, the family consultants interview family members and administer relevant assessments (e.g., rating scales, functional assessment interviews). This initial meeting has a primary focus of building rapport between the family consultant and parents, engaging family members in the process, and identifying key values that can be related to building a support plan tailored to the needs of the family and student.

> The process of gathering information is also a time to build momentum among school personnel toward working together with the family and building an effective plan for the student.

At the same time, the school-based team conducts observations and performs relevant interviews and assessments with teachers and relevant school personnel. During meetings with teachers and other school personnel, the school-based team should consider the use of engagement and MI strategies discussed throughout this book. The process of gathering information is also a time to build momentum among school personnel toward working together with the family and building an effective plan for the student. The school-based team can identify resources, assess potential barriers, and identify strengths within the school that can be used during the action-planning phase of the team meeting.

Often, much of this assessment information is already available within schools. Consider all the data routinely collected on students to track progress and determine eligibility for special education. Or, consider the comprehensive psychoeducational evaluations that are conducted in community clinics and the lengthy reports that are generated from these assessments. Rarely is this information used in a way to build motivation. See Box 8.1 for an example of how to capitalize on this rich source of data.

---

### BOX 8.1 USING PSYCHOEDUCATIONAL EVALUATIONS TO BUILD MOTIVATION

Traditional psychoeducational evaluations (broad measures of academic achievement and behavioral and emotional functioning) are a routine part of assessment and service delivery to students. Despite the prevalence of these evaluations in both clinical and educational practice, however, little evidence exists regarding their utility for increasing positive outcomes. Although there is widespread agreement that assessment data should be used to guide intervention planning and to monitor progress, rarely is the data used to build motivation of parents or students. Assessment feedback provided to parents, students, or even school personnel following student evaluations is a critical yet underused opportunity for school professionals to bridge the gap between assessment and intervention and to influence positive outcomes.

---

*(continued)*

Toward this end, a colleague recently developed a modified Family Check-Up (FCU) to capitalize on all the data that are regularly collected as part of child assessments. Borden (2012) developed and piloted a feedback process based on the FCU and evaluated a protocol for consultants in facilitating feedback sessions. Essentially, she used the data that was collected as part of the assessment to create the feedback part of the FCU. She then trained graduate-level consultants to arrange meetings with parents to present them with the findings, using the MI approach described in this book.

A pilot study found that both parents and consultants perceived the modified FCU-style feedback sessions as important and helpful. Consultants reported increased MI self-efficacy following the trainings and demonstrated greater MI-consistent than inconsistent language during feedback sessions that was significantly related to subsequent change talk from parents. Findings demonstrated that trained graduate student consultants were capable of effectively implementing MI in an assessment feedback context. Additionally, a modified FCU framework may be a useful approach for maximizing the impact of naturally occurring assessment and feedback procedures. Considering that current assessment feedback practices for parents of referred children are individual- and deficit-focused (Wright & Fletcher, 1982) and often neglect critical components of parent engagement (Tharinger et al., 2008), the use of a modified FCU approach could significantly improve the ability of comprehensive evaluation services to improve parents' motivation to change, treatment attendance, and educational outcomes.

## Family Feedback Meeting

All the information is then compiled and the family consultants present the information to the parents in a feedback format. The family meeting follows the same format as described in the Family Check-Up (Chapter 7) and serves the purpose of moving the family through the MI processes of focusing, evoking, and planning.

Following the feedback, the consultants work collaboratively with the family to identify target areas for intervention and begin planning potential home-based and school-based supports. The family consultant utilizes MI strategies, working to connect back to parent values identified during the interview to evoke change talk, all the while staying focused on building supports for the child.

At the same time, the school-based team works with data gathered from the school. The school-based team may also discuss the data prior to coming together with the parents. However, it is good practice to not share family data with the school-based team prior to gaining explicit permission from the family. This may seem counterintuitive, but the reason for doing so is to gain trust from families members and to respect that not all information about family circumstances are pertinent to supporting the student.

### Developing the Plan

Once all information is gathered and shared with the family, a combined meeting with parents, problem-solving team members, and other relevant school personnel (e.g., classroom teacher) is convened. A member of the problem-solving team leads and mediates the meeting, using the strategies for leading meetings discussed below. Together this team, which actively includes the parents, uses their knowledge of what is feasible, effective, and contextually relevant to devise the plan and decide who will implement each component of the plan, what resources are needed, how data will be gathered on how well the plan is implemented, how data will be gathered to determine whether the plan is effective, and when to revisit the plan to revise or work toward a new goal as a team.

## ARRANGING AND LEADING SCHOOL MEETINGS

One possible outcome of the second family meeting and the action-planning stage is a meeting between the family and school personnel. The purpose of this meeting is to create a support team to develop and finalize a plan for supporting the student at home and at school. Invite any adults who have ongoing contact with the student to the meeting. It is important to note that the individual leading the meeting needs to keep a neutral stance, ensuring he or she does not take sides (school vs. family). Often, having an agenda, outlining the purpose of the meeting, and describing the process and expected outcomes can help to keep the meeting productive and goal oriented. The meeting should begin by emphasizing that all team members have come together to work collaboratively to develop a plan that will support the student both at home and school. Emphasizing the shared goal to support the student helps diffuse past experiences and potentially negative attitudes between school personnel and parents. The family consultants work to ensure that the goals and ideas that were developed during the second family meeting are shared. Below, we describe the strategies that help ensure a successful meeting

### Preparation

In this section below, we shift from a third-person to a second-person narrative style "you" because we intend it to be a "how-to" approach for leading meetings.

Preparation for the meeting begins from the first moment the *team* process is initiated. From your first contact with the school personnel and with the child and family, avoid any ongoing negative dialogue about the other. It is common for school personnel and parents of children with recurrent behavior problems to experience discord. Parents may complain that the school is neglecting or unfairly targeting their child (e.g., labeling them, enforcing inconsistent rules for other students). Some parents may feel the problem is with the school or with the teacher because the child does not misbehave at home. Teachers may express concerns about the parent's level of motivation, commitment, or involvement with school. They may also describe the child as willfully disobedient and believe that the child or family situation is hopeless.

In all of your contacts with all participants, avoid communicating your agreement with these perceptions, tacitly or otherwise. Likewise, discourage lengthy conversations of these perceptions. It can be a difficult balance to strike. On the one hand, you want to acknowledge such perceptions through reflective listening to show empathy and concern (e.g., "That's really frustrating to sense that the school is not supporting your child"). When reflecting such statements, be sure to distinguish these as beliefs of the person expressing them and not as your own. On the other hand, it would be a mistake to spend the entire interview encouraging extended discussion about negative perceptions. After a reflection or two, it may be helpful to shift the focus either by reframing what was said or by changing the topic (e.g., "That's disappointing to feel like the parents don't care. First, I wanted us to start by focusing on how Jacob is doing in school").

## Building Positive Perceptions

In addition to minimizing negative conversations, it is also a good idea to plant new positive perceptions for each participant about one another. In the situation in which both the parents and school personnel already have favorable views of each other, it is helpful to strengthen these perceptions. The way to build positive perceptions is to actively express them during your meetings with parents and teachers. For instance, when you meet with parents, make positive statements about specific actions the school is taking or observations you have made. These can include steps the school has taken to improve the situation, comments teachers have made to you about the student, or simply the amount of time they are spending on helping the child. These observations are not shared to directly counter or dismiss the parent's perception (e.g., don't express them immediately after the parent has made a negative comment about the school). Rather, they should be offered at various points in your meetings to emphasize collaboration and shared commitment. For instance, you can take time at the beginning or end of the feedback session to share information about the strengths of the school or teacher: "I've had several contacts with his teacher and she's been very supportive. I can tell she is really concerned and has been working hard to come up with a new plan."

In the same way, it is important to share favorable comments about the family with teachers and other school personnel: "I visited them last week and I am impressed with how open they are to the work we're doing. They really are committed to helping Alex succeed." As with any feedback and new information, it is essential that you believe the things you say (i.e., they are genuine) and that you be as specific as possible. Building these new, more positive perceptions for parents and schools facilitates a more successful partnership.

## Arranging the Meeting

If a school meeting is part of the action plan, save time at the end of the family feedback meeting to identify some possible times for the family to come to school. You can also ask the teacher prior to the family feedback meeting about best times and days for a subsequent school meeting. Explain the purpose of school meetings for the parents and teachers in your early contacts with them. Once you have found an agreed-upon time, schedule the meeting and arrange the location.

In advance of the meeting, create an agenda and share it with participants. The agenda items should be centered on the child. Decide who will lead the meeting. Ideally, this person will be an unbiased third party using MI skills to help guide the meeting in a positive direction.

Prior to meeting with a family, meet with school personnel who will attend the school–family meeting to discuss the purpose and goals. Ask them to identify issues and concerns they would like addressed in the meeting, and to write specific goals they would like to see accomplished as a result. Prepare participants for how the meeting will proceed, including clarifying who will lead the discussion.

It is also helpful to prepare the parents for the full meeting. Ask the parents to identify specific goals and let them know how the meeting will proceed. Encourage parents to write down questions or concerns that they would like to address. It can be helpful to role-play scenarios with parents so that they have more self-confidence to effectively express their concerns and ideas. Discuss any worries the parents have about the meeting and include the child, if appropriate.

One purpose of consulting with participants before the formal meeting is to teach them assertive speaking skills. Share ways for each participant to communicate effectively. These might include thinking and pausing before speaking, acknowledging the efforts and actions of others, keeping a positive perspective, separating facts from feelings, saying what you mean and meaning what you say, separating people from the problem, telling others what you want rather than what you don't like or want, and using "I feel" versus "you" statements.

Finally, arrange a time and place that works for all parties. Give a reminder phone call or e-mail message in advance of the meeting. Distribute the agenda a few days prior to the meeting. Arrive early to the meeting and arrange the space as needed.

## Leading the Meeting

Begin the meeting by welcoming participants. Thank them for coming and comment on their shared commitment to helping the student. Publicly acknowledge the participants for their efforts. Be specific. At a minimum, praise the parents' and teacher's interest and efforts. Be sure also to comment on the student's strengths early in the meeting. For example, "We all want to help Kimo and see him be successful at school. He's a great kid. As a team, we will find the best way to support him and get him back on track. None of us can do this alone. We need each other if this is going to work."

Invite participants to introduce themselves. Provide an overview of the meeting and walk through the agenda. The agenda can either be a handout or written on a board. Ask whether any items need to be added to the agenda.

Next, introduce the ground rules for the meeting. Common ground rules might include the following:

- One person speaks at a time
- Everyone has a right to his or her view. No personal attacks. No blaming.
- Avoid side conversation
- Maintain problem-solving focus, rather than complaint focus
- Stick to the agenda

Ask whether any rules need to be added and gain agreement on the final list of ground rules.

Start the agenda by commenting on the student's positive qualities and signs of growth. Provide specific examples of each quality and ask others to provide input. Then, ask each participant to share goals, both for the student and for the meeting. Reflect and summarize each goal and try to identify connections and themes among the goals. Write these on a board for review and consideration. Refer back to the goals throughout the meeting.

As the meeting progresses, use group facilitation and MI skills to reflect comments and identify any sticking points. Try to anticipate any barriers that may arise as you listen to the discussion. If the conversation starts to drift, steer it back to the agenda item. If tensions rise, redirect the focus back to the needs of the student.

Encourage everyone to participate. Keep the pulse of the room by continuously scanning the group. If nonverbal cues indicate negativity or confusion, stop and check with the individual (e.g., "Mrs. Smith, I see you're frowning right now"). If a lot of negatives are discussed about an issue, comment that there is always something positive and ask for suggestions. Conversely, if all responses to an issue are positive, ask for any concerns that have not been mentioned, or you may not hear these until there is not enough time left in the meeting.

## Managing Conflict

If at any time during the meeting a participant is verbally attacked or put in the "hot seat" by others, intervene immediately to diffuse the tension and redirect the focus to the agenda and goals. Steer the conversation back to the goal and solution needed, rather than toward the past or toward blaming others. If you have written the goals on a board, it may help to physically point to the goals. It can also help to post the ground rules and refer to them when you need to redirect the conversation (e.g., "I just wanted to remind everyone about our ground rules about listening and not interrupting others"). Keep the discussion focused on the future, not on the past.

When conflicts or arguments arise

- Listen. Show respect and empathy to reduce defensive behavior.
- Clarify the desired outcome.
- Clarify both sides' opinions. Positions may not be as different as originally thought.

- Determine the common ground between the two opinions.
- Do not permit blaming. Remain solution oriented, working toward a win–win resolution.

## Managing Common Behavior Problems in Meetings

It can be helpful to anticipate some common problem areas that may arise during meetings. One common pattern is to have someone in the meeting who prefers to complain rather than to focus on solving the problem. One way to respond to this pattern is to first repeat the person's concern and verify understanding of the issue. Then ask others if they have similar feelings. Reflect any responses and summarize. Finally, redirect the group to problem solving and goal planning on the issue (if it is an important issue that needs to be addressed). Otherwise, redirect the focus back to the topic at hand.

Another common pattern is for someone to dominate the conversation. When this occurs, first thank the person for the contribution and then say, "Let's hear what others have to say on the issue." Encourage responses from others. If the behavior persists, remind the person of the ground rules.

Uncomfortable emotions may arise during these meetings. Expect a range of emotions to occur because everyone at the meeting often has much at stake in the outcome. Additionally, sometimes the problems that preceded the meeting have been long-standing unresolved issues, so many participants may have deep, lingering frustrations and grievances. It is important to recognize common and predictable emotions (e.g., a parent may express a range of frustration, sadness, and grief when coming to terms with new perspectives about their child). It is important for you to feel comfortable helping people identify and process upsetting feelings. It can be helpful to clarify emotions and connect them to the thoughts that preceded them. Helping people reach new insights about their emotions and precipitants can empower them. On the other hand, do not let venting emotional expression dominate the meeting. Keep the agenda moving forward.

## Working Toward Resolution

As the meeting progresses, keep the discussion focused on common interests rather than positions. Deal with one issue at a time. Save the most challenging issues for later in the meeting so that the group can experience success before tackling the biggest issues. Continue to ensure that everyone separates the person from the problem behaviors. Take time to listen and hear everyone's perspectives. Finally, develop a plan of action to succeed.

## Concluding the Meeting

Announce that the meeting will be ending soon (15 minutes or so before the end) and check to see whether there are any issues that must be considered during the meeting that have not yet been addressed. Summarize what has been accomplished and what needs to be done by whom and when. Put this action plan into writing (see examples that follow). Review any items that were not addressed and create a plan for resolving these items in the future. Finally, ask for participant feedback on the process of the meeting and thank everyone for his or her time and participation. Schedule future meetings, if needed.

### Meeting Follow-Up

After the meeting, summarize the discussion in a written format that includes what was accomplished and who will do what and when. Distribute the summary to members who attended the meeting. Follow-up on decisions made during the meeting to make sure they are enacted. Also, follow-up on unsettled items and create an action plan for resolving them.

### Happily Ever After

Keep in mind that you cannot always come to consensus but that you can move forward to support the student. It is important to determine what is working and what is not working. This may require additional meetings. Some meetings may need to end without clear resolution. However, all meetings should end only after a clear action plan for next steps has been developed.

### CASE EXAMPLES

The following section provides case examples of using this problem-solving team approach with students who have very challenging and persistent behavior and academic problems.

---

## STUDENT WITH PROMINENT DEPRESSION AND SCHOOL BEHAVIOR PROBLEMS

### FAMILY CONTEXT

Sarah and Bill are biological parents to Kenny. Kenny is 8 years of age. Both parents and the child live in the same household. Kenny is a third-grade student in a rural elementary school. He has attended this school for his entire school career.

---

*(continued)*

# STUDENT WITH PROMINENT DEPRESSION AND SCHOOL BEHAVIOR PROBLEMS (*continued*)

## PRESENTING PROBLEM

The family was referred because Kenny has been having behavioral difficulties at school, which include being sent to the office regularly for disruptive behavior. Specifically, Kenny talks out of turn, argues with the teacher, and has difficulty completing assignments in a timely manner.

## FAMILY AND SCHOOL ASSESSMENT

The family consultant from the problem-solving team contacted Kenny's parents. They were both interested in supporting Kenny at school. The family agreed to complete family assessments, which consisted of parent and child interviews, a battery of questionnaires for the parents, teachers, child, and a classroom observation. The measures used for the family and school assessments were

- Behavior Assessment System for Children (BASC; Reynolds & Kamphaus, 2004), parent, teacher, and child
- Teacher Observation of Classroom Adaptation (TOCA; Koth, Bradshaw, & Leaf, 2009)
- A structured parent interview
- A structured child interview
- A structured teacher interview
- 60-minute direct observation of classroom behavior

The family consultants met with the family in their home after school to complete the parent interview and family assessments. Kenny and both parents were available for the assessment. The assessment lasted approximately 90 minutes. During the assessment both parents actively participated, providing detailed information about strategies that both the school and they had employed in the past to help support Kenny. Major concerns identified during the structured parent interview included Kenny's difficulty completing tasks (especially schoolwork), few friendships, and difficulty paying attention and following directions. Both parents stated that Kenny was kind and helpful around the house.

From the family interview, the family consultant learned that one strategy the classroom teacher had been using to encourage Kenny to complete his schoolwork was to send all incomplete work home. He was then expected to complete all the work he didn't finish at school at home that night. This led to Kenny sitting at the table all night after dinner while his parents argued with him about completing his work. The father stated that Kenny seemed depressed because he was unable to be successful at school. In addition, he noted that they had a high level of conflict with Kenny because they struggled with supporting his work completion at home. Further, they noted

(*continued*)

that Kenny had no free time after school, leaving little time to enjoy peer friendships.

Kenny was also an active participant. The second family consultant met with Kenny as the first family consultant met with the parents. Rapport was easily established and Kenny answered questions on the structured child interview and BASC self-report questionnaire. During the completion of the child BASC, the consultant observed that Kenny had difficulty identifying an answer to concrete questions, often changing his mind or stating that he would need to think about the answer further. Additionally, he asked questions throughout the interview.

## CLASSROOM OBSERVATION

The school-based team conducted a structured teacher interview to identify what the teacher perceived to be problem behaviors, when they occurred, how often, with whom, and how severe the problem behaviors were. In addition, the school-based team participated in a 60-minute observation of Kenny's third-grade classroom. The observation took place at the start of the day. Kenny arrived 15 minutes late to the classroom. Kenny got out of his seat several times to obtain materials when prompted by the teacher to get out an assignment. The teacher provided several opportunities to respond to the class with the expectation that the students would raise their hands. During teacher-led instruction, Kenny called out answers nine times in the first 5 minutes of the observation. The teacher provided attention to 44% of these talk-outs. When the teacher began to consistently ignore Kenny's talk-outs, he placed his head on his desk and then asked to go to the restroom. The teacher allowed him to go to the restroom, stating that he had 3 minutes and she was timing him. Kenny left to use the restroom and did not return until 10 minutes later when the teacher left the room to find him. During the observation, Kenny was off task the majority of the time. At the end of the observation, Kenny had not completed his independent seatwork. In comparison, most students in the classroom had completed the worksheet and moved on to other activities.

## RATING SCALES

Both of Kenny's parents and his classroom teacher each completed rating scales. The measures indicated significant concern with attention problems characterized by being easily distracted, forgetting things, and having trouble concentrating. Additionally, Kenny's mother's responses did not reveal concerns about hyperactivity, aggression, conduct problems, anxiety, depression, or social withdrawal. However, his father's and teacher's responses both revealed concerns about hyperactivity, characterized by disrupting others' activities, acting without thinking, interrupting others when they were speaking,

*(continued)*

## STUDENT WITH PROMINENT DEPRESSION AND SCHOOL BEHAVIOR PROBLEMS (*continued*)

and showing poor self-control. Additionally, Kenny's teacher's responses revealed concerns in several additional areas that his parents did not identify, including problems with aggressive behavior, such as arguing, annoying others on purpose, defying his teacher, and losing his temper. His teacher also documented concerns about conduct problems, such as breaking rules, deceiving others, getting into trouble, and being disobedient. Kenny's teacher's responses indicated depression-related concerns, such as being sad, feelings of negativity, pessimism, loneliness, and Kenny saying that he hates himself. See Table 8.1 for summary of mother, father, and teacher reported ratings.

**Table 8.1 Summary of Mother, Father, and Teacher Rating of Kenny's Behaviors**

| BASC Clinical Scale | Mother Rating | Father Rating | Teacher Rating |
|---|---|---|---|
| Hyperactivity | 54 | 67 | 78 |
| Aggression | 40 | 42 | 70 |
| Conduct problems | 48 | 48 | 69 |
| Anxiety | 59 | 65 | 55 |
| Depression | 43 | 45 | 74 |
| Somatization | 36 | 53 | 43 |
| Attention problems | 67 | 64 | 66 |
| Atypicality | 68 | 73 | 76 |
| Withdrawal | 47 | 51 | 76 |

*Note:* A score of 60 or higher is indicative of an area of concern, whereas a score of 70 or higher indicates a problem in the clinical range. BASC = Behavior Assessment System for Children.

With regard to adaptive functioning, Kenny's parent responses indicated no concerns. However, Kenny's teacher's responses indicated concerns in the areas of social skills, leadership (not working well under pressure, not making decisions easily), and adaptability (not adjusting well to routines, not recovering quickly after a setback, becoming upset when things are changed, not being easily soothed when becoming angry).

The BASC self-report form was given to Kenny to complete. This rating form examines self-perceptions of adjustment in school, clinical, and personal domains as well as emotional symptoms. The family consultant read questions out loud to Kenny to ensure comprehension. Kenny's self-ratings revealed difficulties in the area of locus of control, such as feeling that others blame him for circumstances he can't help; situations going wrong even when he tries; not being able to control what happens to him; difficulties with anxiety, such as worrying about little things, worrying about what is going to happen, and being afraid he might do something bad. Regarding Kenny's self-report of

(*continued*)

depression, he indicated feeling like nothing ever goes right for him, feeling depressed and that no one understands him, and feeling sad. See Tables 8.2 and 8.3 for a summary of Kenny's self-reported ratings.

**Table 8.2** Summary of Kenny's Self-Reported Behaviors

| BASC Clinical Scale | T-Scores Self-Rating |
| --- | --- |
| Attitude toward school | 50 |
| Attitude toward teachers | 55 |
| School problems | 53 |
| Atypicality | 51 |
| Locus of control | 62 |
| Social stress | 52 |
| Anxiety | 61 |
| Depression | 61 |
| Sense of inadequacy | 58 |
| Attention problems | 71 |
| Hyperactivity | 65 |
| Inattention/hyperactivity | 70 |

Note: A score of 60 or higher is indicative of an area of concern, whereas a score of 70 or higher indicates a problem in the clinical range. BASC = Behavior Assessment System for Children.

**Table 8.3** Summary of Kenny's Self-Report of Adaptive Behaviors

| BASC Adaptive Scale | T-Scores Self-Rating |
| --- | --- |
| Relations with parents | 38 |
| Interpersonal relations | 47 |
| Self-esteem | 44 |
| Self-reliance | 50 |

Note: A score below 50 is considered an area of concern. BASC = Behavior Assessment System for Children.

The most significant difficulties indicated by Kenny's responses were attention problems and hyperactivity. Kenny indicated that he has a short attention span, that he forgets things, he has trouble paying attention to what he is doing and to his teacher, that he often acts without thinking, that he has trouble sitting still, and talks without waiting for others to say something. Kenny did not endorse items indicative of a negative attitude toward school or his teacher, school problems, atypicality, social stress, or a sense of inadequacy.

(continued)

## STUDENT WITH PROMINENT DEPRESSION
## AND SCHOOL BEHAVIOR PROBLEMS (continued)

Kenny's responses to items on the adaptive scales indicated a good relationship with his peers, good self-esteem, and good self-reliance. He did indicate that he felt his parents did not enjoy helping him with his homework.

### FAMILY FEEDBACK SESSION

Consultants conducted the feedback session approximately a week following the family assessment. The feedback session occurred at the family's home. Both parents were in attendance. The feedback session lasted for approximately 90 minutes. In this meeting, the consultants presented the major findings of the assessment and discussed implications for addressing any presenting problems. Feedback on both the positive protective factors of the family and risk factors or area of concern was provided. Protective factors identified from the assessment included the strong family relationship and commitment shared by both parents; both parents were child focused and had high levels of parental monitoring of child activities; and both parents were motivated. Despite these strengths, the family assessment revealed concerns in several areas. The identified risk factors included ratings by both parents, Kenny's teacher, and Kenny in the clinical range for problems with inattention. In addition, other externalizing behavior areas of concern included disruptive behavior at school and difficulty completing assignments. Kenny was also rated as having affective difficulties, particularly anxiety and depression, and as having few relationships with peers.

| Feedback Session Dialogue | Comments |
|---|---|
| **Family Consultant (FC):** We've compiled all this information and I'm going to share it with you using this form. We have lots of information and as we walk through it what I want us to think about are things that stand out to you and things you think we should focus on, and any ideas for next steps. I'll write them down and at the end, we'll come up with a solid plan. | Summary and preview |
| So, when we are looking at this form, you'll see it starts here in the green and then moves over to the red. So all this is telling us is that if you see something in the green, that's good—that's something we don't want to change. If you see something in the red, those are things we want to pay attention to and develop a plan to help with. | Introducing feedback form |

(continued)

| Feedback Session Dialogue | Comments |
|---|---|
| The first category is defiance. You don't see a problem with it, but the teacher feels like he's a little bit disrespectful. Same thing with conduct. He's being sent to the principal's office a lot. But you don't see that at home, so it is primarily a school thing. Now problems with attention, this is way up in the red. This is across the board. You see it, he sees it, and his teacher sees it. So this is definitely something we'll want to talk about more. Another one standing out is anxiety. You are both seeing him worry a lot, so that is in the yellow. But his depression is really high. | Feedback<br><br><br><br><br><br><br><br><br><br>Selectively highlighting a key finding |
| **Dad (D):** (Nodding) | |
| **Mom (M):** Is that like self-esteem? | |
| **FC:** It means sad, lonely, feeling like things are bad and not going to get better. | |
| **D:** (to consultant) I told you about that. | |
| **FC:** Yes. | Affirmation |
| **D:** The teachers are constantly leaning on him. I mean you got 4 years of it. | |
| **FC:** So it's building up over time. You (Dad) are definitely seeing it. The teacher sees it, and he's telling us too.<br><br>Any surprises about that? The depression? | Personalized feedback<br>Reflection<br>Check in |
| **D:** I thought the anxiety would be higher. | |
| **FC:** Yeah, it was the depression. They do go together. | |
| **M:** I'm worried about that. I knew he was having problems at school, but I didn't know it was affecting him that way. | Change talk |
| **FC:** So that bothers you. You really don't like to hear he's suffering. | Reflection |
| **M:** Not at all. | |

*(continued)*

## STUDENT WITH PROMINENT DEPRESSION AND SCHOOL BEHAVIOR PROBLEMS (continued)

| Feedback Session Dialogue | Comments |
|---|---|
| **FC:** Let's put that on our list of things to come back to (writes it down). So the family. You guys are doing great. You are both involved, you both communicate well, and have clear expectations at home. Your use of encouragements is good. I put it in the green but a little higher because you told me you used incentives in the past and haven't recently so that is something that we may want to tweak. Any surprises there? | Creating menu<br><br>Feedback and affirmations<br><br>Check in |
| **D:** No. | |
| **FC:** You knew you were doing well. | Reflection |
| **D:** We try. We hoped so. | |
| **FC:** Even one of the first things I noticed was at school you were both at the meeting, right at 3 o'clock. So involved and supportive. Just trying so many things. | Affirmations |
| **M:** It's just hard. And when you offered to help, how could we say no to help? With the problems we're having. I mean we are out of ideas. | |
| **FC:** Even so. The fact you are open to meeting with us in the middle of the night and that you are really open to feedback. It just shows you really want help. You really want to find ways to support him. We are just going to build off that strength. That's a huge core strength and we are going to use it. | Affirmations<br><br>Instilling hope |
| **FC:** And so with the school, I'm sure you won't be surprised by this. Attendance is in the red. It's really about his being on time. When we observed in his classroom, he was about 20 minutes late. And this just puts him behind. So right there, he had missed 15 minutes of instruction, so he was already starting his day behind. And with his attention problems that's just a setup for him to have a bad day. | Feedback |
| **D:** I don't understand how the school is structured where he can be late. When I was in school, we were literally ushered into class. | |
| **FC:** Do you have any idea of what he does? | Open-ended question |

(continued)

| Feedback Session Dialogue | Comments |
|---|---|
| **M:**  Yeah, he just lollygags in the hall. He just moseys. He gets distracted. I mean I usually drop him off at 7:30 and maybe that gives him too much time. Maybe he would be more on time if we had breakfast here and then I dropped him off. | |
| **FC:**  So that's definitely something we want to figure out. Let's put that down and see how we can work with the school to get on top of this. | |

The family meeting concluded with a specific action plan for supporting Kenny at home. Based on the feedback, one option the parents elected to pursue was to arrange a meeting with the school team to address the problems at school.

## TEAM MEETING WITH PARENTS

At the meeting, the team developed a plan to address Kenny's ongoing behavioral difficulties at school. They determined that a school-based intervention with home reward components would be developed. Further, the parents expressed an interest in a medication consult with a child psychiatrist to potentially address some of Kenny's clinically significant attention problems. The problem-solving team worked with the teacher who, in collaboration with Kenny, came up with a checklist of activities he needed to do daily (e.g., arrive in the classroom on time, put away jacket, get to work right away). For each item that Kenny completed, he earned a point. These points could then be traded for a school-based reward. Kenny developed a list of possible reinforcers with the teacher. One of the rewards that Kenny came up with was helping the custodian. At home, Kenny received a reward if he completed 85% of all tasks on the list. The parents rewarded Kenny with free time before completing homework, playing a game as a family, or watching a favorite show.

The problem-solving team monitored the implementation of the daily checklist token economy by observing the process between the teacher and Kenny and gathering the checklists to monitor the number of points received and ensuring that the checklist was being implemented daily. The problem-solving team also monitored progress to determine when and how frequently Kenny cashed in his points for a school-based reward. At school, the intervention was implemented with high fidelity and increased Kenny's ability to complete work and stay on task in the classroom.

The family consultants met with the family to evaluate the effectiveness of the home component of the intervention. One identified problem was that on occasion Kenny misplaced the checklist or the parents were unable to locate the checklist when he arrived home. They needed to review the checklist to determine whether he earned a home reward each day. The family consultant worked on establishing a routine for Kenny in which his checklist went into a folder, he placed the folder into his backpack, and when he came home, his

*(continued)*

## STUDENT WITH PROMINENT DEPRESSION AND SCHOOL BEHAVIOR PROBLEMS (*continued*)

parents would go into the backpack to find the folder. Although seemingly simple, Kenny's need for support with organizational skills was vital to the success of the program. The family was able to successfully implement the intervention at home. They reported that Kenny felt more successful. Further, the rewards he earned often included spending time as a family. Thus, family cohesion increased as a result.

## STUDENT WITH MILD DEVELOPMENTAL DISABILITIES

### PRESENTING PROBLEM

Sarah is an 8-year-old third-grade student diagnosed with mild mental retardation, displaying disruptive classroom behaviors. She has explosive behaviors when frustrated. When asked to do something she did not want to do, she would often throw objects and scream. This frequently resulted in the school administrator coming to the classroom to escort Sarah to the office.

### ASSESSMENT AND FEEDBACK

The family consultants set up a time to meet with the parents in the family's home after school. At the first meeting with the family, one of the family consultants completed an interview with both parents, and the parents each completed the BASC-Parent Report (Reynolds & Kamphaus, 2004). The second consultant met with Sarah and asked her questions about what she thought was challenging for her at school, including what usually happened right before and right after she became upset. Next, the school-based team scheduled a classroom observation and asked the teacher to complete the TOCA Revised (Koth, Bradshaw, & Leaf, 2009) and the BASC-Teacher Report Scale (Reynolds & Kamphaus, 2004). The family consultants summarized this information and shared the feedback with Sarah's parents at a second session in the family's home. At the feedback session, the family consultants discussed the family's strong positive relationship with Sarah as well as good home–school communication. The family wanted to work on Sarah's coping skills, anger management, and social skills.

### TEAM MEETING AND ACTION PLAN

Additionally, a school meeting was held with the principal, general education classroom teacher, special education teacher, school consultant, Sarah's parents, and the family consultants to develop a behavior plan for Sarah.

(continued)

## SCHOOL

During the meeting, the team developed a reinforcement schedule to implement at the school. The schedule involved a brief visit from Sarah's mother (who worked at the school) at lunchtime if Sarah had no outbursts in the morning and being picked up by her mother at the end of the day if Sarah had no outbursts in the afternoon. If she had no outbursts all week, Sarah's reward was having her father join her for lunch. The second strategy implemented was a visual schedule to help support Sarah with transitions and schedule changes during the school day. Sarah and the consultants developed the visual schedule by taking pictures of her doing various activities throughout the school day. The third strategy implemented was a daily behavior chart that Sarah took from class to class to receive feedback on her behavior. The behavior chart had three categories that followed the school's behavior support model (safe, respectful, responsible). Sarah could earn a smiley face, a neutral face, or a sad face in each category for each class.

## PARENTS

The family consultants met with Sarah and her mother at school to work on strategies for improving emotional regulation and social skills. The family consultants provided updates on the effectiveness of the school interventions and gave the parents ideas as well as activities to use at home with Sarah.

## OUTCOME

The school reported several notable incidents that illustrated a change in Sarah's behavior. The first incident occurred when she got upset in class. Instead of throwing objects as she had in the past, she pulled on her own hair for a moment and then recovered. A second incident is when she chose not to go on the school bus with her class to practice for the school play; instead, she chose to stay with one of her teachers to make up work she missed when she was home ill the day before. In the past, Sarah had gotten overwhelmed by the noise on the bus, so deciding she would stay behind was a big step for her. The third event was earning a weekly award for good behavior from her general education teacher for the first time. Although there were positive changes, Sarah did continue to have some outbursts at school.

Sarah's mother and father consistently reported that they felt the intervention was *very effective,* the information provided by the family consultants was *very helpful,* and that they felt *very confident* that they would be able to effectively implement this intervention in the future. The special education and classroom teacher both reported that they believed the goals of the intervention were *very important* and they both felt *very confident* that they would be able to effectively implement this type of intervention in the future.

## SUMMARY

The purpose of this chapter was to demonstrate how a problem-solving team could use effective engagement and MI strategies to develop, implement, and monitor support plans for students, particularly those presenting with complex behavioral and/or academic challenges in school. In some ways, the problem-solving team model we described is a combination of methods using strategies discussed in Chapter 5, in which we described using MI with teachers, and Chapters 4 and 7, in which we described using MI with families. This model of problem solving attends to the underlying processes that can interfere with truly effective plans, including low levels of engagement and lack of motivation among school staff, team members, and family members, and setbacks that occur naturally when working across the school and family contexts. Competing values, expectations, skill deficits, resource limitations, issues with engagement and motivation, and contextual challenges will always be present. Finding ways to overcome these factors within a problem-solving model by bringing them forward as a point of intervention that can help toward improving outcomes for the students in our schools.

**III**

# Implementation and Dissemination

# Integrating Motivational Interviewing With Other Evidence-Based Programs and Practices

The emphasis on using evidence-based practices in schools has mushroomed in recent years. Given the push for accountability in schools during the past several decades, there has been pressure for schools to deliver proven practices that have a high likelihood of helping them meet objectives set by state and national requirements. Along with this growing interest in evidence-based practices, come questions about how best to get school personnel and parents to use the practices as intended. These are questions of implementation fidelity or quality. Fidelity is focused on the real-world challenge that even when schools select high-quality practices to use, there is no guarantee that they will use them in the correct way to ensure the positive outcomes that were found in research studies.

> The application of MI to support implementation of specific programs and practices is a reasonable extension of the approach.

A logical question is whether methods can be developed to help school professionals and parents become more effective at implementing evidence-based practices. A few researchers have turned to motivational interviewing (MI) as a tool for assisting with this process. The application of MI to support implementation of specific programs and practices is a reasonable extension of the approach. Here we focus on several school-based applications that have used MI to help support the delivery of classroom curriculum and behavior management programs at home and school.

## USING MI TO SUPPORT TEACHER IMPLEMENTATION PRACTICES

There are many well-established programs for teaching social and emotional skills to students in schools. Some of these are social–emotional curriculum such as the program Providing Alternative THinking Strategies (PATHS). PATHS is an evidence-based teacher-delivered curriculum focused on teaching students an array of social and coping skills (see Domitrovich et al., 2010). Others are structured classroom-management programs such as the Good Behavior Game (GBG), also known as PAX. GBG is a strategy whereby the teacher divides his or her classroom into two or more teams and then keeps a tally of behavior infractions that occur during a specified period. The team with the fewest tallies wins the game and receives a small reward. Much research supports the impact of GBG on student achievement and social–emotional development (see Domitrovich et al., 2010). PAX is a more comprehensive approach that uses the GBG as the foundation for classroom management and augments it with other strategies for enhancing children's social–emotional skills. Recently, PATHS and PAX have been combined into a single integrated program called PATHS to PAX.

> Teachers receive feedback based on standardized observations of their classrooms and their self-reports of measures of their behavior management practices.

During the past several years, Drs. Reinke and Herman have been working with colleagues at Johns Hopkins University Center for Prevention and Early Intervention (CPEI) to use an MI-based coaching model to support the implementation of PATHS to PAX (Reinke et al., 2012). In this effort, they collect data on teacher implementation practices of both components (PATHS and PAX) including procedural details (how often they deliver the curriculum or play the game) as well as process skills (how well they use the tools and strategies of each program). Teachers who implement the programs with high fidelity are supported with a basic coaching model, which involves some classroom visits and modeling of skills when needed. Teachers with low-implementation frequency or fidelity, on the other hand, are offered a structured MI intervention. In this approach, the coach collects detailed information about the implementation through direct observations and then delivers this feedback using a structured feedback form (similar to the one described in Chapter 5). The coach then invites the teacher to discuss goals and next steps for improving implementation.

Drs. Reinke and Herman have piloted this approach in several urban elementary schools. Available evidence suggests teachers who receive this added MI intervention are more likely to improve their classroom atmosphere than those who receive a standard coaching model.

Finally, Dr. Shepard and her colleagues have been using program- and classroom-level Check-Ups to engage school staff (i.e., classroom staff, school counselors, and administrators) in another evidence-based program, the Incredible Years Teacher Classroom Management Program (IY-TCM; Webster & Reid, 2010). IY-TCM is designed to improve classroom climate and strengthen classroom-management strategies to include greater use of positive behavioral supports and to reduce use of harsh, critical practices, in turn promote children's social competence, emotional regulation, academic engagement, and school readiness skills and reduce aggressive and disruptive behavior in the classroom. The program is a substantial investment of time and energy at all levels, involving participation in six full-day workshops along with working with an IY-TCM coach in the classroom between sessions. We find that school settings, with their multiple competing demands, often vary with respect to leadership "buy-in" and support for IY-TCM and find it challenging to meet the needs required to adopt the program (e.g., capacity to release classroom staff to participate in workshops and to protect time for consultation with IY-TCM coaches, maintain appropriate program dosage and sequencing, support delivery of all program components, and integrate the program with other school and classroom initiatives). Also, both seasoned and new teaching staff approach the training at varying levels of readiness and motivation to participate and adopt new skills.

Dr. Shepard uses staff self-reports on questionnaires and standardized classroom observations to assess organizational capacities to adopt evidence-based programs (i.e., existing infrastructure and availability of required resources, service system priorities, leadership and supervision, school culture and climate, staff competencies, and staff openness and readiness to adopt IY-TCM), and then provides data-based feedback to administrators within an MI framework to facilitate decision making and goal setting around ways to support the ongoing implementation of IY-TCM and to build leadership "buy-in" to the process. In parallel, teachers receive feedback based on standardized observations of their classrooms and their self-reports of measures of their behavior management practices. A structured feedback form is completed collaboratively with the IY-TCM coach to highlight strengths and areas of growth based on the information provided, and teachers are supported in setting targeted goals for their classroom that are linked to IY-TCM learning objectives. They also choose from a menu of options for their work with the IY-TCM coach during daily practice. Dr. Shepard has been piloting this approach in one large Head Start agency, and the data she has collected is promising, demonstrating substantial improvements in classroom practices and staff engagement that are sustained within and across school years.

## USING MI TO SUPPORT PARENT ENGAGEMENT IN PARENTING PROGRAMS

There are many well-established parenting programs for improving parent behavior management practices. When parents participate in these programs, abundant research over the past several decades demonstrates that parents improve their management skills and their children benefit (National Research Council & Institute of Medicine, 2009). These programs have been shown to reduce and prevent even the most severe forms of disruptive behavior problems. The challenge is getting more parents to be willing to participate in such programs. We describe two efforts to achieve this goal.

## MI Plus Coping Power

Over the past few years, Drs. Herman and Reinke have attempted to use MI to increase parent involvement in parenting sessions that are part of the Coping Power (CP) program. CP is an empirically supported indicative preventive intervention for elementary school children showing early signs of aggressive and disruptive behaviors (Lochman & Wells, 1996). The school-based program includes child and parent group interventions to address the sociocontextual risk factors for youth aggression. Although CP is a well-established intervention, engaging parents in the intervention can be difficult, particularly in urban settings. Prior research indicates that parents' participation in three or more sessions is associated with significant improvements in child outcomes; however, the overall level of parent participation tends to be rather low (Wells, Lochman, & Lenhart, 2008).

> They used the Family Check-Up as a platform for delivering the content of Coping Power Parent.

To overcome this problem, Drs. Herman and Reinke worked with colleagues at CPEI to integrate the Family Check-Up (FCU) with the CP Parent program. In particular, they used the FCU as a platform for delivering the content of CP Parent. The goal was to use the FCU as a method for increasing parent engagement in the parenting program. In this model, parents first attend two sessions of the FCU. At the second meeting, the parent receives tailored feedback about his or her parenting behaviors and family communication. The meeting ends with an invitation to select one or more CP Parent modules that fits with the parent's preferences and needs based on the feedback.

A pilot study conducted in a large urban school district with low-income families revealed that parents and school-based consultants found the integrated model to be effective, helpful, and culturally responsive (Herman et al., 2012). Nearly all parents who completed the two-session FCU went on to complete at least one CP module. This contrasted with virtually no parent participation in the CP Parent program in this setting prior to the FCU integration.

## MI Plus Incredible Years Parenting Series

Like CP, the Incredible Years Parenting Series (IY-PS) is a well-established program for intervening with the parents of children who have severe behavior problems. Additionally, IY-PS has been adapted and used as a preventive intervention and shown to prevent severe behavior problems. Dr. Shepard has been working to integrate an MI approach with IY (Shepard, Armstrong, Silver, Berger, & Seifer, 2012) to address the significant problems that also plague this parenting program: low enrollment, poor attendance, and premature program dropout. Rather than tailoring sessions to parent preferences as in the CP integration, Dr. Shepard has left the IY intervention format, dosage, and sequencing of core components intact. Instead, she used MI strategies to bolster parent participation in the entire IY-PS program. The rationale for this is that IY is a group intervention, and reducing it to an individually delivered program to allow parents to attend only specifically selected modules may reduce some of its therapeutic benefits. In Dr. Shepard's model, parents complete a two-session FCU that has been adapted to explicitly assess and target parent readiness to change, including careful assessment of parent beliefs that could undermine engagement (i.e., beliefs about their child, about their role as parents, and about services) and tailored feedback to address those beliefs and attitudes that are serving as barriers to participation. As in the traditional FCU, parents are supported in setting goals for their children and family based on the feedback they receive, and the IY-PS group is then introduced as an option for meeting their goals. The action plan targets IY-PS attendance, including identifying potential barriers to participation like lack of transportation, competing demands, lack of support from family members, and then developing plans to overcome those identified barriers. A randomized pilot trial is currently under way. Initial evidence suggests that the FCU significantly increased parent participation in IY compared to typical enrollment and also compared to a control group.

## USING MI TO BOLSTER ENGAGEMENT AND IMPLEMENTATION IN MULTICOMPONENT INTERVENTIONS

### First Step to Success

Many interventions, including the ones described above, have multiple components that involve parents, teachers, and students. One such program, First Step to Success, is an empirically supported intervention for young children exhibiting early behavior problems at school. First Step includes a school program and a home program. Under the leadership of First Step's senior author (Dr. Hill Walker), Dr. Frey and colleagues (2012) have recently developed enhancements to the original intervention so that the First Step intervention more effectively alters home and school ecologies for more severely impacted students, and increases the likelihood that change is maintained following the intervention. First Step to Success was originally designed as a secondary prevention intervention to target primary grade students with emerging to moderate behavior disorders, rather than students whose challenging behavior is severe and already entrenched across home, school, and community settings. First Step has three modular components: (a) a universal screening and early identification procedure, (b) an adapted school intervention procedure called CLASS (Contingencies for Learning Academic and Social Skills; see Walker & Hops, 1979), and (c) homeBase, which is a family intervention in which parents learn from a coach how to teach school success skills at home. The enhancements Dr. Frey made to the existing First Step to Success intervention components were developed so that the First Step intervention more effectively alters home and school ecologies for more severely impacted students, and increases the likelihood that change is maintained following the intervention.

The enhancements to the First Step intervention include a new home component, called Enhanced homeBase, and the First Step Classroom Check-up

(CCU). The curricula for Enhanced homeBase and the First Step CCU include instructions and resources to assist the coach in implementation. Enhanced homeBase typically takes two to five 60-minute sessions (i.e., home visits), whereas the First Step CCU is typically completed in two to three brief interviews with the teacher in the classroom. The development of the Enhanced homeBase procedures was guided by Dishion and Stormshak's (2007) FCU, and the First Step CCU is based on Reinke, Lewis-Palmer, & Merrell's (2008) CCU model.

Process data indicate the Enhanced homeBase procedures can be implemented with fidelity, are perceived as socially valid by parents and coaches, and are associated with decreases in parental stress and parenting efficacy (Frey, Lee, et al., 2013b). Additionally, process data on the First Step CCU indicate the procedures can be implemented with fidelity, are perceived as socially valid by teachers and coaches, and are associated with increases in teacher rates of attention to positive behavior and improved teacher–student relationships (Lee et al., in press). The extent to which coaches practice MI with proficiency is an important aspect of implementation fidelity for the enhancements. Across parents and teachers, behavior coaches demonstrated acceptable levels of MI proficiency, both with regard to the MI spirit and the use of microskills (Frey, Lee, et al., in press). Finally, pilot study results provide compelling evidence that the First Step intervention, when implemented with the Enhanced homeBase and First Step CCU enhancements, is promising for improving student outcomes on social–behavioral indices, decreasing problem behavior, and improving academic engaged time (Frey, Small, et al., 2013).

## MI Navigation Guide

The application of MI in both the Enhanced homeBase and First Step CCU components of the intervention were based on the MI Navigation Guide (MING; Frey et al., 2013a; Lee et al., in press). The MING is a process for increasing motivation to adopt and implement evidence-based practices in school settings. The MING is a five-step process, illustrated in Figure 9.1, intended to increase parent and teacher motivation to implement the universal principles on which the First Step intervention was designed. The five-step MING process was used as a guide to create procedures, resources, and tools to assist coaches in using MI techniques to increase parent and teacher motivation to adopt and implement these universal principles within the home and school settings, respectively.

> The MING is a process for increasing motivation to adopt and implement evidence-based practices in school settings.

## PRINCIPLES FOR INTEGRATING MI WITH OTHER INTERVENTIONS OR PRACTICES

Based on our experiences described above using MI as an entrée into other programs and practices, we have derived several principles for how to accomplish

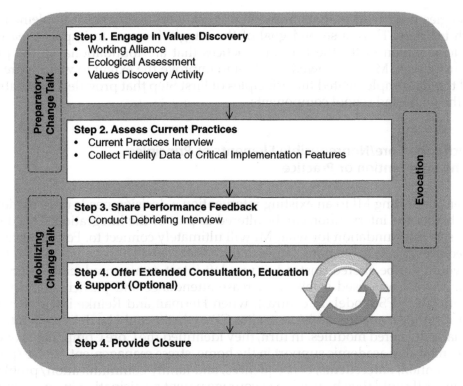

**Figure 9.1** Motivational interviewing navigation guide. Reprinted from Lee et al. (in press) by permission of Eddie McNamara.

Modified from Miller and Moyers (2012).

a successful integration. For illustrative purposes, we describe the First Step enhancements in more detail.

### Identify the Rationale and Goal of the Integration

It is easy to view MI as a panacea for any compliance- or engagement-related problem, but actually it is not. If you are considering using MI to improve implementation of another practice, it is important to take time to reflect on what the existing problem is that MI will be used to overcome, and to carefully consider the goal of integration.

> If you are considering using MI to improve implementation of another practice, it is important to take time to reflect on what the existing problem is that MI will be used to overcome, and to carefully consider the goal of integration.

The initial rationale for First Step enhancements was provided by evidence that the intervention's effects were more variable for children with more severe problems, and that booster sessions were sometimes necessary for the effects to be maintained at 1-year follow-up. Thus, the original goal of using MI was to fortify the home component and to reach families that had perhaps not been represented in research data because they did not agree to participate in homeBase. It became apparent during the project that the motivational strategies used with parents had a high likelihood of success if implemented with teachers. Thus, a second goal of the integration was to improve teacher implementation skills, the teacher practices that are foundational to the program. Overall, MI was viewed as a tool to improve the extent to which parents and teachers implemented the principles of First Step that provide a foundation for the home and school components.

## Specify the Core/Nonreducible Elements or Principles of the Intervention or Practice

When connecting MI to an existing intervention a decision needs to be made as to whether the intervention can be altered as part of the integration. This decision sets the foundation for what MI will ultimately connect to. For instance, as noted previously, in Shepard's integration of MI with IY-PS, it was decided that IY would not be altered. Instead, it was left intact as a nonreducible intervention, and MI was used solely to increase attendance and participation in the traditional IY-PS model. In contrast, when Herman and Reinke integrated MI with CP, they made the decision to alter CP so that it could be delivered in individually delivered modules. In turn, they identified the Core Components of CP as six modules: academic support in the home, stress management, praise/positive attention, antecedents, consequences, and family communication/problem solving. MI could then be used to encourage parent participation in one or more of these modules that matched their preferences and needs. In the First Step enhancements, the home component was modified entirely, but in the school component, the program procedures remain unchanged, and the First Step CCU is an optional supplement. Five universal principles of positive behavior support were identified as central to the First Step intervention: (a) establish clear expectations, (b) directly teach the expectations, (c) reinforce the display of expectations, (d) minimize attention for minor inappropriate behaviors, and (e) establish clear consequences for unacceptable behavior (Frey et al., 2013). Dr. Frey used these in his adapted model.

## Specify the Structure and Assessments for the Integration

The assessment information collected in MI should map onto feedback that is delivered and ultimately effect the intervention options that are available. In the CP integration, therefore, after specifying the modules of CP, assessments were identified that could inform parent decisions about which modules to participate in. Thus, they collected interview, rating scale, and observation assessments that targeted home–school communication, family communication, parent stress management, and parent behavior management. See Table 9.1 for examples of data that were collected that mapped onto the intervention domains of CP.

> The assessment information collected in MI should map onto feedback that is delivered and ultimately effect the intervention options that are available.

**Table 9.1 Core Components of Coping Power and Corresponding Measures**

1. Academic support in the home
   - Structured Interview of Parenting Practices
     - Home-Learning Environment (7 items)
     - Parent–Teacher involvement (7 items)
2. Stress management
   - Daily Hassles (20 items)
   - Life Events Questionnaire (12 items)
3. Positive attention/praise
   - Structured Interview of Parenting Practices
     - Praise (2 items)
     - Play and Involvement (3 items)
   - Alabama Parenting Questionnaire–9
     - Positive Parenting (3 items)
4. Antecedents
   - Structured Interview of Parenting Practices
     - Clear Instructions (2 items)
     - Monitoring/Knowing (6 items)
   - Alabama Parenting Questionnaire–9
     - Supervision (3 items)
5. Consequences
   - Structured Interview of Parenting Practices
     - Consistency (4 items)
   - Alabama Parenting Questionnaire–9
     - Inconsistent Discipline (3 items)
6. Family cohesion and problem solving
   - Structured Interview of Parenting Practices
     - View of Child (4 items)
   - Child Parent Relationship Scale (15 items)
   - Family Relation Scale (5 items)

In Enhanced First Step, the assessments mapped onto the five universal principles. Frey and colleagues created rating forms that tapped each of these domains for parents and teachers. His team then created feedback and planning forms connected to these principles (see Handouts 9.1 to 9.6). The developers made an intentional decision to exclude standardized, norm-referenced instrumentation, instead relying on researcher-developed tools to assess and facilitate the self-assessment of the five universal principles. All measures and tools are provided within the procedural manual (Frey et al., 2013). For instance, in Enhanced homeBase and the First Step CCU assessment process parents and teachers complete a self-assessment of how well they were doing on each of the universal principles (Handouts 9.1 and 9.2). Additionally, a consultant conducts classroom observations focused on assessing these principles using the tool in Handout 9.3. Frey and colleagues also use a case conceptualization form (Handout 9.4) to integrate their assessment data and to prepare for feedback meetings. In these meetings, they use the change plan forms given in Handouts 9.5 and 9.6 for guiding the planning process with parents and teachers, respectively. Each of these forms illustrates how the principles of MI and the forms for each MI process can be tailored to any new application.

## Collect Data to Determine Whether the Integration Addressed Your Goal

After implementing the integrating model, it is important to collect process data to determine whether the integration accomplished your goal. Often these are proximal outcomes believed to mediate the main outcomes the intervention is designed to impact. Some examples of process data and proximal outcomes that could be collected include: (a) parent attendance, (b) teacher implementation of the universal principles, (c) coach–parent, alliance and (d) parental efficacy. Additionally, it is a good idea to collect social validity data from participants (teachers, consultants, parents, and students) to get their perceptions of the integrated model in terms of goals of the intervention, acceptability and feasibility of the procedures, perceptions of effectiveness (helpful, useful, impactful), and overall satisfaction.

## Refine the Integrated Model as Needed Based on the Data

Use the data you collected to guide improvements to your model. In all of the examples described previously, the integrated models went through an iterative process in which the assessments, interviews, and feedback components were repeatedly improved based on consultant and consultee feedback. Final forms and procedures were then documented in structured intervention manuals that others could use and duplicate.

## SUMMARY

MI can be used to support the implementation process for any new school-based intervention. As the examples in this chapter illustrate, MI provides a solid foundation and framework for guiding the integration of existing interventions or simply increasing adherence to an established program or set of practices. For any practice that does not directly address the motivational aspects of its use or implementation, MI is a logical and compatible approach to enhance motivation.

# Handouts and Forms

### HANDOUT 9.1 ENHANCED FIRST STEP:
### UNIVERSAL PRINCIPLES PARENT SELF-ASSESSMENT

| Establish Clear Expectations | |
|---|---|
| ✓ Expectations are clear (specific behaviors).<br>✓ Expectations are explained positively and reviewed frequently.<br>✓ Expectations are reviewed just before difficult times (visits to the store, important events, at the beginning of a game). | Rate Yourself:<br><br>How well do you make use of clear expectations?<br><br>○ Not very well at all　○ Could do better　○ Well enough　○ Very well |

| Directly Teach the Expectations | |
|---|---|
| ✓ Expectations are taught in small steps, with very clear definitions.<br>✓ Role-play, demonstrations, examples of the right and wrong way, and make-believe play are used to teach expectations. | Rate Yourself:<br><br>How well do you teach your expectations?<br><br>○ Not very well at all　○ Could do better　○ Well enough　○ Very well |

| Reinforce the Display of Expectations | |
|---|---|
| ✓ Praise is used to reinforce the expectations when you notice appropriate behavior (even small steps).<br>✓ Reward activities are used (one-on-one time, special events, fun activities).<br>✓ More praise is used than reprimands. | Rate Yourself:<br><br>How well do you reinforce expectations?<br><br>○ Not very well at all　○ Could do better　○ Well enough　○ Very well |

## Minimize Attention for Minor Inappropriate Behaviors

| | |
|---|---|
| ✓ Behavior that is just a little annoying or irritating is ignored, in favor of... <br> ✓ Appropriate behavior is noticed more often than inappropriate behavior. | **Rate Yourself:** <br><br> Do you minimize attention for inappropriate behavior? <br><br> ○    ○    ○    ○ <br> No, not at all   Could do better   Well enough   Very much so |

## Establish Clear Consequences for Unacceptable Behavior

| | |
|---|---|
| ✓ Consequences are planned for ahead of time. Everyone knows the consequences for inappropriate behavior. <br> ✓ There are different consequences depending on how severe the inappropriate behavior is. <br> ✓ Consequences are logical and thoughtful. Not created when emotions are running high. | **Rate Yourself:** <br><br> How well do you make use of clear consequences? <br><br> ○    ○    ○    ○ <br> Not very well at all   Could do better   Well enough   Very well |

## HANDOUT 9.2 ENHANCED FIRST STEP: UNIVERSAL PRINCIPLES TEACHER OVERVIEW AND SELF-ASSESSMENT

| Establish Clear Expectations | |
|---|---|
| ✓ Expectations are clear (specific behaviors).<br>✓ Expectations are stated positively and reviewed periodically (e.g., class meetings).<br>✓ Expectations are restated prior to potentially difficult times (transitions, special events). | **Rate Yourself:**<br>How well do you make use of clear expectations?<br><br>○     ○     ○     ○<br>Not very   Could do   Well   Very well<br>well at all   better   enough |

| Directly Teach the Expectations | |
|---|---|
| ✓ Expectations are explicitly and directly taught in the settings in which they occur.<br>✓ Expectations are taught through role-play and demonstrations using positive and negative examples. | **Rate Yourself:**<br>How well do you teach your expectations?<br><br>○     ○     ○     ○<br>Not very   Could do   Well   Very well<br>well at all   better   enough |

| Reinforce the Display of the Expectations | |
|---|---|
| ✓ Expectations are positively reinforced informally (e.g., personal notes, one to one, notes home) to reinforce new skills.<br>✓ Expectations are reinforced formally (e.g., graphs, charts, reward activities).<br>✓ More praise is used than reprimands. | **Rate Yourself:**<br>How well do you reinforce expectations?<br><br>○     ○     ○     ○<br>Not very   Could do   Well   Very well<br>well at all   better   enough |

| Minimize Attention for Minor Inappropriate Behaviors | |
|---|---|
| ✓ Minor rule infractions are precorrected through reviews of the expectations.<br>✓ Behavior that is just a little annoying or irritating is ignored, in favor of . . .<br>✓ Appropriate behavior is noticed more often than inappropriate behavior. | **Rate Yourself:**<br>Do you minimize attention for inappropriate behavior?<br><br>○     ○     ○     ○<br>Not very   Could do   Well   Very well<br>well at all   better   enough |

| Establish Clear Consequences | |
|---|---|
| ✓ A systematic plan exists for the entire class that consists of a hierarchy of consequences for when expectations are violated.<br>✓ Consequences for inappropriate behavior are individualized (when appropriate).<br>✓ Consequences are logical and thoughtful. Not created when emotions are running high. | Rate Yourself:<br><br>How well do you make use of clear consequences?<br><br>○　　　　○　　　　○　　　　○<br>Not very　Could do　Well　Very well<br>well at all　better　enough |

# HANDOUT 9.3 ENHANCED FIRST STEP: TEACHER OBSERVATION OF THE UNIVERSAL PRINCIPLES CODING FORM

**Reinforce the Display of Expectations** (Attending to Appropriate Behaviors)

|  |  | Focus Student | Peer | Class |
|---|---|---|---|---|
| **General** | *Verbal* |  |  |  |
|  | *Non-verbal* |  |  |  |
| **Specific** | *Verbal* |  |  |  |

Behaviors in conflict with **Minimize Attention for Minor Inappropriate Behaviors** (Attending to Inappropriate Behavior)

|  |  | Focus Student | Peer | Class |
|---|---|---|---|---|
| **General** | *Verbal* |  |  |  |
|  | *Non-verbal* |  |  |  |
| **Specific** | *Verbal* |  |  |  |

**Establish Clear Expectations:** ____Yes ____No
**Comments:**

**Directly Teach the Expectations:** ____Yes ____No
**Comments:**

**Establish Clear Consequences for Unacceptable Behavior:** ____Yes ____No
**Comments:**

Student & Family Name: _____

School: _____

Teacher: _____

Date: _____

## HANDOUT 9.4 ENHANCED FIRST STEP: CASE CONCEPTUALIZATION SHEET

Family Values:

Strengths of the **Student**:

Strengths of the **Family**:

Family Check-Up Assessment Results/Notes:

Caregiver Assessment of Important Student Behaviors:

Teacher Assessment of Important Student Behaviors:

Self-Assessment of Important Caregiver Behaviors:

Student & Family Name: _____

Possible Change Plan Focus:

Assessment of Importance:

    1   2   3   4   5   6   7   8   9   10

Assessment of Confidence:

    1   2   3   4   5   6   7   8   9   10

Barriers:

Resources:

## HANDOUT 9.5 ENHANCED FIRST STEP: PARENT CHANGE PLAN

| | |
|---|---|
| Establish Clear Expectations | |
| Directly Teach the Expectations | |
| Reinforce Displays of the Expectations | |
| Minimize Attention for Inappropriate Behavior | |
| Establish Clear Consequences | |

| Teacher Values: | |
| --- | --- |
| Specific Goals: | |
| **Maintenance Observations (Schedule and Notes)** | |
| The most **important** reason for making this change and meeting this goal is:<br><br><br>**Importance Rating (1 to 10)** | One reason that I am **confident** is:<br><br><br>**Confidence Rating (1 to 10)** |
| **Resources Support:** | |

# 10

# Learning Motivational Interviewing and Monitoring Implementation Quality

Where are you now in terms of reflecting on your own skills in using motivational interviewing (MI)? How would you like to use MI in the future and continue to develop your skills? For many of you, the answers to these questions will be that you are in the early stages of learning MI and want to continue practicing using the skills in everyday conversations. For others who came to this book with some background in MI or for those committed to using MI in more advanced applications, the answers to these questions will be in line with becoming more fluent in MI.

> How do we ensure that we are doing MI correctly or at least doing it well enough to make a difference?

Using a program or a practice like MI as it was intended is referred to as implementation fidelity. A key fidelity question for all of us is how do we ensure that we are doing MI correctly or at least doing it well enough to make a difference? In this chapter, we explore the range of ways to assess and monitor fidelity and to move you forward in your skill development.

School professionals who intend to become fully fluent in the method, beyond simply engaging in everyday conversations about change, will need to use tools for monitoring their MI skills. School administrators may decide to assign one or two people in a building to develop this level of proficiency in MI. School systems will need to establish socially valid infrastructures that produce personnel who can practice MI competently. Unfortunately, as important as implementation quality is to affecting behaviors, many questions remain: How much training, supervision, and practice are required to practice MI proficiently? What level of competence is "good enough?" and What standards should be used to evaluate proficiency? These are all long-standing questions that apply to any evidence-based intervention or practice, like MI.

A variety of resources exist for learning MI and for monitoring implementation quality. However, many of the resources that exist were developed by and for substance abuse and mental health counselors and health professionals and, therefore, are not specific to the application of MI in school settings. Fortunately, many relevant lessons about learning and monitoring implementation quality have been gleaned from over a decade of research in the fields of substance abuse, mental health, and health. Additionally, a few school-based research teams have begun developing and modifying existing interventions based on the MI approach. New professional development systems to train school personnel are emerging as are resources to support ongoing supervision and professional development efforts and evaluate quality of implementation. This chapter addresses learning MI and measuring quality of implementation, or MI proficiency in school-based settings. The tools in this section range from simple and brief self-assessments to intensive video-based review and coding of MI skills. You may elect to use any or all of these based on your own level of MI skills and your goals for continued development.

As you read this chapter, reflect on your stage of development with regard to MI skills. If you are a beginner, completely new to MI, consider the next steps you would like to take to incorporate the method into your daily interactions. This might involve setting goals for yourself to use one or more MI methods over time. Focus on additional training or resources you would like to access to support your goal and any tools you might use to assess your progress. If you are an advanced MI user, you might consider setting goals for yourself as well. However, your attention will be on using some of the implementation quality tools to self-assess and also to get feedback on your MI-skill development. Use Handout 10.1 MI Professional Development Planning Sheet to self-assess your progress and develop a plan for improvement.

## LEARNING MI

Although easy to understand conceptually, practicing MI proficiently (i.e., accurately and when indicated) requires ongoing practice and feedback. The use of MI in school settings is relatively new. The context of schools is substantially different from the medical and clinical–mental health contexts in which consultants using this approach have traditionally worked. Lee et al. (in press) identified the following challenges in school-based applications of MI: (a) the identification of teacher target behaviors for change, (b) lack of training in client-centered skills, and (c) time constraints of teachers. Regarding target behaviors, evocation requires a specific target behavior, and identifying and focusing on appropriate target behaviors for teachers can be a difficult task. Additionally, unlike medical or counseling settings, where people come prepared to talk about themselves and their own behavior problems, in schools, adults (teachers and parents) generally want to focus on a child's behavior problems and are not initially interested in changing

> Although easy to understand conceptually, practicing MI proficiently (i.e., accurately and when indicated) requires ongoing practice and feedback.

their own behavior. Further, the foundational skills discussed in the next section may be common for those learning MI in human service settings to have mastered, but less common among school personnel. Finally, teachers and other school professionals have many demands on their time and are often unable to schedule lengthy or frequent meetings to discuss change plans; thus it is not only important to be able to use MI proficiently, it is important to be able to use it efficiently.

## Training Options

The Motivational Interviewing Network of Trainers (MINT) serves as a primary vehicle to create a pool of qualified instructors using a Train the Trainers model. A brief review of the research on training in MI finds medical personnel and community mental health and substance abuse counselors to be common participants in MI trainings. These trainings frequently use lecture and interactive methods such as role-plays, group work, and modeling. Systematic reviews of MI trainings are mixed, with some (see Madson, Loignon, & Lane, 2009; Walters, Matson, Baer, & Ziedonis, 2005) suggesting trainings yield only moderate gains in practice skills, and that these skills degrade rapidly following MI-training workshops, and others (see Söderlund, Madson, Rubak, & Nilsen, 2011) suggesting the results are generally favorable. All of these reviews, however, are critical of the existing literature because prior studies provide minimal descriptions of training methods, limited measurement of participant change over time, and use pre–post designs without psychometrically validated measures. Further, few studies report on individual performance feedback and coaching to improve the acquisition of clinical skills, which may be a necessary element for the maintenance of MI skills learned in these settings and for the improvement of the clinical skill necessary for application in authentic practice settings (Miller, Sorensen, Selzer, & Brigham, 2006). A unique feature of systems that include individual performance feedback and coaching is that learning MI is viewed as an active process that involves practicing, reflecting, and applying the skills in authentic practice settings.

Training methods to maximize the likelihood that consultants learn to use empirically supported mental health treatments with competency have been the focus of policy (Miller et al., 2006; Reickmann, Kovas, Fussell, & Stettler, 2009) and training evaluations (Beidas & Kendall, 2010; Madson et al., 2009). Current literature regarding various training methodologies for learning to implement mental health treatments competently provides a distinction between those that are effective and those that may not be. Self-study and even full-day workshops are not enough to become fully fluent in a method (Baer et al., 2004; Davis, 1998; Miller et al., 2004; Miller, Yahne, Moyers, Martinez, & Pirritano, 2004; Sholomskas et al., 2005; Walters et al., 2005). These methods can lead to perceptual or attitudinal changes and initial skill development. But to become fully fluent, expert-led workshops followed by supervised supervision comprised of feedback and coaching are generally needed (Andrzejewski, Kirby, Morral, & Inguchi, 2001; Miller et al., 2004; Morgenstern, Morgan, McCrady, Keller, & Carroll, 2001). Train the trainer is another method that has shown promise for the successful teaching and learning of empirically supported practices (Addis, Wade, & Hatgis, 1999; Fixsen, Naoom, Blasé, Freidman, & Wallace, 2005). With this method, practitioners from an agency are trained by experts and they then return to their agency to train, supervise, and monitor staff members' use of the method. Both the expert training and train-the-trainers approaches using 15 hours within a workshop format, followed by four to six individual training and coaching sessions, have been effective in teaching community practitioners to use MI proficiently (Martino et al., 2011).

Although there are currently no published studies evaluating training systems to train educators, it is reasonable to assume educators with basic counseling skills will likely need a similar amount and type of training and coaching as consultants in mental health settings and more if their foundational skills are less developed. Using the examples and resources from *motivationalinterviewing.org*, a few training resources have been developed and pilot tested for assisting school personnel to learn MI. Although the general approach is similar to that promoted by MINT, these trainings include examples and activities relevant to school-based consultation and coaching, and can be easily adapted depending on the extent to which participants have the foundational skills of MI practice. For example, a Motivational Interviewing Training and Support (MITS) program was recently implemented with 12 early-childhood consultants in Louisville, KY, via a Head Start Mental Health Consultation contract. The purpose of the MITS is to increase school-based consultants' MI proficiency. The MITS includes the following components: (a) 15 hours of interactive instruction (i.e., workshops) as endorsed by MINT (Miller & Rollnick, 2002) that involved, among other learning activities, watching and discussing audio- and video-recorded examples of interventionists implementing MI within the context of educational consultation followed by structured role-plays (Lane, Hood, & Rollnick, 2008); (b) three individual consultations within the expert consultation framework (Martino et al., 2011); and (c) one group debriefing session. Participants completed several instruments that were revised for use within the context of school-based consultation. These measures include (a) Motivational Interviewing Knowledge and Attitudes Test (MIKAT; Leffingwell, 2006), (b) the Written Assessment of Simulated Encounters–School-Based Applications (WASE-SBA; Lee, Frey, & Small, 2013), and (c) the Video Assessment of Simulated Encounters–School-Based Applications (VASE-SBA; Lee, Small, & Frey, 2013). A revised version of the Motivational Interviewing Treatment Integrity (MITI) code (Moyers et al., 2007) was used to provide individualized feedback to participants using the elicit–provide–elicit framework. Although the intensity and training required to have school personnel become proficient requires further study, this initial attempt suggests: (a) baseline MI proficiency was quite low among participants, (b) the MITS is socially valid, and (c) the procedures resulted in substantial increases from baseline to post-test on the revised versions of the MIKAT, WASE-SBA, and VASE-SBA.

## MONITORING MI QUALITY

Fortunately, a variety of evaluation tools exist to monitor proficiency and to provide feedback during individual and group supervision meetings. These strategies are discussed in this section. Fidelity, or the extent to which an intervention is delivered as intended, was once believed to be one dimensional, either people used a method correctly or not. However, it is now widely recognized as a more nuanced construct with many different aspects (Dane & Schneider, 1998; Fixsen et al., 2005; Jones, Clarke, & Power, 2008). One popular way of thinking about fidelity describes it as being composed of five different qualities (adherence, exposure, quality, participant responsiveness, and program differentiation), any of which can be done well or done poorly (Dane & Schneider, 1998). The key idea here is that it is important to reflect on your MI practice.

Focus on the tools themselves and ways you might use one or more to evaluate your skill development or that of your colleagues.

Below, we describe several tools that you might find useful to assess your MI skill development over time, including available options to measure knowledge and MI quality. The details regarding how these tools have been modified for use in school settings are provided when available. We provide extensive descriptions of each tool, including its psychometric properties (e.g., research showing how reliable and valid it is) for readers to make informed decisions about their use of existing measures of MI fidelity. If your interest is more cursory, feel free to skim over the psychometric details. Instead, focus on the tools themselves and ways you might use one or more to evaluate your skill development or that of your colleagues.

## Knowledge

The MIKAT is a brief, paper-and-pencil test containing 14 true/false questions representing a combination of myths and MI-consistent principles and concepts and multiple-choice questions. Additionally, Martino, Haeseler, Belitsky, Pantalon, and Fortin Iv (2007) developed a nine-item, multiple-choice test to evaluate students' knowledge, attitude, confidence, and commitment of brief MI principles and practices. This measure has been modified for school professionals. See Handout 10.2 for an example of an MI knowledge measure and Handout 10.3 for the answer key.

## MI Quality or Proficiency

The evaluation of MI quality can be done with global ratings scales, but most often requires coding of practice samples, conducted via live observation, videotape, or audiotape of interactions between a consultant and a "client" (e.g., teacher, parents, or children); standardized protocols have also been used to control for confounding variables (i.e., client differences) that can affect MI quality. When coding video- or audio-recordings for supervision, the entire session should be coded. However, when completed for research, it is standard practice to randomly select the starting point and code for 20 minutes. Although self-ratings have been used (see Hartzler, Baer, Dunn, Rosengren, & Wells, 2007), having one or more experts in MI (who are independent of the research project) code practice samples is ideal. We have divided the presentation of tools to evaluate MI proficiency, whether for performance feedback or research, into those we believe are best suited for assessing proficiency for those who are using foundational skills and MI spirit in everyday conversations about change or advanced applications of MI that involve use of the foundational skills strategically within the context of the four MI processes.

*Foundational Skills and MI Spirit*

In our experience, we have found that certain foundational skills and the spirit that encompasses the use of MI can be applied during everyday conversations about change in a variety of settings and with teachers, administrators, parents, and students. The foundational skills, discussed in Chapter 3, are represented by the acronym OARS: Open-ended questions, affirmations, reflections, and summaries, and also include informing and advising. The MI spirit includes partnership, acceptance, compassion, and evocation. Although using these skills and adopting the MI spirit alone does not constitute proficient MI practice, MI cannot be done well without these important aspects of the approach.

> The take-home message from this finding is that it is a good idea to focus first on your basic listening and relationship skills as you are learning MI.

There is some empirical support for the importance of foundational skills and the MI spirit. For example, two randomized controlled trials found that baseline counseling skills were highly predictive of learning MI and later using it (Miller, Yahne, Moyers, Martinez, & Pirritano, 2004; Moyers et al., 2009). These results are likely to be just as important in educational settings, and this is consistent with our experiences. Additionally, empathy, an important aspect of acceptance, is highly related to the successful use of MI (Miller, Hedrick, & Orlofsky, 1991). The take-home message from this finding is that it is a good idea to focus first on your basic listening and relationship skills as you are learning MI.

Three common and well-established instruments for monitoring basic MI proficiency include the (a) Motivational Interviewing Treatment Integrity Tool (MITI; Moyers, Martin, Manuel, Hendrickson, & Miller, 2005), (b) Video Assessment of Simulated Encounters–Revised (VASE-R; Bell & Cole, 2008), and (c) Helpful Response Questionnaire (HRQ; Martino et al., 2007).

*MITI Tool*

The MITI (Moyers et al., 2005) is designed for providing evaluative performance feedback and to measure fidelity in the context of applied research and supervision. Descriptions, examples, and scoring rubrics are used to more rigorously define the exact nature of directive use. The MITI allows for independent coding of MI across five global dimensions (evocation, collaboration, autonomy/support, direction, and empathy); evocation, collaboration, and autonomy/support are frequently combined to produce a global spirit rating. Additionally, each consultant utterance is coded as one of the following: (a) close-ended question, (b) open-ended question, (c) simple reflection, (d) complex reflection, (e) MI-adherent, (f) MI-nonadherent, and (g) information. Beginning proficiency and competency thresholds are provided for five summary scores: (a) global spirit rating, (b) percentage of complex reflections, (c) percentage of open questions, (d) reflection-to-question ratio, and (e) percentage of MI Adherence. It is important to note that these thresholds are based on expert opinion. These benchmarks lack normative or other validity data to support them and have been established within the context of clinical counseling contexts, largely in the field of substance use/abuse treatment. The MITI demonstrates adequate psychometric properties (Moyers et al., 2005).

### VASE-R

The VASE-R only contains global ratings and does not require audio- or videotaped interactions. Instead, the VASE-R is a group-administered measure for assessing MI skills. It consists of three video-recorded vignettes of actors portraying substance abusers (Rosengren, Baer, Hartzler, Dunn, & Wells, 2005). Each vignette includes a number of statements by a hypothetical client, between which the recording is paused and respondents are asked to provide written responses to six questions that are consistent with MI principles. Responses are coded on a 3-point system, with response options including: 0, *confrontational or likely to engender resistance*; 1, *neutral or inaccurately represents the content of the client's speech*; and 2, *accurately reflects the content of the client's speech*. After evaluating the VASE-R's psychometric properties, Rosengren, Hartzler, Baer, Wells, and Dunn (2008) suggested an 18-item scale with five subscales: reflective listening, responding to resistance, summarizing, eliciting change talk, and developing discrepancy; although they recommended that scale interpretation for the vignettes and subscale components be made cautiously. Recently, the VASE-R was modified for school personnel. In addition to creating vignettes of school-based consultations, the coding structure was modified to improve what has traditionally been poor interrater reliability and to reflect the latest conceptualization of MI (Lee, Frey, & Small, 2013).

### HRQ

Like the VASE-R, the HRQ does not require audio- or videotaped sessions from the learners' actual practice. The HRQ presents six hypothetical client statements in written form, and asks the respondent to write down what he or she would say next. Each response is rated based on the occurrence or nonoccurrence of open- and close-ended questions, reflections, and MI nonadherent statements. Additionally, each response is rated, using a 5-point scale, based on the quality of empathy and the omission or presence of communication roadblocks. The scale has high interrater agreement (Martino et al., 2007). The HRQ has also recently been revised. The revised version, the WASE-SBA, is relevant to school consultants and updated to reflect more recent conceptualizations of MI (Lee, Small, & Frey, 2013).

### Advanced MI Applications

A few more sophisticated systems, designed to evaluate the strategic use of MI skills, include the (a) Motivational Interviewing Skills Code (MISC; Moyers, Martin, Cately, Harris, & Ahluwalia, 2003), (b) Behaviour Change Counselling Index (BECCI; Lane, 2002; Lane, Hood, & Rollnick, 2008), (c) Independent Tape Rating Scale (ITRS; Gibbons et al., 2010), and (d) *Motivational Interviewing Assessment: Supervisory Tools for Enhancing Proficiency* (*MIA: STEP*; Martino et al., 2006).

### MISC 2.1

The MISC uses two methods for quantifying therapist–client interactions, which are assessed during independent evaluations of a segment of audio- or videotape. During the first evaluation, the evaluator assigns a global score for several dimensions related to consultant behavior and client behavior. Consultants are rated on three dimensions, acceptance, empathy, and overall adherence to the spirit of MI. Clients are rated on self-exploration, which the authors note is a dimension closely related to the construct of experiencing found in the client-centered therapy literature. During the second evaluation, frequency counts of specific behaviors (15 consultant behaviors, 4 of which have subcategory ratings) and the categorization of client language within change and sustain talk categories are rated. The detailed client language coding structure of the MISC 2.1 includes content definitions for the client's language parsing client utterances into subcodes for reason (desire, ability, need), commitment (other, taking steps, neutral), and assigning a rating of the relative strength of the talk (high, medium, low). During the second evaluation, or "pass," the complexity of these behavior codes often requires attention to coding consultant utterances first, and an additional "pass" for the categorization of client language. Moyers, Martin, Catley, Harris, and Jasjit (2003) report that psychometric support for the MISC is adequate.

### BECCI

The BECCI is a measure of behavior-change counseling, developed in 2002 by a group of MI practitioners and trainers. The BECCI is a brief measure of practitioner skillfulness using MI strategies. It was created to assess consultations in health care settings. Unlike the MITI and MISC, the BECCI contains only global ratings, as opposed to global ratings and behavior counts. The BECCI contains 11 items that are evaluated on a Likert-type scale from 0 *not at all* to 4 *a great extent*. An overall composite score may also be obtained. The rater judges whether the practitioner speaks for *more than half the time, about half the time,* or *less than half the time.* To use the BECCI, the evaluator should have knowledge of behavior-change counseling and be well versed in the BECCI checklist; the manual provided required readings and a video that is required. It has acceptable levels of internal consistency (Lane et al., 2008).

That the instrument was developed for health care-based consultations is an advantage, as this context is more consistent with school-based consultations than are clinical counseling sessions. It is also possible that higher interrater reliability scores can be attributed to comprising only global ratings.

### ITRS

The ITRS (Martino, Ball, Nich, Frankforter, & Carroll, 2009) is a 39-item scale adapted from the Yale Adherence and Competence Scale (Carroll, Nich, Sifry, Nuro, & Frankforter, 2000). It was originally developed to evaluate community program therapists' adherence and competence in implementing motivational enhancement therapies (MET), a manualized version of MI (Miller & Rollnick, 2002) that was originally developed for Project MATCH (Miller, Zweben, DiClemente, & Rychtarik, 1992). The ITRS measures consultants' frequency of use and competence in implementing MI (Ball, Martino, Corvino, Morganstern, & Carroll, 2002; Gibbons et al., 2010). The measure consists of 10 MI-consistent items, rated along two 7-point Likert-type scales; the extent to which the therapist delivered the intervention (adherence; 1 = *not at all,* to 7 = *extensively*) and, the skill with which the therapist delivered the intervention (competence; 1 = *very poor,* to 7 = *excellent*). In previous studies (i.e., Ball et al., 2007; Carroll et al., 2006), consultants who were rated average or above on five or more of the items were considered competent.

### MIA: STEP

The *MIA: STEP* consists of 10 MI-consistent behaviors and six MI-inconsistent behaviors that are assigned a rating along two continuums: frequency/extensiveness and competence/skill. There are also two general ratings of client motivation. The manual also includes guidance for providing feedback to consultants based on their performance.

### SCHOOL-BASED MI FIDELITY MEASURES

There have only been a few examples of fidelity measures being applied within the context of school-based adaptations of MI research. Specifically, an adapted version of the MITI was used to evaluate the proficiency of behavioral coaches as part of an IES-funded development and innovation grant to create an enhanced version of the First Step to Success early intervention program. Fidelity measures specific to the Family Check-Up (FCU) and Classroom Check-Up—which also rely on MI—have also been used.

## MI Proficiency for First-Step Coaches

Researchers at the University of Louisville and Oregon Research Institute used a revised version of the MITI to evaluate MI proficiency of behavioral coaches implementing the Tertiary First Step to Success intervention. This version of the intervention includes a new home component, called Tertiary homeBase, and was also implemented with an additional school component, called the First Step Classroom Check-Up. To capture the MI proficiency of the behavioral coaches, the coaches were assessed using a modified version of the MITI[1] (see Frey et al., 2013). Interclass correlations (ICC) were computed for 20 (67%) of the audio recordings. The ICC for the global spirit rating was .47. The ICCs for closed and open-ended questions were .91 and .90, respectively. Simple, complex, and total reflections yielded ICCs of .51, .27, and .73, respectively.

Coaches exceeded the competency criteria for the global spirit rating ($M = 4.33$, $SD = .57$). Mean scores for five of the global dimensions ranged from 4.07 (Understand and Reflect; $SD = .74$) to 4.26 (Expert Role and Collaboration; $SD = .76$). Additionally, coaches met the beginning proficiency level for Reflection-to-Question Ratio with a mean ratio of 1.82 ($SD = 1.49$) and for Percentage of Open-Ended Questions with an average of 56% ($SD = .24$) across the 30 audio-recorded sessions.

## Implementation Fidelity to Check-Ups

In addition to assessing MI implementation, Check-Ups usually include procedural checklists that ask coaches to self-assess whether they completed each of the Check-Up components. Recently, Smith, Dishion, Shaw, and Wilson (in press) developed a more specific approach to considering fidelity to the FCU. They refer to the five essential elements of FCU fidelity with the acronym COACH: (a) Conceptual understanding of the model, (b) Observant and responsive to client interactions, (c) Actively structures sessions, (d) Carefully teaches and provides corrective feedback, and (e) Harnesses motivation and hope. This team has developed an extensive coding manual to assess implementation of each of these qualities. The coding system includes specific types of language that would occur during meetings that would indicate compliance with each element. For instance, an example of speech demonstrating conceptual understanding of the FCU model during a family meeting would be, "based on our observations and information we collected from you, increasing your use of positive strategies with Juan makes a lot of sense."

## SELF-REFLECTION

Miller and Moyers defined eight tasks for learning MI. Learning these tasks need not occur in sequence as some of them you may have already mastered

---

[1] For this version, the revised global dimensions were as follows: (a) Expert Role and Collaboration; (b) Control, Autonomy, and Choice; (c) Direct Client Language; (d) Understand and Reflect; and (e) Evocation.

prior to reading this book. To be fluent in MI, however, requires that you learn to do each of these tasks well. We have altered the language of some of these tasks here:

1. Conveying the MI spirit
2. Using OARS
3. Catching yourself (rolling with resistance)
4. Recognizing/reinforcing change talk
5. Evoking change talk
6. Developing a change plan
7. Consolidating commitments
8. Integrating MI with other treatments.

There are many ways you might continue to improve your skills related to each of these tasks. First, explore the wide range of MI resources that are readily available. MI-related websites offer excellent resources, including training manuals, handouts, videos, and self-development tools (http://www.motivationalinterviewing.org and http://www.motivationalinterview.org). There are also many excellent books on the topic of MI. You might start by rereading this book and, if you haven't already, actually do some of the recommended exercises this time! Second, consider attending a 1- or 2-day training on MI. The MI websites can give you training dates. Third, you might identify colleagues who share your interest in MI and establish a learning group. This might include reading and discussing MI books and/or giving each other feedback about your MI skill development. Fourth, consider taping and coding some of your consultation conversations. Try using one or more of the fidelity tools described previously to help with your coding and understanding of MI skills. You might try this on your own or in partnership with a colleague. Fifth, observe others doing MI and coding their behaviors for MI-consistent and MI-inconsistent responses. You can order reasonably priced videos from MI websites, purchase "The Method of Motivational Interviewing" by Stephen Rollnick (DVD), or you can watch examples on YouTube by searching for "MI." Finally, you might also contact an MI expert and ask him or her to be a consultant for you. You can find the names and contact information for MI trainers on various websites.

Now take a moment to reflect on your personal development of MI skills for each of the MI tasks. Use Handout 10.1 to identify your strengths and areas of growth. Also, consider which training opportunities might best be suited to helping you in your development. Finally, set a goal for yourself to continue to advance your MI skills.

*One word of caution*: As you set your own goals for skill development, be mindful of the research on what is necessary for people to become fluent in MI. One study found that consultants could learn the spirit of MI and apply basic MI skills from a range of professional development approaches, including full-day workshops and reading books. However, high-quality use of MI over time required a period of ongoing consultation or supervision with an MI trainer. Additionally, although many people were able to increase their use of MI-consistent responses (OARS) even in relatively brief training experiences, few people were able to reduce the use of MI-inconsistent responses (e.g., the righting reflex, educating, directing) without some form of ongoing feedback). The lesson from this research is that to improve your MI skills it will take a concerted effort for you to learn to undo your intuitive, MI-inconsistent responses. Recall from earlier chapters that our gut response to sustain talk (formerly called resistance) is usually counterproductive and inconsistent with MI. To unlearn this you will likely need some form of ongoing feedback that includes listening to tapes of your conversations. We refer to this key stage of learning MI as the catch yourself phase. This is when you first start becoming aware that in the midst of conversation your intuitive response will not be MI consistent; you will then be able to successfully interrupt it. At first it may be an awkward and external (e.g., with you saying aloud, "Wait" or "I'm not going to ask that" or simply having an extended pause during which you decide on an alternate response; see the example in Chapter 5); gradually with practice this becomes an easier and more internal process.

> The lesson from this research is that to improve your MI skills it will take a concerted effort for you to learn to undo your intuitive, MI-inconsistent responses.

> After reading an MI book or attending a training session, many people overestimate their MI skills and underestimate their need for additional training or practice. Try to avoid that trap as you reflect on your next steps.

One other important note from prior research is that experiencing MI through books or trainings comes with one potential downside. Miller et al. (2004) found that people who received some form of MI training (via books or workshops) were actually less likely to seek out additional MI training in the future than those not exposed to the training. Miller and Rollnick (2013) refer to this as the overconfidence trap. That is, it appears that after reading an MI book or attending a training session, many people overestimate their MI skills and underestimate their need for additional training or practice. Try to avoid that trap as you reflect on your next steps.

## SUMMARY

The ability of school personnel to learn to use the MI approach competently is an area of research that is likely to receive a great deal of attention over the next decade. As a result, careful and systematic attention must be given to systems that can support school personnel in learning this approach. Efforts to develop and evaluate the effectiveness of systems to teach school personnel the foundational skills and MI spirit, as well as advanced applications of MI, are currently in process. Additionally, the fidelity measures described in this chapter provide a solid foundation.

# Handouts and Forms

## HANDOUT 10.1 MI PERSONAL DEVELOPMENT PLANNING SHEET

| MI Strengths? | MI Areas for Growth? |
|---|---|
| ☐ MI Spirit<br>    ☐ Partnership<br>    ☐ Acceptance<br>    ☐ Compassion<br>    ☐ Evocation<br>☐ OARS<br>    ☐ Asking open-ended questions<br>    ☐ Giving affirmations<br>    ☐ Using reflections<br>        ○ Simple<br>        ○ Complex<br>    ☐ Providing summaries<br>☐ Change talk<br>    ☐ Hearing change talk<br>    ☐ Evoking change talk<br>☐ Developing discrepancies<br>☐ MI Processes<br>    ☐ Engaging<br>    ☐ Focusing<br>    ☐ Evoking<br>    ☐ Planning | ☐ MI Spirit<br>    ☐ Partnership<br>    ☐ Acceptance<br>    ☐ Compassion<br>    ☐ Evocation<br>☐ OARS<br>    ☐ Asking open-ended questions<br>    ☐ Giving affirmations<br>    ☐ Using reflections<br>        ○ Simple<br>        ○ Complex<br>    ☐ Providing summaries<br>☐ Change talk<br>    ☐ Hearing change talk<br>    ☐ Evoking change talk<br>☐ Developing discrepancies<br>☐ MI Processes<br>    ☐ Engaging<br>    ☐ Focusing<br>    ☐ Evoking<br>    ☐ Planning |

### What training opportunities or experiences can improve my areas for growth?

☐ Reread sections of this book related to that growth area
☐ Complete exercises and use forms in this book related to that growth area
☐ Use one or more of the fidelity assessment tools described in Chapter 11
☐ Start a reading and resource group on MI in your school
☐ Look for resources on motivationalinterviewing.com related to that growth area
☐ Read additional books on MI
☐ Attend workshops on MI
☐ Other _____

### Goals and Plan

*My goal to improve my MI skills is to focus on the following growth area_____.*
*To achieve this goal I will use the following training opportunity_____.*
*I will achieve this goal by _____(date) and will reassess my plan.*

# HANDOUT 10.2 MITS: MI QUIZ—REVISED[2]

*In an MI approach, these statements are either factually true or false or consistent with the truth ("true") or inconsistent with the truth ("false"). Indicate your response by circling the appropriate item to the right.*

1. A coach's expectation for a teacher's ability to change has no effect on whether change occurs.
2. If a teacher resists talking about behavioral change, direct confrontation and persuasion are necessary.
3. Coaches should emphasize personal choice over teachers' behaviors, including what the coach views as inappropriate classroom management.
4. Readiness to make change is the teacher's responsibility—no one can help him or her until the teacher decides he or she is ready.
5. Proficiency in MI requires the coach to use more reflections than questions.
6. An indication of a successful motivational interview is the amount of change talk produced by the teacher.
7. Differentially responding to change versus sustain talk is only necessary during the final phases of a motivational interview.

Select the responses that best answer each of the following questions. Multiple responses may be selected.

8. Which of the following represent the spirit of an MI approach to dealing with behavior change? (Select all that apply).

|  | Fostering partnerships |  | Directing the conversation |
|---|---|---|---|
|  | Demonstrating acceptance |  | Persuading with logic |
|  | Providing compassion |  | Judging proficiency |
|  | Maintaining evocation |  | Promoting ideas |

9. Which of the following represent the processes of an MI approach to dealing with behavior change? (Select all that apply).

|  | Reassuring |  | Questioning |
|---|---|---|---|
|  | Engaging |  | Evoking |
|  | Approving |  | Deciding |
|  | Focusing |  | Planning |

---

[2] Based on the Motivational Interviewing Knowledge and Attitudes Test (MIKAT; Leffingwell, 2006).

10. Which of the following represent the core interviewing skills of an MI approach to dealing with behavior change? (Select all that apply).

| | | | |
|---|---|---|---|
| | Asking open-ended questions | | Moralizing |
| | Interpreting behavior | | Summarizing |
| | Affirming | | Defending |
| | Analyzing | | Informing and advising |
| | Reflecting | | Consoling |

# HANDOUT 10.3 MI QUIZ—REVISED ANSWER KEY

The following statements are either factually true or false or consistent with ("true") or inconsistent with ("false") an MI approach. Indicate your response by circling the appropriate item to the right.

1. A coach's expectation for a teacher's ability to change has no effect on whether change occurs. **FALSE**
2. If a teacher resists talking about behavioral change, direct confrontation and persuasion are necessary. **FALSE**
3. Coaches should emphasize personal choice over teachers' behaviors, including what the coach views as inappropriate classroom management. **TRUE**
4. Readiness to make change is the teacher's responsibility—no one can help the teacher until the teacher decides he or she is ready. **FALSE**
5. Proficiency in MI requires the coach to use more reflections than questions. **TRUE**
6. An indication of a successful motivational interview is the amount of change talk produced by the teacher. **TRUE**
7. Differentially responding to change versus sustain talk is only necessary during the final phases of a motivational interview. **FALSE**

Select the responses that best answer each of the following questions. Multiple responses may be selected.

8. Which of the following represent the spirit of an MI approach to dealing with behavior change? (Select all that apply).

| | | | |
|---|---|---|---|
| x | Fostering partnerships | | Directing the conversation |
| | Persuading with logic | x | Demonstrating acceptance |
| x | Providing compassion | | Judging proficiency |
| | Promoting ideas | x | Maintaining evocation |

9. Which of the following represent the processes of an MI approach to dealing with behavior change? (Select all that apply).

| | | | |
|---|---|---|---|
| | Reassuring | | Questioning |
| x | Engaging | x | Evoking |
| | Approving | | Deciding |
| x | Focusing | x | Planning |

10. Which of the following represent the core interviewing skills of an MI approach to dealing with behavior change? (Select all that apply).

| | | | |
|---|---|---|---|
| x | Asking open-ended questions | | Moralizing |
| | Interpreting behavior | x | Summarizing |
| x | Affirming | | Defending |
| | Analyzing | x | Informing and advising |
| x | Reflecting | | Consoling |

# 11

# The Future of Motivational Interviewing in Schools

Addressing the motivational aspects of academic and behavior supports at home and school represent the next frontier of school-based practices. For too long, we have ignored this critical aspect of behavior change or assumed it was beyond our role or capacity to influence. As this book and the extensive literature about motivational interviewing (MI) clearly demonstrate, consultants can and should attend to motivation as part of any activity connected to behavior change.

How do we make these MI practices more commonly available in schools? In other words, how do we best disseminate this new best practice for intervening in academic and behavior problems? This book is intended as a first step toward that broader goal. By making more school professionals aware of MI and by equipping them with the basic knowledge and expertise needed for MI practice, we hope to begin spreading the word. Beyond this, we hope to improve training methods for MI by capitalizing on online education and distance supervision.

> MI is intended to complement school-based initiatives and maximize their impact.

## HOW DOES MI FIT WITH OTHER SCHOOL INITIATIVES?

As we are all too familiar, most schools have many competing initiatives at any given moment in time. Pressures mount for implementing new and improved academic and behavioral curriculum and staff development. It is easy for any one of these initiatives to get lost in the shuffle if collectively they are competing for the same limited time, resources, and attention. MI is intended to comple-ment these initiatives and maximize their impact.

Some of the applications of MI fit well within the widely disseminated tiered models of academic and behavior supports. Specific models such as the Classroom Check-Up (CCU) and the Family Check-Up (FCU) can be viewed as second- or third-tier preventive interventions. As described in Chapter 8, we see the application of elements of the FCU as a key component for improving the impact of behavior support teams. Depending on school resources, students could be screened into receiving an FCU-type intervention based on their own behavior or academic symptoms or simply by a parent seeking additional fam-ily services or supports.

In a similar way, the CCU can be used as selective or indicated intervention for teachers who are not responding to available coaching or staff development opportunities in a given district. Teachers who continue to struggle after receiv-ing the CCU and some additional coaching may then be given daily personal-ized feedback to improve targeted behavior performance.

## OTHER APPLICATIONS

With a little reflection, it is easy to imagine other extensions of the MI strat-egies to schools. We envision a School or District Check-Up that can assess and give feedback to administrators on important district goals such as improving staff morale, increasing family participation, meeting per-formance expectations, and imple-menting school-wide academic and behavior support initiatives. Recall that to be consistent with MI, the applica-tion must include a compassionate beginning; that is, starting with the goal of enhancing the welfare of the individuals exposed to MI, not to be used in a punitive fashion.

> One innovative application of MI has been to improve the cultural responsiveness of teachers.

One innovative application of MI has been to improve the cultural respon-siveness of teachers. The achievement gap between White students and stu-dents of color in the United States is a major concern for the educational system. Additionally, children of color are disproportionately represented in special education and have much higher rates of office discipline referrals. This is true even in schools with high-quality implementation of school-wide behavior sup-ports. One solution to these problems is to promote culturally responsive educa-tion whereby educators are trained to be aware of their biases and to develop appreciation of cultural variations.

Over the past several years, Dr. Catherine Bradshaw and colleagues (2012) developed a model called Double Check for understanding and promoting cul-turally responsive education. They reviewed extant literature regarding cultur-ally responsive education and identified five defining components: (a) *reflective thinking about children and their "group" membership,* (b) *effective communication,* (c) *authentic relationships,* (d) *connection to curriculum,* and (e) *sensitivity to stu-dents' cultural and situational messages.* After defining each of these elements, they then produced professional development workshops for educators to promote awareness and application of these elements.

As with any quality professional development, however, Dr. Bradshaw added a coaching component to help ensure educators could actually enact the behaviors and attitudes associated with the model. She drew on MI and the CCU in particular to support teachers in acquiring these skills. After the professional development, teachers meet with a coach who assesses their classroom management, classroom atmosphere, and the five components of Double Check through an interview, rating scales, and classroom observations. The coach then meets with the teacher to deliver feedback on these domains in the manner that has been described throughout the book. The feedback meeting ends with the development of a goal-setting plan.

Initial evidence suggests that the model is well received by teachers and coaches. It is currently being tested in a randomized trial to determine whether the model not only promotes culturally responsive education but also whether it leads to reductions in disproportionality and the achievement gap.

## FUTURE RESEARCH

Although we have presented school-based MI as an approach with some evidence and much potential, we hope we have also communicated that this burgeoning line of research is in its infancy. In fact, researchers and practitioners in the field of substance abuse have been working over three decades to understand the nuanced application of this effective practice. It is our hope that we can build on their work and thereby expand the knowledge-base, promise, and effectiveness of this practice within the context of schools. The following are a few lines of research we believe are important toward this end.

### Deepening Our Understanding of Motivation

Although several lines of research are currently focusing on supporting teacher behavior through consultation (e.g., direct teacher training, joint intervention development and treatment integrity assessment, instructional consultation, and MI), little is known about the "active ingredients" or paths linking consultant–teacher behavior, teacher behavior change, and student outcomes. It is important to examine how the underlying mechanisms of change associated with MI as applied to the consultant–teacher relationship are working by examining in great detail the links among the delivery of consultation services, teacher behavior change, and student behavior change. Establishing this connection would be informative for the professional preparation of administrators and specialized instructional support personnel. It would also have implications for consultation and coaching models and strategies in school settings. As research related to the application of MI in the context of school-based consultation advances, we will need to (a) determine which components of MI are critical and which are supplementary (Noell, 2008);

(b) identify which components of MI should be adhered to rigidly, which require flexibility and adaptation (Durlack & DuPre, 2008), and which employ reliable and valid processes to evaluate and document treatment integrity of the MI-based consultation process (Noell & Gansle, 2006); and (c) establish whether there are any subgroups for whom the critical threshold of MI implementation varies (Durlack & DuPre, 2008).

## Examining and Scaling Up Existing Interventions

Throughout the book, we have presented evidence for a number of stand-alone interventions (e.g., CCU, the SE-FCU), supplements to existing interventions (First Step CCU and Enhanced homeBase), as well as adaptations of MI integrated with intervention systems (e.g., Providing Alternative THinking Strategies [PATHS] to Good Behavior Game [GBG], also known as PAX). Although the evidence is very encouraging, it needs to be expanded in several ways. First, we need additional information about the efficacy and effectiveness of these approaches, primarily through the implementation of more rigorous research designs capable of making causal attribution, and determining for whom MI is effective and under what conditions. A particularly important aspect of this work will be to understand the extent to which coaches or interventionists are required to implement MI with proficiency for desired outcomes to be obtained.

## The Creation of Sustainable Infrastructures to Train School Personnel

If school-based coaches and researchers are to use MI effectively, relevant training and supervision structures must be created to support school staff. Thus, there is a need for effective training and supervision structures that can efficiently develop MI skills among the wide variety of school-based professionals who might become coaches. Efforts to develop school-based training procedures are under way. As mentioned in Chapter 10, there are currently efforts to develop and evaluate a professional development system to train school-based consultants to use MI. It will be important to learn more about this process. Additionally, preparing those in school settings to use MI will likely reveal other possible applications for the practice.

## A NEW DIMENSION

We are only beginning to scratch the surface of innovative applications of MI in schools. The take-home message from this book is that too often we ignore a fundamental aspect of human growth and development—motivation—assuming it is beyond our sphere of influence. Given the progress of extending MI applications throughout the world and in a wide variety of settings, the next generation of academic and behavior interventions in schools will surely attend to the motivational context of interventions. In the meantime, embrace the ideas set forth in this book and continue to examine your own assumptions about how you can best help parents, teachers, and students change and grow. Although the prospect of having to address the motivation of another can be daunting, MI gives us a model for intervening in motivation. In this way, rather than contributing to a sense of helplessness or burden, MI empowers us by reminding us of our vast influence and potential. It gives us a new lens through which to view academic

> Too often we ignore a fundamental aspect of human growth and development, motivation, assuming it is beyond our sphere of influence. MI empowers us by reminding us of our vast influence and potential.

and behavior problems, compliance, and engagement, one in which we are co-creators of the world in which motivation can flourish or be dampened by our attitudes and actions. Given this new insight, we are now all positioned to act with others in ways that call forth their own motivations to change.

# Bibliography

Abidin, R. A. (1995). *Parenting Stress Index professional manual* (3rd ed.). Lutz, FL: Psychological Assessment Resources.

Achenbach, T. M. (2001). *Manual for the ASEBA school-age forms and profiles*. Burlington, VT: Department of Psychiatry, University of Vermont.

Achenbach, T. M., & Edelbrock, C. S. (1983). *Manual for the Child Behavior Checklist and Revised Child Behavior Profile*. Burlington, VT: University of Vermont Dept. of Psychiatry.

Adamson, R., & Mitchell, B. (2011). *Using FBA/BSP and FCU to increase appropriate behavior across academics settings for an escape-maintained student*. Poster presented at the 3rd Annual Educational, School, & Counseling Psychology Conference, Columbia, MO.

Addis, M. E., Wade, W. A., & Hatgis, C. (1999). Barriers to dissemination of evidence-based practices: Addressing practitioners' concerns about manual-based psychotherapies. *Clinical Psychology: Science & Practice, 6*, 430–441.

Affronti, M. L., & Levison-Johnson, J. (2009). The future of family engagement in residential care settings. *Residential Treatment for Children and Youth, 26*, 257–304.

Amador, X. F., & Johanson, A. L. (2000). *I am not sick I don't need help!: Helping the seriously mentally ill accept treatment*. Peconic, NY: Vida Press.

Amrhein, P. C., Miller, W. R., Yahne, C. E., Palmer, M., & Fulcher, L. (2003). Client commitment language during motivational interviewing predicts drug use outcomes. *Journal of Consulting and Clinical Psychology, 71*, 862–878.

Andrzejewski, M. E., Kirby, K. C., Morral, A. R., & Inguchi, M. Y. (2001). Technology transfer through performance management: The effects of graphical feedback and positive reinforcement on drug treatment counselors' behavior. *Drug and Alcohol Dependence, 63*, 179–186.

Armitage, C. J., Harris, P. R., Hepton, G., & Napper, L. (2008). Self-affirmation increases acceptance of health-risk information among UK adult smokers with low socioeconomic status. *Psychology of Addictive Behaviors: Journal of the Society of Psychologists in Addictive Behaviors, 22*(1), 88–95.

Baer, J. S., Rosengren, D. B., Dunn, C. W., Wells, E. A., Ogle, R. L., & Hartzler, B. (2004). An evaluation of workshop training in motivational interviewing for addiction and mental health clinicians. *Drug and Alcohol Dependence, 73*, 99. doi:10.1016/j.drugalcdep.2003.10.001

Ball, S. A., Martino, S., Corvino, J., Morganstern, J., & Carroll, K. M. (2002). *Independent tape rater guide*. Unpublished psychotherapy tape rating manual.

Ball, S. A., Martino, S., Nich, C., Frankforter, T. L., Van Horn, D., Crits-Christoph, P.,...Carroll, K. M. (2007). Site matters: Motivational enhancement therapy in community drug abuse clinics. *Journal of Consultation in Clinical Psychology, 75,* 556–567.

Beidas, R. S., & Kendall, P. C. (2010). Training therapists in evidence-based practice: A critical review of studies from a systems-contextual perspective. *Clinical Psychology: Science & Practice, 17,* 1–30. doi:10.1111/j.1468–2850.2009.01187.x

Bell, K., & Cole, B. (2008). Improving medical students' success in promoting health behavior change: A curriculum evaluation. *Journal of General Internal Medicine, 23,* 1503–1506. doi:10.1007/s11606–008-0678-x

Bergin, A. E., & Garfield, S. L. (Eds.). (1994). *Handbook of psychotherapy and behavior change* (4th ed.). New York, NY: John Wiley & Sons.

Berry, J. O. (1995). The parental stress scale: Initial psychometric evidence. *Journal of Social and Personal Relationships, 12*(3), 463–472.

Biglan, A., Flay, B. R., Embry, D. D., & Sandler, I. N. (2012). The critical role of nurturing environments for promoting human well-being. *American Psychologist, 67,* 257–271.

Blom-Hoffman, J., & Rose, G. S. (2007). Applying motivational interviewing techniques to further the primary prevention potential of school-based consultation. *Journal of Educational & Psychological Consultation, 17,* 151–156.

Borden, L. (2012). *Project arches: An evaluation of a modified Family Check-up intervention in an assessment setting* (Unpublished dissertation). University of Missouri.

Bradshaw, C., Rosenberg, M., Debnam, K., Hardee, S., Bates, L., & Hershfeldt, P. (2013). *Double Check: A model of cultural proficiency and student engagement.* Program Manual. Baltimore, MD: Johns Hopkins Center for the Prevention of Youth Violence.

Brown, R. A., Ramsey, S. E., & Sales, S. (2008). *Therapist manual: MI+ intervention* (Unpublished training manual). Providence, RI: Brown University.

Capaldi, D. M., & Patterson, G. R. (1994). Interrelated influences of contextual factors on antisocial behavior in childhood and adolescence for males. In D. Fowles, P. Sutker, & S. Goodman (Eds.), *Psychopathy and antisocial personality: A developmental perspective* (pp. 165–198). New York, NY: Springer Publishing Company.

Carroll, K. M., Ball, S. A., Nich, C., Martino, S., Frankforter, T. L., Farentinos, C., ..., Woody, G. E. (2006). Motivational interviewing to improve treatment engagement and outcome in individuals seeking treatment for substance abuse: A multisite effectiveness study. *Drug and Alcohol Dependence, 81,* 301–312.

Carroll, K. M., Nich, C., Sifry, R. L., Nuro, K. F., & Frankforter, T. L. (2000). A general system for evaluating therapist adherence and competence in psychotherapy research in the addictions. *Drug and Alcohol Dependence, 57,* 225–238.

Center for the Study and Prevention of Violence. (2007). *Blueprints for violence prevention.* Boulder, CO: Institute of Behavioral Science, University of Colorado, Boulder.

Chaparro, E. (2011). *District-wide implementation of school-wide behavior support and reading models.* Keynote address presented at the 3rd Annual Educational, School, & Counseling Psychology Conference, Columbia, MO.

Cohen, G. L., Garcia, J., Apfel, N., & Master, A. (2006). Reducing the racial achievement gap: A social-psychological intervention. *Science, 313*(5791), 1307–1310.

Conduct Problems Prevention Research Group. (1999). Initial impact of the Fast Track prevention trial for conduct problems: II. Classroom effects. *Journal of Consulting and Clinical Psychology, 67,* 648–657.

Connell, A., & Dishion, T. (2008). Reducing depression among at-risk early adolescents: Three-year effects of a family-centered intervention embedded within schools. *Journal of Family Psychology, 22,* 574–585.

Connell, A., Dishion, T., Yasui, M., & Kavanaugh, K. (2007). An adaptive approach to family intervention: Linking engagement in family-centered intervention to reductions in adolescent behavior. *Journal of Consulting and Clinical Psychology, 75*(4), 568–579.

Corcoran, K., & Fischer, J. (2000). *Measures for clinical practice: A sourcebook* (2 Vols., 3rd ed.). New York, NY: Free Press.

Crnic, K. A., & Greenberg, M. T. (1990). Minor parenting stresses and young children. *Child Development, 61,* 1628–1637.

Dane, A. V., & Schneider, B. H. (1998). Program integrity in primary and early secondary prevention: Are implementation effects out of control? *Clinical Psychology Review, 18,* 23–45.

Davis, D. (1998). Does CME work? An analysis of the effect of educational activities on physician performance or health care outcomes. *International Journal of Psychiatry Medicine, 28,* 21–39.

Dishion, T., & Kavanagh, K. (2003). *Intervening in adolescent problem behavior: A family-centered approach.* New York, NY: Guilford Press.

Dishion, T., Shaw, D., Connell, A., Gardner, F., Weaver, C., & Wilson, M. (2008). The Family Check-Up with high-risk indigent families: Preventing problem behavior by increasing parents' positive behavior support in early childhood. *Child Development, 79,* 1395–1414.

Dishion, T. J., & Stormshak, E. A. E. (Eds.). (2007). *Intervening in children's lives: An ecological, family-centered approach to mental health care.* Washington, DC: American Psychological Association.

Dishion, T. J., Stormshak, E. A., & Kavanagh, K. A. (2007). *Everyday parenting: A professional's guide to building family management skills.* Champaign, IL: Research Press.

Dishion, T. J., Stormshak, E. A., & Kavanagh, K. A. (2011). *Everyday parenting: A professional's guide to building family management practices.* Champaign, IL: Research Press.

Dishion, T. J., Stormshak, E., & Siler, C. (2010). An ecological approach to interventions with high-risk students in schools: Using the Family Check-Up to motivate parents' positive behavior support. In M. R. Shinn & H. M. E. Walker (Eds.), *Interventions for achievement and behavior problems in a three-tier model including RTI* (pp. 101–124). Bethesda, MD: National Association of School Psychologists.

Domitrovich, C. E., Bradshaw, C. P., Greenberg, M. T., Embry, D., Poduska, J. M., & Ialongo, N. S. (2010). Integrated models of school-based prevention: Logic and theory. *Psychology in the Schools, 47,* 71–88.

Driscoll, K., & Pianta, R. C. (2011). Mothers' and fathers' perceptions of conflict and closeness in parent-child relationships during early childhood. *Journal of Early Childhood and Infant Psychology, 7,* 1–24.

Duran, E., & Duran, B. (1995). *Native American postcolonial psychology.* Albany, NY: State University of New York.

Durlak, J. A., & DuPre, E. P. (2008). Implementation matters: A review of research on the influence of implementation on program outcomes and the factors affecting implementation. *American Journal of Community Psychology, 41*(3–4), 327–350.

Dusenbury, L., Brannigan, R., Hansen, W. B., Walsh, J., & Falco, M. (2005). Quality of implementation: Developing measures crucial to understanding the diffusion of preventive interventions. *Health Education Research, 18,* 308–313.

Elgar, F., Waschbusch, D., Dadds, M., & Sigvaldason, N. (2007). Development and validation of a short form of the Alabama Parenting Questionnaire. *Journal of Child and Family Studies, 16*(2), 243–259.

Epstein, J. (1995). School/family/community partnerships: Caring for the children we share. *Phi Delta Kappan, 76,* 701–712.

Epstein, J., & Lee, S. (1995). National patterns of school and family connections in the middle grades. In B. Ryan, G. Adams, T. Gullotta, R. Weissberg, & R. Hampton (Eds.),

*The family–school connection: Theory, research, and practice* (pp. 108–154). Thousand Oaks, CA: Sage.

Fauber, R. L., & Long, N. (1991). Children in context: The role of the family in child psychotherapy. *Journal of Consulting and Clinical Psychology, 59*(6), 813–820.

Festinger, L. (1957). *A theory of cognitive dissonance*. Evanston, IL: Row, Peterson.

Fixsen, D. L., Naoom, S. F., Blase, K. A., Freidman, R. M., & Wallace, F. (2005). *Implementation research: A synthesis of the literature*. Tampa, FL: Louis de la Parte Florida Mental Health Institute.

Frey, A., Cloud, R., Lee, J., Small, J. W., Seeley, J. R., Feil, E. G., … Golly, A. (2011). The promise of motivational interviewing in school mental health. *School Mental Health, 3*, 1–12. doi:10.1007/s12310–010-9048-z

Frey, A. J., Lee, J., Small, J. W., Seeley, J. R., Walker, H. M., & Feil, E. G. (2013a). Motivational Interviewing Navigation Guide: A process for enhancing teacher's motivation to adopt and implement school-based interventions. *Advances in School Mental Health Promotion*. doi: 10.1080/1754730X.2013.804334

Frey, A. J., Lee, J., Small, J. W., Seeley, J. R., Walker, H. M., & Feil, E. G. (2013b). Transporting motivational interviewing to school settings to improve the engagement and fidelity of tier 2 interventions. *Journal of Applied School Psychology, 29*(2), 183–202.

Frey, A. J., Small, J., Lee, J., Walker, H. M., Seeley, J., Feil, E., & Golly, A. (2013). *Expanding the range of the First Step to Success intervention: Tertiary-level support for teachers and families*. Manuscript submitted for publication.

Frey, A. J., Walker, H. M., Seeley, J., Lee, J., Small, J., Golly, A., et al. (2013). *First step to success enhancements*. Retrieved from http://www.firststeptosuccess.org

Gibbons, C. J., Carroll, K. M., Ball, S. A., Nich, C., Frankforter, T. L., & Martino, S. (2010). Community program therapist adherence and competence in a motivational interviewing assessment intake session. *American Journal of Drug and Alcohol Abuse, 36*, 342–349. doi:10.3109/00952990.2010.500437

Gibson, J., Pennington, R., Stenhoff, D., & Hopper, J. (2010). Using desktop videoconferencing to deliver interventions to a preschool student with autism. *Topics in Early Childhood Special Education, 29*(4), 214–225.

Gill, A., Hyde, L., Shaw, D., Dishion, T., & Wilson, M. (2008). The Family Check-Up in early childhood: A case study of intervention process and change. *Journal of Clinical Child & Adolescent Psychology, 37*, 893–904.

Glynn, L. H., & Moyers, T. B. (2010). Chasing change talk: The clinician's role in evoking client language about change. *Journal of Substance Abuse Treatment, 39*, 65–70.

Greenberg, M. T., Domitrovich, C. E., & Bumbarger, B. (2001). The prevention of mental disorders in school-aged children: Current state of the field. *Prevention and Treatment, 4*(1), 1–62.

Hartzler, B., Baer, J. S., Dunn, C., Rosengren, D. B., & Wells, E. (2007). What is seen through the looking glass: The impact of training on practitioner self-rating of motivational interviewing skills. *Behavioural and Cognitive Psychotherapy, 35*, 431–445.

Hawkins, J. D., & Catalano, R. F. (2004). *Communities that care: Prevention strategies guide*. South Deerfield, MA: Channing Bete.

Herman, K. C., Borden, L., Schultz, T., Hsu, C., Brooks, C., Strawsine, M., & Reinke, W. (2011). Motivational interviewing applications with families. *Residential Treatment for Children and Youth, 28*, 102–119.

Herman, K. C., Bradshaw, C., Reinke, W. M., Lochman, J., Boxmeyer, C., Powell, N.,… Ialongo, N. (2012). Integrating the Family Check-Up and the Parent Coping Power Program. *Advances in School Mental Health Promotion, 5*, 208–219.

Herman, K. C., Lambert, S. F., Reinke, W. M., & Ialongo, N. S. (2008). Academic incompetence in first grade as a risk factor for depressive cognitions and symptoms in middle school. *Journal of Counseling Psychology, 55*, 400–410.

Herman, K. C., Reinke, W. M., Bradshaw, C., Lochman, J., Borden, L., & Darney, D. (2012). Increasing parental engagement in school-based preventive interventions: The integration of the Family Check-Up and the Parent Coping Power Program. In M. Weist, N. Lever, C. Bradshaw, & J. Owens (Eds.), *Handbook of school mental health* (2nd ed., pp. 223–236). New York, NY: Springer.

Hershfeldt, P. A., Pell, K., Sechrest, R., Pas, E. T., & Bradshaw, C. P. (2012). Lessons learned coaching teachers in behavior management: The PBISplus Coaching Model. *Journal of Educational and Psychological Consultation: The Official Journal of the Association for Educational and Psychological Consultants, 22*(4), 280–299.

Hirschstein, M. K., Estrom, L. V., Frey, K. S., Snell, J. L., & MacKenzie, E. P. (2007). Walking the talk in bully prevention: Teacher implementation variable related to initial impact of the Steps to Respect program. *School Psychology Review, 36*, 3–21.

Hohman, M. (2011). *Motivational interviewing in social work practice.* New York, NY: Guilford Press.

Jaccard, J., Dodge, T., & Dittus, P. (2002). Parent-adolescent communication about sex and birth control. *New Directions for Child & Adolescent Development, 97*, 9–41.

Jones, H. A., Clarke, A. T., & Power, T. J. (2008). Expanding the concept of intervention integrity: A multidimensional model of participant engagement. *In Balance, 23*, 4–5.

Kohl, G. O., Lengua, L. J., & McMahon, R. J. (2000). Parent involvement in school: Conceptualizing multiple dimensions and their relations with family and demographic risk factors. *Journal of School Psychology, 38*, 501–523.

Koth, C. W., Bradshaw, C. P., & Leaf, P. J. (2009). Teacher observation classroom adaptation-checklist: Development and factor structure. *Measurement and Evaluation in Counseling and Development, 42*, 15–30.

Kumpfer, K. L., & Collings, S. J. (2003). Effectiveness of family-focused interventions for school-based prevention. In K. Robinson (Ed.), *Advances in school-based mental health: Best practices and program models* (pp. 7.1–7.11). Kingston, NJ: Civic Research Institute.

Lane, C. (2002). *The Behaviour Change Counselling Index (BECCI): Manual for coding behaviour change counselling.* Cardiff, South Glam, UK: University of Wales. Retrieved from http://www.motivationalinterviewing.org/content/becci-manual

Lane, C., Hood, K., & Rollnick, S. (2008). Teaching motivational interviewing: Using role play is as effective as using simulated patients. *Medical Education, 42*, 637–644. doi:10.1111/j.1365–2923.2007.02990.x

Lee, J., Frey, A. J., Seeley, J., Small, J., Walker, H. M., Golly, A.,…Rutledge, A. (in press). Adapting motivational interviewing to an early intervention addressing challenging behavior: Applications with teachers. In E. McNamara (Ed.), *Motivational interviewing with children and young people: Issues and further applications.* United Kingdom: Positive Behaviour Management.

Lee, J., Frey, A. J., & Small, J. W. (2013). *The Video Assessment of Simulated Encounters–School-Based Applications.* Cincinnati, OH: University of Cincinnati.

Lee, J., Small, J. W., & Frey, A. J. (2013). *Written Assessment of Simulated Encounters–School-Based Applications.* Cincinnati, OH: University of Cincinnati.

Leffingwell, T. R. (2006). Motivational Interviewing Knowledge and Attitudes Test (MIKAT) for evaluation for training outcomes. *MINUET, 13*, 10–11.

Lochman, J. E., Boxmeyer, C., Powell, N., Qu, L., Wells, K., & Windle, M. (2009). Dissemination of the Coping Power Program: Importance of intensity of counselor training. *Journal of Consulting and Clinical Psychology, 77*, 397–409.

Lochman, J. E., Boxmeyer, C., Powell, N., Roth, D. L., & Windle, M. (2006). Masked intervention effects: Analytic methods addressing low dosage of intervention. *New Directions for Evaluation, 110*, 19–32.

Lochman, J. E., & Wells, K. (1996). A social-cognitive intervention with aggressive children: Prevention effects and contextual implementation issues. In R. D. Peters & R. J. McMahon (Eds.), *Preventing childhood disorders, substance abuse and delinquency* (pp. 111–143). Thousand Oaks, CA: Sage.

Lochman, J. E., & Wells, K. C. (2004). The Coping Power Program for preadolescent aggressive boys and their parents: Outcome effects at the one-year follow-up. *Journal of Consulting and Clinical Psychology, 72*, 571–578.

Lochman, J. E., Wells, K., & Lenhart, S. (2008). *Coping power: Child facilitators guide.* New York, NY: Oxford University Press.

Lunkenheimer, E., Shaw, D., Gardner, F., Dishion, T., Connell, A., & Wilson, M. (2008). Collateral benefits of the Family Check-Up on early childhood school readiness: Indirect effects of parents' positive behavior support. *Developmental Psychology, 44*, 1737–1752.

Madson, M. B., Loignon, A. C., & Laine, C. (2009). Training in motivational interviewing: A systematic review. *Journal of Substance Abuse Treatment, 36*, 101–109.

Martino, S., Ball, S. A., Gallon, S. L., Hall, D., Garcia, M., Ceperich, S., . . . Hausotter, W. (2006). *Motivational interviewing assessment: Supervisory tools for enhancing proficency.* Salem, OR: Northwest Addiction Technology Transfer Center, Oregon Health and Science University.

Martino, S., Ball, S. A., Nich, C., Canning-Ball, M., Rounsaville, B. J., & Carroll, K. M. (2011). Teaching community program clinicians motivational interviewing using expert and train-the-trainer strategies. *Addiction, 106*, 428–441. doi:10.1111/j.1360–0443.2010.03135.x

Martino, S., Ball, S., Nich, C., Frankforter, T. L., & Carroll, K. M. (2009). Correspondence of motivational enhancement treatment integrity ratings among therapists, supervisors, and observers. *Psychotherapy Research, 19*, 181–193.

Martino, S., Haeseler, F., Belitsky, R., Pantalon, M., & Fortin 4th, A. H. (2007). Teaching brief motivational interviewing to year three medical students. *Medical Education, 41*, 160–167. doi:10.1111/j.1365–2929.2006.02673.x

McKay, M., Atkins, M., Hawkins, T., Brown, C., & Lynn, C. (2003). Inner-city African American parental involvement in children's schooling: Racial socialization and social support from the parent community. *American Journal of Community Psychology, 32*(1/2), 107–114.

McKay, M., & Bannon, W. (2004). Engaging families in child mental health services. *Child and Adolescent Psychiatric Clinics of North America, 13*(4), 905–921.

McKay, M. M., Hibbert, R., Hoagwood, K., Rodriguez, J., Murray L., Legurski, J., & Fernandez, D. (2004). Increasing evidence-based engagement interventions into "real world" child mental health setting. *Brief Treatment and Crisis Intervention, 4*, 177–186.

McMahon, R. J., & Forehand, R. L. (2005). *Helping the noncompliant child: Family-based treatment for oppositional behavior* (2nd ed.). New York, NY: Guilford Press.

Mesa, J., Lewis-Palmer, T., & Reinke, W. M. (2005, Fall). Providing teachers with performance feedback on praise to reduce student problem behavior. *Beyond Behavior*, 45–55.

Miller, W., & Moyers, T. (2006). Eight stages in learning motivational interviewing. *Journal of Teaching in the Addictions, 5*, 3–17.

Miller, W. R. (1983). Motivational interviewing with problem drinkers. *Behavioural Psychotherapy, 11*, 147–172.

Miller, W. R., Benefield, R. G., & Tonigan, J. S. (1993). Enhancing motivation for change in problem drinking: A controlled comparison of two therapist styles. *Journal of Consulting and Clinical Psychology, 61*, 455–461.

Miller, W. R., C'de Baca, J., Matthews, D. B., & Wilbourne, P. L. (2001). Alberquerque, NM: University of New Mexico. Retrieved from http://www.motivationalinterview. net/library/valuescardsort.pdf

Miller, W. R., Hedrick, K. E., & Orlofsky, D. R. (1991). The Helpful Responses Questionnaire: A procedure for measuring therapeutic empathy. *Journal of Clinical Psychology, 47*, 444–448.

Miller, W. R., & Moyers, T. (2012, April). *Advanced workshop in motivational interviewing.* Paper presented at Sheraton Albuquerque Uptown Hotel, Albuquerque, NM.

Miller, W. R., Moyers, T. B., Ernst, D., & Amrhein, P. (2008). *Manual for the Motivational Interviewing Skill Code (MISC), version 2.1.* Unpublished manuscript, University of New Mexico.

Miller, W. R., Moyers, T. B., & Rollnick, S. (2012). *Motivational interviewing: Helping people change* (DVD). Carson City, NV: The Change Companies.

Miller, W. R., & Rollnick, S. (2002). *Motivational interviewing: Preparing people for change* (2nd ed.). New York, NY: Guilford Press.

Miller, W. R., & Rollnick, S. (2013). *Motivational interviewing: Preparing people for change* (3rd ed.). New York, NY: Guilford Press.

Miller, W. R., & Rose, G. S. (2009). Toward of theory of motivational interviewing. *American Psychologist, 64*, 527–537.

Miller, W. R., Sorensen, J. L., Selzer, J. A., & Brigham, G. S. (2006). Disseminating evidence-based practices in substance abuse treatment: A review with suggestions. *Journal of Substance Abuse Treatment, 31*, 25–39.

Miller, W. R., Yahne, C. E., Moyers, T. B., Martinez, J., & Pirritano, M. (2004). A randomized trial of methods to help clinicians learn motivational interviewing. *Journal of Consulting and Clinical Psychology, 72*, 1050–1062. doi:10.1037/0022–006x.72.6.1050

Miller, W. R., Zweben, A., DiClemente, C. C., & Rychtaric, R. (1992). *Motivational enhancement therapy manual: A clinical research guide for therapists treating individuals with alcohol abuse and dependence* (Project MATCH Monograph Series, Vol. 2). Rockville, MD: National Institute on Alcohol Abuse and Alcoholism.

Minke, K. (2005). Family–school collaboration and positive behavior support. *Journal of Positive Behavior Interventions.*

Minke, K. M., & Anderson, K. J. (2005). Family–school collaboration and positive behavior support. *Journal of Positive Behavior Interventions, 7*(3), 181–185.

Moilanen, K., Shaw, D., Dishion, T., Gardner, F., & Wilson, M. (2010). Predictors of longitudinal growth in inhibitory control in early childhood. *Social Development, 19*(2), 326–347.

Morgenstern, J., Morgan, T. J., McCrady, B. S., Keller, D. S., & Carroll, K. M. (2001). Manual-guided cognitive behavioral therapy training: A promising method for disseminating empirically supported substance abuse treatments to the practice community. *Psychology of Addictive Behaviors, 15*, 83–88.

Moyers, T., Martin, T., Catley, D., Harris, K. J., & Ahluwalia, J. S. (2003). Assessing the integrity of motivational interviewing interventions: Reliability of the Motivational Interviewing Skills Code. *Behavioral and Cognitive Psychotherapy, 31*, 177–184.

Moyers, T., Martin, T., Manuel, J., Hendrickson, S., & Miller, W. (2005). Assessing competence in the use of motivational interviewing. *Journal of Substance Abuse Treatment, 28*, 19–26.

Moyers, T., Martin, T., Manuel, J., Miller, W., & Ernst, D. (2007). *The Motivational Interviewing Treatment Integrity (MITI) code manual: Version 3.0.* Retrieved from http://casaa.unm.edu/download/miti.pdf

Moyers, T. B., Martin, T., Christopher, P. J., Houck, J. M., & Tonigan, J. S. (2009). From in-session behavior to drinking outcomes: A causal chain for motivational interviewing. *Journal of Consulting and Clinical Psychology, 77*, 1113–1124.

Moyers, T. B., & Martino, S. (2006). *What's important in my life.* Alberquerque, NM: University of New Mexico. Retrieved from http://www.motivationalinterview.net/library/valuesschizophrenia.pdf

Naar-King, S., & Suarez, M. (2011). *Motivational interviewing with adolescents and young adults.* New York, NY: Guilford Press.

National Research Council & Institute of Medicine. (2009). *Preventing mental, emotional, and behavioral disorders in young people.* Washington, DC: National Academies Press.

Nock, M. K., & Ferriter, C. (2005). Parent management of attendance and adherence in child and adolescent therapy: A conceptual and empirical review. *Clinical Child and Family Psychology Review, 8*, 149–166.

Nock, M., Ferriter, C., & Holmberg, E. (2006). Parent beliefs about treatment credibility and effectiveness: Assessment and relation to subsequent treatment participation. *Journal of Child and Family Studies, 16*, 27–38.

Nock, M. K., & Kazdin, A. E. (2001). Parent expectancies for child therapy: Assessment and relation to participation in treatment. *Journal of Child and Family Studies, 10*, 155–180.

Nock, M. K., & Kazdin, A. E. (2005). Randomized controlled trial of a brief intervention for increasing participation in parent management training. *Journal of Consulting and Clinical Psychology, 73*, 872–879.

Nock, M. K., & Photos, V. (2006). Parent motivation to participate in treatment: Assessment and prediction of subsequent participation. *Journal of Child and Family Studies, 15*, 345–358. doi:10.1007/s10826–0006-9022–4

Noell, G. H. (2008). Appraising and praising systematic work to support systems change: Where we might be and where we might go. *School Psychology Review, 37*, 333–336.

Noell, G. H., & Gansle, K. A. (2006). Assuring the form has substance: Treatment plan implementation as the foundation of assessing response to intervention. *Assessment for Effective Intervention, 32*, 32–39.

Olin, S., Hoagwood, K. E., Rodriguez, J., Ramos, B., Burton, G., Penn, M., . . . Jensen, P. S. (2010). The application of behavior change theory to family-based services: Improving parent empowerment in children's mental health. *Journal of Child & Family Studies, 19*, 462–470.

Park, E., Pullis, M., Reilly, T., & Townsend, B. (1994). Cultural biases in the identification of students with behavioral disorders. In R. L. Peterson & S. Ishii-Jordan (Eds.), *Multicultural issues in the education of students with behavioral disorders* (pp. 14–26). Cambridge, MA: Brookline Books.

Prokhorov, A. V., Pallonen, U. E., Fava, J. L., Ding, L., & Niaura, R. (1996). Measuring nicotine dependence among high-risk adolescent smokers. *Addictive Behaviors, 21*(1), 117–127.

Reed, M. B., & Aspinwall, L. G. (1998). Self-affirmation reduces biased processing of health-risk information. *Motivation and Emotion, 22*, 99–132.

Reid, J. B., Patterson, G. R., & Snyder, J. J. (2002). *Antisocial behavior in children and adolescents: A developmental analysis and the Oregon model for intervention.* Washington, DC: American Psychological Association.

Reinke, W. M., Herman, K. C., Darney, D., Pitchford, J., Becker, K., Domitrovich, C., & Ialongo, N. (2012). Using the Classroom Check-Up to support implementation of PATHS to PAX. *Advances in School Mental Health Promotion, 5*, 220–232.

Reinke, W. M., Herman, K. C., & Sprick, R. (2011). *Motivational interviewing for effective classroom management: The Classroom Check-Up.* New York, NY: Guilford Press.

Reinke, W. M., Lewis-Palmer, T., & Martin, E. (2007). The effect of visual performance feedback on teacher use of behavior-specific praise. *Behavior Modification, 31*(3), 247–263.

Reinke, W. M., Lewis-Palmer, T., & Merrell, R. (2008). The Classroom Check-Up: A classwide teacher consultation model for increasing praise and decreasing disruptive behavior. *School Psychology Review, 37*(3), 315–332.

Reinke, W. M., Splett, J., Robeson, E., & Offutt, C. (2009). Combining school and family interventions for the prevention and early intervention of disruptive behavior problems in children: A public health perspective. *Psychology in the Schools, 46*, 33–43.

Reinke, W. M., Sprick, R., & Knight, J. (2009). Coaching classroom management. In J. Knight (Ed.), *Coaching: Approaches & perspectives* (pp. 91–112). Thousand Oaks, CA: Corwin Press.

Reynolds, C., & Kamphaus, R. (2004). *Behavioral Assessment System for Children* (BASC-2). (2nd ed.). Circle Pines, MN: AGS.

Rieckmann, T. R., Kovas, A. E., Fussell, H. E., & Stettler, N. M. (2009). Implementation of evidence-based practices for treatment of alcohol and drug disorders: The role of the state authority. *Journal of Behavioral Health Services & Research, 36*, 407–419.

Rogers, C. R. (1959). A theory of therapy, personality, and interpersonal relationships as developed in the client-centered framework. In S. Koch (Ed.), *Psychology: The study of a science: Formulations of the person and the social contexts* (Vol. 3., pp. 184–256). New York, NY: McGraw-Hill.

Rollnick, S., Miller, W., & Butler, C. C. (2007). *Motivational interviewing in health care: Helping patients change behavior.* New York, NY: The Guilford Press.

Romanelli, L. H., Ramos, B., & Burton, G. (2008). Listening, engagement, and collaboration skills. In P. S. Jensen & K. E. Hoagwood (Eds.), *Improving children's mental health through parent empowerment: A guide to assisting families* (pp. 23–34). New York, NY: Oxford University Press.

Rosengren, D. B., Baer, J. S., Hartzler, B., Dunn, C. W., & Wells, E. A. (2005). The Video Assessment of Simulated Encounters (VASE): Development and validation of a group-administered method for evaluating clinician skills in motivational interviewing. *Drug and Alcohol Dependence, 79*, 321–330.

Rosengren, D. B., Hartzler, B., Baer, J. S., Wells, E. A., & Dunn, C. W. (2008). The Video Assessment of Simulated Encounters–Revised (VASE-R): Reliability and validity of a revised measure of motivational interviewing skills. *Drug and Alcohol Dependence, 97*(1/2), 130–138. doi:10.1016/j.drugalcdep.2008.03.018

Sanetti Hagermoser, L., & Kratochwill, T. R. (2009). Toward developing a science of treatment integrity: Introduction of the special series. *School Psychology Review, 38*, 445–459.

Schroeder, C.M., & Prentice, D.A. (1998). Exposing pluralistic ignorance to reduce alcohol use among college students. *Journal of Applied Social Psychology, 28*, 2150–2180.

Sellman, J. D., MacEwan, I. K., Deering, D. D., & Adamson, S. J. (2007). A comparison of motivational interviewing with non-directive counseling. In G. Tober & D. Raistrick (Eds.), *Motivational dialogue: Preparing addiction professionals for motivational interviewing practice.* New York: Routledge.

Sellman, J. D., Sullivan, P. F., Dore, G. M., Adamson, S. J., & MacEwan, I. (2001). A randomized controlled trial of motivational enhancement therapy (MET) for mild to moderate alcohol dependence. *Journal of Studies on Alcohol, 62*, 389–396.

Shaw, D. S., Dishion, T. J., Supplee, L., Gardner, F., & Arnds, K. (2006). Randomized trial of a family-centered approach to the prevention of early conduct problems: 2-year effects of the Family-Check-Up in early childhood. *Journal of Consulting and Clinical Psychology, 74*(1), 1–9.

Shepard, S., Armstrong, L. M., Silver, R. B., Berger, R., & Seifer, R. (2012). Embedding the Family Check-Up and evidence-based parenting programs in Head Start to increase parent engagement and reduce conduct problems in young children. *Advances in School Mental Health Promotion, 5*, 194–207.

Sholomskas, D. E., Syracuse-Siewert, G., Rounsaville, B. J., Ball, S. A., Nuro, K. F., & Carroll, K. M. (2005). We don't train in vain: A dissemination trial of three strategies of training clinicians in cognitive—Behavioral therapy. *Journal of Consulting and Clinical Psychology, 73*, 106–115. doi:10.1037/0022–006x.73.1.106

Smith, J. D., Dishion, T. J., Shaw, D. S., & Wilson, M. N. (in press). Indirect effects of fidelity to the Family Check-Up on changes in parenting and early childhood behavior problems. *Journal of Consultation and Clinical Psychology.*

Söderlund, L. L., Madson, M. B., Rubak, S., & Nilsen, P. (2011). A systematic review of motivational interviewing training for general health care practitioners. *Patient Education & Counseling, 84*, 16–26. doi:10.1016/j.pec.2010.06.025

Sprauge, J., & Golly, A. (2013). *Best behavior. Building positive behavior support in schools* (2nd ed.). Longmont, CO: Sopris Learning.

Sprick, R. (2008). *Discipline in the secondary classroom: A positive approach to behavior management* (2nd ed.). Eugene, OR: Pacific Northwest Publishing.

Sprick, R. (2010a). *CHAMPS: DVD inservice* (2nd ed.). Eugene, OR: Pacific Northwest Publishing.

Sprick, R. (2010b). *Teacher planner for the secondary classroom.* Eugene, OR: Pacific Northwest Publishing.

Sprick, R. (2010c). *When every second counts: Mini inservices for handling common classroom behavior problems.* Eugene, OR: Pacific Northwest Publishing.

Sprick, R., Garrison, M., & Howard, L. (1998). *CHAMPS: A proactive and positive approach to classroom management.* Longmont, CO: Sopris West.

Sprick, R., Garrison, M., & Howard, L. (2009). *CHAMPS: A proactive and positive approach to classroom management* (2nd ed.). Eugene, OR: Pacific Northwest Publishing.

Sprick, R., & Howard, L. (1996). *The teacher's encyclopedia of behavior management: 100 problems/500 plans.* Longmont, CO: Sopris West.

Sprick, R., Knight, J., Reinke, W. M., Skyles, T., & Barnes, L. (2010). *Coaching classroom management: Strategies and tools for administrators and coaches.* (2nd ed.). Eugene, OR: Pacific Northwest Publishing.

Sprick, R., Sprick, M., & Garrison, M. (1992). *Foundations: Developing positive school discipline policies.* Longmont, CO: Sopris West.

Stormshak, E. A., & Dishion, T. J. (2002). An ecological approach to child and family clinical and counseling psychology. *Clinical Child and Family Psychology Review, 5*(3), 197–215.

Strait, G. G., Smith, B. H., McQuillin, S., Terry, J., Swan, S., & Malone, P. S. (2012). A randomized trial of motivational interviewing to improve middle school students' academic performance. *Journal of Community Psychology, 40*, 1032–1039.

Tharinger, D. J., Finn, S. E., Hersh, B., Wilkinson, A., Christopher, G. B., & Tran, A. (2008). Assessment feedback with parents and preadolescent children: A collaborative approach. *Professional Psychology: Research and Practice, 39*(6), 600–609. doi: 10.1037/0735-7028.39.6.600

Thevos, A. K., Kaona, F. A. D., Siajunza, M. T., & Quick, R. E. (2000). Adoption of safe water behaviors in Zambia: Comparing educational and motivational approaches. *Education for Health, 13*, 366–376.

Wagner, M., Friend, M., Bursuch, W., Kutash, K., Duchmowski, A.., Sumi, W.C., et al. (2006). Educating students with emotional disturbance: A national perspective on school programs and services. *Journal of Emotional and Behavioral Disorders, 14*, 12–30.

Wagner, M., Kutash, K., Duchnowski, A. J., Epstein, M. H., & Sumi, W. C. (2005). A national picture of the characteristics of students with emotional disturbances receiving special education. *Journal of Emotional and Behavioral Disorders, 13*, 79–96.

Walker, H. M., & Hops, H. (1979). The class program for acting out children: R&D procedures, program outcomes, and implementation issues. *School Psychology Review, 8*(4), 370–381.

Walters, S. T., Matson, S. A., Baer, J. S., & Ziedonis, D. M. (2005). Effectiveness of workshop training for psychosocial addiction treatments: A systematic review. *Journal of Substance Abuse Treatment, 29*, 283–293.

Webster-Stratton, C. (1998a). Parent training with low-income families: Promoting parental engagement through a collaborative approach. In J. R. Lutzker (Ed.), *Handbook of child abuse research and treatment* (pp. 183–210). New York, NY: Plenum.

Webster-Stratton, C. (1998b). Preventing conduct problems in Head Start children: Strengthening parent competencies. *Journal of Consulting and Clinical Psychology, 66,* 715–730.

Webster-Stratton, C., & Reid, M. J. (2010). The Incredible Years parents, teachers and child training series: A multifaceted treatment approach for young children with conduct problems. In A. E. Kazdin & J. R. Weisz (Eds.), *Evidence-based psychotherapies for children and adolescents* (pp. 194–210). New York, NY: Guilford Press.

Wells, K. C., Lochman, J. E., & Lenhart, L. (2008). *Coping power: Parent group facilitator's guide.* New York, NY: Oxford University Press.

Westra, H. A. (2011). *Motivational interviewing in the treatment of anxiety.* New York, NY: Guilford Press.

White, M. (1988, Summer). The externalization of the problem and the reauthoring of lives and relationships. *Dulwich Centre Newsletter,* 3–21.

White, M. (1995). *Re-authoring lives: Interviews and essays.* Adelaide, South Australia: Dulwich Centre.

White, M., & Epston, D. (1990). *Narrative means to therapeutic ends.* New York, NY: W. W. Norton.

Winslow, E. B., Poloskov, E., Begay, R., & Sandler, I. N. (2011). *Theory-based strategies for engaging parents into preventive parenting interventions: Results of a randomized experimental study.* Manuscript submitted for publication.

Wright, B. A., & Fletcher, B. L. (1982). Uncovering hidden resources: A challenge in assessment. *Professional Psychology, 13*(2), 229–235. doi: 10.1037/0735-7028.13.2.229

# Index